Walk with Us

Walk With Us

Triplet Boys,
Their Teen Parents
& Two White Women
Who Tagged Along

Elizabeth K. Gordon

Crandall, Dostie & Douglass Books, Inc.
Roselle, New Jersey

Published by:
Crandall, Dostie & Douglass Books, Inc.
245 West 4th Avenue, Roselle, NJ 07203-1135
(908) 241-5439
www.cddbooks.com

ISBN-10 1-934390-30-5
ISBN-13 978-1-934390-30-6
LCCN 2007924913

First printing 2007

Grateful acknowledgment is made to the following:

Excerpt from "O, Yes" from Tell Me A Riddle by Tillie Olsen, copyright © 1961 by Tillie Olsen; reprinted by permission of the Author's Agents, the Elaine Markson Agency.

Excerpts from "My Life as I Know It" by Tahija Ellison (pseudonym), copyright © 2007 by Tahija Ellison; reprinted by permission.

Excerpt from Beloved by Toni Morrison copyright © 1987 by Toni Morrison and the publisher Alfred A. Knopf, a division of Random House, Inc., New York.

"Ella's Song," composer, Bernice Johnson Reagon, Songtalk Publishing, 1986. The lyrics for "Ella's Song" and "We All Everyone of Us" are compositions of Bernice Johnson Reagon, Songtalk Publishing, © 1986, www.bernicejohnsonreagon.com.

Lucille Clifton, "blake" from The Terrible Stories. Copyright © 1996 by Lucille Clifton. Reprinted with permission of BOA Editions, Ltd., www.boaeditions.org.

Lucille Clifton, "note to my self" from Quilting: Poems 1987-1990. Copyright © 1991 by Lucille Clifton. Reprinted with permission of BOA Editions, Ltd., www.boaeditions.org.

Lucille Clifton, "won't you celebrate with me" from The Book of Light. Copyright © 1993 by Lucille Clifton. Reprinted with permission of Copper Canyon Press, www.coppercanyonpress.org.

Excerpt from "The Ones Who Walk Away from Omelas" by Ursula K. Le Guin, copyright © 1973, 2001 by Ursula K. Le Guin; first appeared in New Dimensions 3; from the Author's collection, The Wind's Twelve Quarters; reprinted by permission of the author and the author's agents, the Virginia Kidd Agency, Inc.

Reading Group Guide available at **http://www.walkwithus.info**

Cover design by Ellen Moore Osborne, www.TrinityArts.com

COVER PHOTOS:
Row houses and red wall - Eugene Martin © 2007
Babies, adults, and dangling shoes – Jamarr Sturgis © 2007
Girls jumping rope and boy running – Kaki Sjogren © 2007

NOTE: Teen parents not pictured.

iv

Dedicated to each of the triplets

and in memory of
Joseph Scott Gordon
1974-1990

. . . caring asks doing. It is a long baptism into the seas of humankind, my daughter. Better immersion than to live untouched. . . . Yet how will you sustain?

— from "O Yes" by Tillie Olsen

Introduction

I came back to Philadelphia because I could not run away again. Twice I'd lived on the affordable edge of its inner city, and twice left. The first time I was twenty and sharing a house with five University of Pennsylvania students. Not a student myself, I was nevertheless learning. It was the late seventies. I went to open mikes in storefronts painted Peter Max style, crashed a poetry class at Penn, and relished a workshop at the Jewish Y with Sonia Sanchez. Money I earned selling leather coats at the downtown mall.

I enjoyed the tree-shaded enclave of the Penn campus, with its modern sculpture and fortunate young people, but the streets drew me too: vendors and preachers, the suddenly shifting compositions of fountain and child, spire and cloud, "angels in the architecture" (as Paul Simon sings it), genius in the graffiti. A street musician played his plastic recorder out to the side as if it were a silver flute. When I heard the same man's music not long ago, almost thirty years later — "Greensleeves" echoing in the portico of City Hall — I felt I knew Philadelphia well, and loved it.

But I did not always love it. The noise and the pollution, the poverty and my reaction to the poverty, and most of all the racial tension made me eager to leave. Growing up white in South Florida I had seen how violently many white people fought school desegregation, how the black students and teachers endured. I knew our Broward

1

County town had two halves, but only one police force, and that one white. The race riots in nearby Liberty City and the rioting beamed contextless into our living room between *Lost in Space* and *Gilligan's Island* left me fearing that the black people on that other, othered side of town would come get us if they could. It seemed only logical. And nobody telling me about King's agape illogic, or showing me the few white people trying to trade in white supremacy for the beloved community King called forth.

At twenty, oblivious to my white privilege and largely ignorant of America's racial history, I yet felt the fear those who expect to be held accountable feel, and guilt that made living on the edge of the inner city a personal dilemma — one I wasn't ready to solve. When it came, I welcomed the chance to get away. The day my first love and I drove her VW bug out of West Philly, with Schuylkill the kitten clawing at the windows to stay near his namesake river, I didn't think I'd ever see Philadelphia again. When I was drawn back for a visit a few years later, I supposed it was out of nostalgia for the college relationship that by then had ended. With a heart somewhat less numb to the relationship the city offered I once again walked its streets. I like to think I crossed the paths of the young parents at the center of this book, Tahija Ellison and Lamarr Stevens*, who were just then beginning their lives, but it's unlikely: They lived in a neighborhood I would have avoided then, though it became my own and precious to me, the very North Philly where this story takes place.

The second time the city of B. Free (Ben) Franklin reeled me in I was thirty. I lived in Germantown, in a cooperative home where the writer Toni Cade Bambara had once lived. Across the street was a rehabilitation program for women in recovery. There I met women who'd nearly drowned in the flood of crack cocaine pouring into the inner cities through channels that seem to have had government sanction, if not

---

*Their names, and most others, have been changed to protect privacy.

downright sponsorship.* It was crack that stole the mothers of Tahija Ellison and Lamarr Stevens, for a time, and stole their chance at a happy childhood forever.

Just as my roots were beginning to take hold, I felt the pull to leave. I told myself I needed more time in nature, that the city was too expensive, that I should move nearer my family, but something else was happening, something simple and human, yet complex and mystical. I was waking up to my membership in the dominant majority; I was hearing a call to change and to work for change. I have met people as young as twenty and certainly many at thirty who have heard and answered such a call. I was not like them. What I heard, faintly, I had neither the confidence nor the hope to respond to in a meaningful way. And so I ran away again. But the people I'd met and the stories I'd heard clung to me like wildflower seeds patient for a chance to take root.

I moved to New York's Hudson River Valley and found part-time work at a community college teaching writing and litera-ture. That's what I was doing when I met the woman who would lure me back to my first city. It was 1997, and I was nearly forty. I didn't know exactly what it was I had been running from all those years but I knew enough to know that, like Jonah, I ran at my own peril. Philadelphia is not, however, my Nineveh; Philadelphia's the whale. And the shore that whale spit me out on is this book.

Sometimes when I'm out walking everything my eye falls on seems luminous, and I give praise from the moment. Sentences stream though my mind, pacing me like a long-legged compan-ion. By the time I reach home I have a list, a litany of gratitude, "For the daffodils, fake or not, on the porch of the yellow house / For the birch sapling bent like an arch / For the bright five o'clock" — like that. Eventually I had a poem for every month of the year, except September. It was August when I moved into the Badlands of North Philadelphia, where, just a few months before, the Presidents' Summit for America's Future had brought one

---

*For the connection between the U.S. government and the crack epidemic, see *Dark Alliance, the Story Behind the Crack Explosion*, by Gary Webb.

3

sitting president, his vice president, two former presidents, a former first lady, a bevy of CEOs, and retired General Colin Powell Jr. to pick up trash and whitewash graffiti.

I confess I did feel a perverse pride at moving to a place whose very trash and graffiti so many dignitaries had failed (as I could plainly see) to prevail against, but I didn't expect its red-brick beauty to yield a September poem. Then one afternoon, with the back wall of a muffler shop, it began. In September I felt gratitude,

> For shadow and shade on a cinderblack wall,
>   and the spray-painted word,
>   the word or name Tokay
> For two boys playing catch and a yellow butterfly
>   passing through
> For in the night a car alarm calling,
>   "I have been tampered with
>   I have been tampered with"
> For the sullen look of a passing youth,
>   for the appeal beneath the sullen look
> For sneakers dangling by their laces from telephone wire,
>   turning like a wind vane in the wind
> For sycamores with dignity lining a street
> For a recitation in Spanish from the prophet Jeremiah
> For the Spanish word *Zion,*
>   so much gentler than the English "Zion"
> For the pigeon grooming itself on a wire,
>   pulling me as ably as did the great blue heron
>   down the groove of tension into immanence
> For a mother calling "Hakim, Hakim"
> For the surf of sound around homes
>   as around homeless shelters, around the sullen youth
>   sitting on a cement wall in the dapple of late afternoon,
>   North Philadelphia, early fall

*   *   *

"September" has more people and signs of people in it than all the other months' poems combined, for in the city inspiration reached me mainly through the people, through three in particular — Damear, Mahad, and Lamarr. I first encountered those names on three strips of masking tape their mother had placed on three blinking, beeping heart monitors. After they were born I shared a house with them and their mother for nearly two years, with their father all but living there too. By the time they moved out, they had moved into my heart, moved in and rearranged all the furniture.

This book is based on my memories, journals, conversations, and written interviews with the key players. I am aware of the myriad mistakes, distortions, and thefts white writers, musicians, and artists have perpetrated on black individuals and communities. I pray I have not added to the ignominious history of expropriation, or, if I have, that in reflecting upon myself and my motives I have thrown some light into the inner workings of that expropriation.

When the narrative enters the thoughts of someone other than myself it is to depict events those who experienced them described to me many times and which I felt I could risk retelling without undue distortion. Many of the conversations are composites built from several conversations. No person is a composite; all are my attempt at accurate depiction, attempts that demanded examination of all that limits and distorts my vision. I realize that while I might unblinker my eyes to some extent and strive to own and expand my perspective, actual transcendence of it is achieved in rare, heightened moments of openness that the rest of life is but an attempt to be faithful to. In the end, this book may be a failure about failure, but it is a failure I did not flee. I can only hope that the light of the people described shines through the clouds of my limited perspective and as the sun does a morning fog, burns it away.

Part One

Monitored Hearts

Chapter 1

That October I thought I was pregnant. I didn't know what to do so I said I would wait to tell my mom, but before I could find my mom my aunt put me out her house at one o'clock in the morning and I had to go to Renee's house and Lamarr didn't know where I was again. At that time I didn't know what to do. Finally I got in touch with Lamarr and I told him where I was, he was glad to know I was all right but he didn't know what to do. A few days later we had to go to an ultrasound appointment and the doctor said "I see one, no two" then she said "wait I see three." When she said that Lamarr passed out. When we told everyone they thought we were lying to them but we weren't. I got in touch with my unreliable dad yet again. This time he was doing ok. By then it was November 7th. He was suppose to come and get me and finally take care of me but the next day I waited as usual and he never showed up. I was left hanging all over again. It was about two weeks later Renee's mom told me I had to leave so that she wouldn't get in trouble for breaking her lease by having me live there.

*My Life as I Know It**

---

*Quotations from this in-progress autobiography of Tahija Ellison are used by permission of the author. See Appendix for the full text.

The marble steps of Dobbins High School ended, with no more buffer than a sidewalk, at Lehigh Avenue — four lanes of traffic that on this cold and drizzly afternoon moved slowly to and from the light at the corner. Had you been driving by you probably wouldn't have noticed her, though she stood at the top of the steps, alone and still within the stream of dismissed students: a short, brown-skinned girl in a black robe and tight black headscarf that gave her the appearance, against the marble wall, of a silhouette.

Her first name was Tahija (pronounced Ta-*hee*-juh), her surname Ellison. Tahija she had chosen herself when she converted to Islam in eighth grade. Her mother had named her Shannon, and some in her family still called her that. Ellison came via her great-grandmother Mary Millicent Ellison from a South Carolina cotton planter.

She offered the traditional Arabic greeting to other Muslim students, "Assalamu alaikum" (peace be to you), and received theirs in turn, "Wa alaikum assalam," (and to you be peace).

Her mind wasn't on her peers, though, and her heart wasn't peaceful. The day before, she had called her father and asked if she could move in with him. Since starting high school a little more than a year before she had lived in five different places. She was staying then with her friend Renee, but Renee's mother was paralyzed and lived in federally subsidized handicapped housing with a strict, strictly enforced lease: no guests longer than a week. If Tahija remained they'd all be put out, and it didn't seem to matter to anyone but her and her boyfriend Lamarr that she was four months pregnant, with triplets.

Triplets. Two boys and a girl the doctor had said. She looked down. The robe hardly showed it. She looked out at the street. It had been almost a year since she'd seen her father, and that time … she didn't like to think about that time. He'd been junking bad. All she could do was pick out the matted mess his hair had gotten into and braid it up nice. He might lie dead to the world in an alley somewhere but at least folks stepping over him on their way to work would know someone cared about him, loved him, quit drill team so she could spend her afternoons searching the streets for him, and her heart racing now, racing, when a man with his profile turned to look at her through a bus window, not smiling a smile not his.

She waited until after all of the students and teachers and staff had gone and the custodian had come to pull shut the big doors one by one, one by one winding a chain through their handles. Then she centered her backpack on her back, walked down the steps, left to the corner, around the puddle and slowly across Lehigh to stand with the others waiting in the rain for the 33 bus — the bus that would take her back to Renee's, where she could stay, she hoped, awhile longer.

It was November 8th, her fifteenth birthday.

When we were living in the same house and I was helping with the triplets, I'd sometimes pick Tahija up after school. Because she had told me about waiting for her father that day and other days, I was anxious to be on time. But I could have been on time a thousand times and early a thousand more and still in some rainy November of her heart Tahija will always be waiting for her father.

Months later she found out what happened to him. In the morning he had gone to help a friend collect scrap from the yard of a house the friend claimed to be living in. But when a police car flew around one corner, that friend (*so-called* friend, Tahija always said when telling the story) tore off around the other, leaving her father with a shopping cart of bent and rusted sheet metal that thanks to the three-strikes law and his stormy youth was going to get him locked up for a very long time.

One in three American black men between the ages of eighteen and thirty in the criminal justice system — an often quoted statistic, but the human reality behind the numbers wouldn't seep toxic waste-like into me until, loving the triplets as I would come to love them, I felt how fiercely they loved and needed their father.

11

Should they lose sight of Lamarr behind a tree, say, in the park: "Where's my daddy" — the pride and proprietorship, the fear, as if they knew, sensed, had breathed in on the polluted air knowledge of the steep drop their young father walked alongside every day of his life. One in three.

"He's right over there, Baby, see?"

How long Lamarr Stevens had been at the front door I didn't know. I was up on the third floor painting my new bedroom (white with dark green trim). A guy from the apartment building across the street was washing his car, blasting brassy salsa like it could blast him a lawn and circular drive. During a quiet interval (was he washing the speakers?) I heard the knocking.

I opened the window on a stream of bus exhaust and looked down to see a big head flanked by broad shoulders, arms very dark against a white t-shirt. Though it was cold enough, he wore no coat, no sweater even, and nothing on his head but the silver curve of headphones. He pushed these back and hung away from the handrail, looking up at me.

"You Kathryn?"

"Yeah."

"I been hearing about you."

"Yeah?"

"A lot."

He smiled, and I saw he was a teenager, fifteen or sixteen.

"I'm Lamarr. Kaki said I could use the shower."

And I said, "What, *now*?"

And he said, "Yeah."

And the salsa music resumed its pinballing up and down the street.

I went down the stairs to find out about this promised shower. Before me, on the other side of the wrought-iron bars of a security door the house's previous owners had put in, was a young black male, on the stocky side, wanting in. His white t-shirt reached low over creased jeans so baggy only the orange tips of his boots showed. I was being seen through the bars too: middle-aged white woman, medium build, ruddy face, small hazel eyes, short hair, jeans and sweatshirt marked by green paint. Hesitating.

I'd been living in that neighborhood known as the Badlands long enough to notice how even the small children formed protective associations. The very postures of the stray dogs and edgy cats said it: don't trust anybody. But he had an open, expressive face, eyebrows like strokes of charcoal on a dark brown canvas, and he spoke in a reassuringly even voice.

"I called Kaki last night," he said, "asked could I use the shower, I have this meeting, with a record producer? She said yeah, she'd tell you."

"She must have forgot," I said.

He smiled, his cheekbones two knobs nudging the outer corners of his eyes upward. "That'd be Kaki."

Kathleen Nelsen became Kaki on the way home from Hawaii. Her missionary brother had invited her there, for a vacation, he said. And the hotel *was* four star, but the trip wasn't a vacation, exactly, it was an Intervention. A born-again former lesbian locked her in earnest conversation and did everything short of kissing her to persuade her that lesbianism was a sin. At the airport, she bought a key chain with the Hawaiian spelling of her name on it: Kaki (sounds, she tells people, like cocky, but with the stress on the second syllable). Perhaps to buffer herself from the family that loved her but couldn't seem to love all of her, she adopted the new name. Back at Penn Mutual her co-workers tripped over it — Khaki, Cookie, Keekee. It just didn't seem the sort of name a mid-level insurance executive ought to have. But she wasn't going to stay a mid-level insurance executive much longer, anyway.

One day a group she'd given a 401(k) presentation to went into the silence: fifty or so middle-aged people sitting, eyes closed, hands in their laps. They were Quakers. Kaki stood before them in her suit set, hose, heels, and gold hoop earrings wondering what to do. What was there to do? She sat down and went into the silence too. Within a year she'd joined a Quaker meeting and begun going with its members into the prisons. She began to facilitate workshops in the Alternatives to Violence Project (AVP),* and before long the disparity between her privilege and the extreme poverty so many of the prisoners had survived struck her as unconscionable. How could she share her faith in Transforming Power when she'd never walked the streets they'd walked, never been asked in the face of death to count on grace instead of a gun?

So she left; left the promising career, the house designed in the style of Frank Lloyd Wright, the relationship of fifteen years. She was forty-one. She rented awhile then bought a row house in the neighborhood whose young men fed the bellies of the upstate prisons. Now when she talked about nonviolence she drew upon real-life encounters set on real-life corners: Broad and Erie, Second and Diamond, Kensington and Allegheny. She told about confronting a man as he beat a woman in front of a grocery store, how he'd been so shocked by her mild "Do you need help here?" that his outburst stalled and he went into an explanation that ended in tears. The prisoners said she was crazy, said she should move out of the neighborhood or at least learn to mind her own business in it, but they had encounters to talk about too — conflicts, fights, crises that might have gone differently.

So much could go differently with peace as an alternative. Asking people to consider that became her work. She lived simply, and much of what she did she did for free. Because "Kaki" sounded to some of her neighbors like a Spanish slang word, many called her *Aki* instead: in English, *here*.

---

*The AVP program was developed in 1975 by lifers in a New York State prison working in collaboration with Quakers.

* * *

I met Kaki Nelsen at the twentieth annual Quaker Lesbian Conference. Like many of the women attending, she lived in Philadelphia. Unlike the rest, she made her home in the inner city. I told her how I'd lived on the edge of Philly's inner city in my early twenties, and again in my thirties; how each time, leaving, I had felt a strong pull to stay, for what exactly I hadn't been sure; and how now, near forty, I had this sense that I should go back to Philly, find out what for.

I might have moved to the city Kaki or no Kaki, but maybe I'm fooling myself. Maybe I needed the anchor of a place to live and the carrot of a good relationship. And it did seem that, except for the fact that a significant portion of our fellow citizens thought our love strange, threatening, or downright sinful — all attitudes that affected me more than I could know. Affected but did not prevent. And so there I was, a year after falling in love with her and an hour after meeting Lamarr Stevens, driving down rush-hour I-95 looking for a prison.

She had told me to watch for pink buildings with windows like the handles of disposable razors. Just north of an older prison's crumbling stone turrets I spotted it — a Pepto-Bismol colored complex that but for the razor wire topped fences might have been a community college. I pulled up just as the doors opened on a dark blue stream of corrections officers (COs). Within it drifted a bright buoy — a tall woman in a red pullover with *Build Community Not Conflict* across the front. A white headband held back her long brown hair, leaving short bangs to bounce as she walked. From one arm hung a straw bag, from the other two striped hula hoops.

I knew those hula hoops. I'd tripped over those hula hoops. They were filled with beads that whirred like skateboarders on a plaza. When she opened the door and tossed them into the back seat they seemed to chuckle — contraband laughter. We kissed hello and told how our day had gone. Hers had been the last in a week-long workshop attended by inmates and CO's. Mine had featured Lamarr's visit.

"Oh that's right," she said, "I forgot to tell you he was coming over."

"Forgot to *ask* me you mean."

Right there in the white Chevy Cavalier her father had left her we had our first argument over Lamarr and Tahija (or Tamarr and Lahija, as we sometimes trippingly call them). Not very heated, it turned into one of the debriefing, self-assessment sessions that was becoming our habit: processing our experience of life in the 'hood, examining, owning, trying to stretch our perspectives.

"So what did you feel," she asked when she'd finished kibitzing with the guard at the front gate, "having a young black male you'd never met before show up telling you he could use the shower?"

"Come on," I said, "I did desegregation in middle school, in the south."

"South Florida's not *The South*."

"It's more south than Minne-*so*-ta."

She smiled, just, but it was enough. Her mother had the same smile: paired hills of the upper lip rising and sloping down again to a point that looked penciled on. But she was so serious. As I drove through the bleak white neighborhood that surrounded the prison, I thought back to that morning.

"I guess it did seem a little ... I mean, I didn't want to be doing something where everybody would say later, 'How could she be so stupid?' You know. But I could see he wasn't one of the addicts who come around selling stuff — "

"Boosting," she said, "selling stolen goods."

"Right. So I open the door, and what comes into my head, when he's standing there in the living room, is this black kid from first grade, the only black kid in the class, probably the whole school. He was tall, reddish hair, serious, angry — I thought. The way the nuns treated him I figured he must be angry. Plus it was 1963, riots on TV, the white people around me all 'talking shit,' like people here say, you know."

16

"Scared, guilty, projecting their own motives onto a people they hardly knew," she said.

"I guess," I agreed, glancing at her to see if she meant me. Here was someone who at sixteen years old left her Methodist church when it refused to invite to services a poor black family the church had been giving charity to, left and never went back.

"So Lamarr's standing there," she prodded.

"Right. And this fear from first grade, fear of this kid, hits me, and it sets off a sort of domino chain … and when the last domino falls, smack, there it is: guilt."

"Guilt," she said.

"About feeling the fear."

"Okay."

"About reacting mainly, or at all, to his skin color."

Kaki turned to me, her knees bumping the gearshift (her 5'-10" height is all in her legs).

"Lamarr's had it hard, I kid you not. Food, clothes, deodorant, a bed, a shower, cash to keep utilities from being cut off — you name it, he's had to provide it off and on for himself and his younger twin brothers since he was small — I mean like five. Sympathetic white people were the only renewable resource around. Watch him, or he'll be playing you like a gosh-darned banjo before you can say Jiminy Cricket."

That's the best cussing Kaki, raised Minnesotan, can manage.

"So I should have feared him?" I asked.

"No. But neither should you let him manipulate you."

"I didn't let him manipulate me."

"Did you give him any money?" she asked.

"No. Well, two subway tokens."

"That's what I mean!" she said.

"You're the one told him, without informing me, that he could use the shower."

"He had a job interview."

"He told me it was a meeting with a record producer," I said.

"For Pete's sake! So did you let him take a shower?"

"Yes. And he knew right where everything was, Miss Banjo."

We were on 95, heading toward the city and not, with the crawling commuters, away from it. Stretching to the right of the elevated highway was Fishtown, the working class white neighborhood separated from ours by the El. I walked there sometimes. The corner bars and football fields felt more familiar to me than the drug corners and basketball courts of my new neighborhood, and I could blend in there, comfortably anonymous for awhile.

To the left, east, flowed the Delaware River. On its New Jersey shore in the shade of the Betsy Ross Bridge hunkered another new prison — rows and rows of the razor-handle window slits.

"At least those prisoners have a river to look out at," I said.

"Unless the windows were placed above eye level," Kaki said.

I didn't want to think about a world in which windows were purposely placed above eye level. Yet here I was in it, as I always had been.

Chapter 2

So Lamarr asked his mom could I stay with them and she said yes, so Kaki and Kathryn picked me up with Lamarr and took me to his mom's house. I really didn't know Kaki and Kathryn back then, but I was glad that they were willing to help me move my things from Renee's mom's house.

My Life as I Know It

"So finally I get to meet the girlfriend," Kaki said, turning to face the back seat.

Lamarr's left eyebrow indicated that he had heard her. He was leaning against the window, palms up and open in his lap, tinny bass leaking from his headphones. He pushed them to the edges of his ears and looked back at her.

I was in the driver's seat. We were parked in the parking lot of a high-rise apartment building. Lamarr had asked Kaki if his pregnant girlfriend could move in with us. He said she was carrying triplets. We said we wanted to meet her before deciding, so we were helping her move from her friend's place, where she couldn't stay any longer, to his mom's house, where she could stay until the threatened eviction.

"The way you use her as an excuse to get out of GED tutoring," Kaki went on, "I wasn't even sure there was a girlfriend. And how do you know it's triplets?"

"Ultrasound," he said, his right eyebrow forming (I swear he could do this) a veritable Nike swoosh. *I'm putting up with a lot here,* it said.

Lamarr and Kaki had known each other since she'd moved to his neighborhood four years before. They'd met at a nonviolence workshop. I was trying to see what was real in their relationship and what was the manipulation she'd warned me against. And I wondered — if he used her, did she use him?

I was seven years younger than Kaki, with a bachelor's to her two master's — one of those the weighty MBA. My parents had always struggled, and my father died at forty-two, leaving my mother with five kids, a mortgage, and a Dodge Dart she didn't know how to drive. Kaki's parents were professionals, and her life, though not easy, and been a good deal more cushioned than mine. I think I sensed as she could not the power gap between her and Lamarr. At any rate, though I was curious to see it, I dearly hoped she didn't ask him to produce the ultrasound.

Just then he pulled a pager from the pocket of his jeans. "That's Tahija."

The car was a two door, so I had to get out first. I asked if he wanted help carrying his girlfriend's things.

"I'm okay," he said, positioning the headphones on his ears and sighing like a middle-aged man. He was wearing a new, dazzling white t-shirt, same big jeans, same orange boots from the famous boot company supposedly owned, he'd told me, by the Klu Klux Klan. A long silver chain swung, pendantless, from his neck.

I got back in and watched him cross the parking lot. He walked slowly, arms out from his sides in a way that seemed both menacing and weary.

"You know who he reminds me of?" I said.

"Who?"

"My brother Joey."

20

I had told Kaki about Joey, who had died six years before. He'd been sixteen, Lamarr's age now.

"So what about Lamarr reminds you of Joey?"

I thought about it as I watched Lamarr disappear through the glass doors of the high-rise.

"Well one thing, Joey was a big guy, like Lamarr. The way Lamarr tugs at the front of his t-shirt, like to get it to drop straight over his belly, but it doesn't?" Kaki laughed. "Joey did that." But it wasn't build or mannerisms so much that made these two — one pale as paper, a redhead, the other dark as teak wood — seem alike to me; it was something deeper, something, I sensed, having to do with absent fathers. Our father, Joey's and mine, had died when Joey was just two. Lamarr's father, though alive, had rarely supported or lived with him and his twin brothers.

A man walking by on the sidewalk glanced our way, and sped up.

"Probably thinks we're drug buyers," Kaki said, "or narcs."

"How *you* doing," I said, trying to smile like neither to an elderly woman in a red wool coat.

"How *you* doin'," she said, and sped up.

Folks here were friendly enough, but it seemed like what many saw first and oftentimes last was our whiteness. If I had a dollar for every time someone confused me with Kaki, who was taller by five inches, with long dark hair to my short light ... But mostly people were polite, just distrustful. Sometimes their distrust felt unfair, but when I thought about it, and remembered books I'd read and stories I'd heard, kept hearing — and it seemed like every person of color who I came to know at all well had terrible stories to tell — the more that distrust made sense. I figured it fell to me, was *on* me, as people here said, to prove myself the exception.

And here, walking slowly toward us, came the very person to put me to the test.

Lamarr had come out of the building with a short girl in a neck-to-ankle black robe. He carried a small Rite-Aid bag. She held a bright yellow stuffed something nearly half as long as she was.

"What ever is she carrying?" Kaki asked.

"Why, I think that's Tweetie Bird," I said.

We'd known Lamarr was Muslim. On him this meant not shaving, which he didn't really need to do yet, while with the girlfriend ... the effect was striking. Covering her head was a cobalt-blue scarf that I'd learn to call a kemar. This came low on her forehead, like a nun's wimple, and crossed under her chin, disappearing into the black robe. She was big bone-ded, as people pronounced it, but she didn't look four months pregnant, and certainly not with triplets.

Kaki got out and pushed the front seat forward for them. Lamarr tossed in the plastic bag (her possessions?) and introduced her,

"This is Tahija."

Tahija got in and slid across the back seat, holding the Tweetie Bird by the waist.

"How you doin'?" Kaki said.

"Fine," Tahija said, "How *you* doin'?"

"Fine, thank you," said Kaki. "This is my partner Kathryn Gordon."

"Hey," I said, turning to face her.

"Hey," she said.

"Nice to meet you."

We looked at each other. Framed by the radiant blue kemar her round hazelnut-brown face seemed to glow. She had very large almond-shaped eyes, light brown, the lashes long and curled.

I started the car and drove where Lamarr and Kaki directed me.

At a light, I looked in the rearview mirror. As if my gaze had clicked audibly into place, Tahija met it. In her face I saw an odd blend of expectation and fear, as in that of a child too small to see over the steering wheel who's somehow gotten a car rolling toward traffic. Her eyes were set in inch-wide rings so regular and so dark, on the lids especially, I thought they must be makeup. They weren't makeup, I'd learn, but a sign of vitamin D deficiency.

"So is it boys or girls, or what?" I asked. (I did the math: four possible combinations.)

"Two boys and one girl," she answered.

"Two boys and a girl."

"That's what I said."

O-kay....I drove. Lamarr jumped in with news of a big record deal he was trying to cut. With a friend who sang bass, he and his twin brothers made up the rhythm and blues group Natural. They performed at area clubs and colleges, with a regular gig at Villanova University.

"But this producer's real shysty," Lamarr explained, leaning forward while Tahija looked out the window. "And my brothers don't trust nobody. You'd be surprised how many groups around here cut two, three albums, dynamite stuff, and end up flat broke, you know?"

"Cheated?" Kaki said.

"Exactly. Awhile back we drove to New York to audition for Puff Daddy's TV show *Make a Star?* Remember Tahija? So we figured we'd all three audition solo, because one of us making it is the same as all three making it, right? But Puff Daddy don't show. Dude going to pull up in a stretch limo and tell us 'cancelled.' Must've been a thousand of us waiting."

We drove awhile in silence. Lamarr pointed out the park that had terrified him when he was little, Needle Park. Except for the plastic bags snagged everywhere on the trees and bushes (urban tumbleweed, Kaki calls it) it seemed okay, to me. Then we went through a tunnel where Lamarr's friend's brother Craig had been jumped and beaten into a coma.

"Punks going to *drive* over him."

"Left him blind in one eye," Tahija said.

"Which eye was blinded?" I asked.

"Excuse me?" she said.

"She say which eye messed up," Lamarr said.

"The left."

The left. I thought about our reasons for not bringing Tahija straight to Kaki's house, then glanced into the rearview. I wish the triplets could see their mother's eyes as they were then, when she was fifteen: so clear, so open, unguarded in a way they would never again be.

We came to a short, narrow one-way street of tiny two-story row houses, most of them redbrick, as on our street, but sagging and leaning, as if gravity pulled harder here. Lamarr's street. Houses abandoned ... few boarded up, leaving the unbroken windows to forever reflect the broken. And not a tree, not a shrub, not a child or a toy in sight. I parked. On the side of one house the outline of a demolished staircase rose through torn wallpaper to a demolished second floor.

"Now this is North Philly," Lamarr said, as if Kaki's neighborhood twenty blocks east wasn't.

In this, the state's poorest census tract, the addiction rate was nearly fifty percent.* More deaths by homicide here than in any other part of the city. Instead of saving for cars and class rings the teens took out life insurance policies on themselves.

Feeling something in my belly like you do at the crest of a roller coaster loop, I looked into Kaki's hazel eyes, saw what I needed to see there, and turned to Tahija.

"You really wanna stay at our place, or is that just Lamarr's idea?"

"I think it would be good," she said. "I need less stress."

How I wanted to drive her right then to the land of no stress, but as Laurel and Hardy say, you can't get there from here.

They got out. From the car it was two steps across the sidewalk, three up and into the house. As they went in, we saw through the open door a livingroom furnished with nothing more than a red vinyl weight-lifting bench and scattered weights.

Fifty percent. A life- and sanity-threatening statistic into which the expectant mother had just disappeared carrying

---

*From the newsletter of New Jerusalem Now, a residential recovery community in the neighborhood for fifteen years. NJN was founded by Sister Margaret McKenna of the Medical Mission Sisters and inspired by Rev. Henry T. Wells' grassroots recovery movement.

nothing more than a bag of clothes, a stuffed animal, and a comet tail of trauma longer than I could know.

We remained parked. The sky roused itself to a stunning orange along the western horizon, deep blue overhead. People say pollution is the cause of beautiful city sunsets but isn't it light acting on pollution?

"Something else may come up," one of us said.

"It may."

The houses on the east side of the street inhaled the sky's orange and breathed out a deep red.

"If they stayed a few months ..." Kaki began.

"Just until the babies came?"

"It'd give Lamarr time to find a job, save for an apartment."

"Buy furniture," I added.

"Cribs."

"*Three.*"

"Lord."

Back on our street of tall narrow three-story houses, trinities they were called, Christmas lights shone already, one house with all its six windows framed in blue blinking lights. The corner store cast a bright carpet of light across the sidewalk and groups stood around front steps talking and laughing. Kids rode razor-scooters in the narrow lane between parked and moving cars, and three sisters we knew, the King girls, jumped rope beneath a streetlight.

Hancock Street was more like the Bronx neighborhood my mother had grown up in and told me about than any place I'd ever lived: sisters moving in near sisters; cousins traveling in tough look-alike groups; corner candy stores; the elevated train tracks, or El, nearby; drunks on the street from time to time, but drunks you knew; the music of other languages; the music of well-handled English; arguments across banisters; block parties; hardships but a sense of sharing them. Of course, the late 90's in Philly were very different from the Bronx of the 30s and 40s, but it made me realize what I had been missing in the rural places and anonymous college towns where I'd lived: community — cross-cultural, intergenerational, complicated, who-keeps-leaving-candywrappers-on-my-front-stoop community.

Standing behind Kaki as she jiggled the finicky lock, I leaned back and looked up, as Lamarr had been looking up the first time I saw him. The night had turned a good, clear dark, dark enough for part of Cassiopeia's "W" to show through.

Inside the house, light from the street played in the tinsel of our unlit tree. For me every Christmastime there is a moment, sometimes not until Christmas Eve itself, when I begin to feel the spirit of the season. Until then, the more so as I get older and my mother is longer gone, I don't believe I will ever feel it again. There in the dark living room, Kaki beside me, Lamarr's neighborhood and Tahija's eyes fresh in my memory, I felt it. A thrill of hope, a weary world rejoicing.

Chapter 3

I was in Lamarr's mom's house for three days and his cousin
nagged that I didn't eat and I was pregnant, and then one of his
uncles said that I was a runaway and his stepfather said I had to
leave so I called my grandmother Agnes and asked her to come
and get me. I stayed with her one week before I had a meeting
with Kaki and Kathryn about me staying there until I could get
something permanent. They agreed and I moved in right away.

My Life as I Know It

Every few minutes I opened the front door and leaned out to
check the street. It was early afternoon, sunny, not too cold. Miss
Tina, the Jehovah's Witness lady who owned the home on the
other side of the rooming house, was sitting on her front stoop
with her little granddaughter, Kesha. I asked how her teacher's
aide job was going and how her daughter's job was going and she
caught me up. When I told her about Tahija coming to live with us
she said, "Triplets! Well God bless her." She called her daughter to
the door and told her and her daughter said the same thing.

The old guys, Dominicans who lived in the rooming house above
the store, were outside, Poppi into some story that had them all laughing. Stan was on his corner across the intersection, night-dark face
deep in a furred hood, hand out for the change that would buy

27

him a bed for the night. Stan seemed to be mentally ill, but it was hard to tell since he was skittish as a deer. Across the street Nareyda stood in her open doorway feeding pigeons polenta from an iron skillet. White Stan was out too, making his way across the intersection with his cane and stroke-frozen side. Though he was not old, the drink had left his skin gray as the sidewalk, his brain slowed. Sober now, he lived in a group home that faced the park, a little cluster of damaged Caucasians, some of whom begged change in the days before their social security checks came in. Struggling to make it around a puddle by the curb, White Stan didn't see me, which was just as well. He'd have wanted to talk, and I was on a mission. My mission was to spot Tahija's grandmother's car and warn Kaki so she could get the vacuum put away in time.

The elementary school down the block let out and in the spill of children I missed them pulling in. Then I saw the blocky black silhouette, the head sheathed in clinging black, like a skin diver's.

"They're here!" I called into the house.

Kaki stowed the vacuum and came to stand beside me. Along with Miss Tina, the Stans, the old guys, and Nareyda we watched the odd pair approach. Leading the way was a stylish, light-skinned woman of sixty-five or so. She wore a flowered pantsuit and shoulder-length steel-gray dreadlocks tipped with bright beads. Looking about her as she strode, she seemed the exact opposite of the somber girl trailing behind her, eyes to the sidewalk. When they reached the steps we shook hands with the grandmother, Agnes Grealy, and invited them in.

Tahija took the rocker in the corner and sat there glum as a park bench in the rain. Agnes Grealy sat very straight and forward on the sofa, shaking her head a little as she spoke, exciting the beads. She had freckles on either side of her nose and a gap between her two front teeth that her smile treated like a diamond.

She hoped we knew that she felt awful, just awful, that just a few years back she'd sold the big house Tahija might have moved into at this time of need. But the problem was her new place, senior housing, had a restricted lease.

"No guests?" I said.

"Yes, and if I had known when I signed the lease...." But, she went on to say, she meant to help in every way possible. And she was grateful, very grateful for all we were considering doing for her granddaughter, who was a polite girl, she wanted us to know, and clean.

Tahija gripped the rocker's arms like she was in a dentist's chair, the color rising in her cheeks. As if she were the one moving in, the grandmother told us all about herself — the chain of beauty parlors she'd owned, the day care center, the divinity degree she was earning, her career as a model, and the woman lover she'd had in her thirties. They were still friends. We could meet her if we liked.

Tahija's grandmother seemed to want to impress us, which was only logical, given that she hoped we would take her granddaughter in, but I got the feeling she would have tried anyway, that she placed great importance on the opinions of people like Kaki and me, white people. Here she was our elder by nearly thirty years, a successful businesswoman dressed like she'd just stepped out of *Essence Senior,* us wearing beat running shoes, jeans, t-shirts, living in a house worth not much more than her car — and still, there she sat being deferential. It embarrassed and confused me. Was it something she'd learned, before learning began, back in East St. Louis? She told us about growing up there, how on festival days the St. Louis fire department barricaded the two bridges across the Mississippi, cutting off the black neighborhoods of East St. Louis.

Had *I* learned, before learning began, an attitude that drew out this attitude in her? Was I forever the little white girl on the festival side of the barricade, she forever the little colored girl with the beaded braids looking through it at me, wishing, maybe, as tragic Pecola in Toni Morrison's *The Bluest Eye* had wished, that she could be me, or complexioned like me, if that's what getting into her city's festivals took?

While this complicated interaction went on, Tahija rocked steadily, sniffling a little when her grandmother spoke of the pregnancy as a tragedy, Lamarr as a lost soul she didn't trust any further than she could throw him, and sure didn't want staying over, *sleeping* over. She promised that if we took Tahija in and let her stay after the babies were born, she, Agnes Grealy, would help in every way. Why, in the first few weeks she'd probably have to sleep right here on the sofa, so as to be up with the babies. If that was okay with us.

Sure it was okay with us, we said, thrilled at the thought of having such an interesting African American woman in our lives. I think we hoped she would give us what so many white people want, what they give themselves in Hollywood fantasies where hip brothers high-five geeky white co-workers and soulful maids/nurses/friends affirm well-to-do white women who will never return the favor: acceptance. We wanted her by her actions to say, *Yes, I may have been barred from my city's festivals, churches, restaurants, stores, and non-domestic jobs, I may have walked past a lake of raw sewage every day on my way to a ramshackle school, my mother in her old age may have screamed and trembled mistaking doctors for the Klansmen who hung her favorite uncle and her best friend's father from a Mississippi tree, but, heck, that's all past, I don't hold it against you. In fact I like you fine.*

Thomas Jefferson said the reason the framers didn't mention slavery in the Constitution was because they believed the ugly weed that had spread through the colonies like five-fingered Virginia creeper would soon die a natural death. Far from dying a natural death, however, slavery required a whole army and the bloodiest war ever just to lay it out flat, and even then it zombied back *Night of the Living Dead* style: sharecropping, chain gangs, lynchings, Jim Crow, Tulsa, anti-bussing riots, white flight, police terror. Perilous: for a man to hold up his head, for a woman to say no, for a child to hope.

Nobel laureate Toni Morrison's novel *Beloved* has in it a redeemed slave and redeeming preacher named Baby Suggs, sometimes called Baby Suggs, holy. At one point Baby Suggs, holy says to the main character, her daughter-in-law Sethe, "There is no bad luck in this world but whitefolks."* I didn't understand at the time what it meant to Tahija to be moving in with such bad-luck strangers. I got an idea a few years later, after she'd moved out and we were talking about our friend Barbara Parnell. Barbara was a hard-drinking, coal-black, big-hearted woman Tahija tried to mother, though Barbara was thirty years her senior. I'll always remember Tahija charging across the street and through the open door of Barbara's apartment shouting like some Old Testament prophet at four or five grown and tetchy women, "This ain't no speakeasy! This ain't no speakeasy!" Chased them right out the door.

So Tahija and I were recalling the winter Barbara's food stamps were cut to twenty dollars a month, and Sam Harpur, the neighborhood handyman and Barbara's live-in boyfriend, went off his meds and was arrested buying crack. He and Barbara had moved into an unheated house with no running water, and with Sam in prison Barbara deteriorated fast. Asthma, diabetes, high blood pressure — chronic poverty's common maladies — she had them all and they all got worse. Kaki and I tried to convince her to move in with us. Tahija did too, but Barbara wasn't having it. Saying she'd be too lonely with us, she moved in with an already overburdened childhood friend, endured one dialysis treatment deep in the bowels of Temple Hospital, and refused a second. As doctors made plans to amputate one of her legs Barbara went into a coma, to die a few days later.

"So why wouldn't she move in with us?" I asked Tahija. "And what did she mean, 'I'd be lonely'?"

"I guess that she felt more comfortable with people she'd known all her life," Tahija answered, diplomatically.

"Yeah, who let her drink and smoke," I said.

"Who didn't get into her business," she added, undiplomatically, a lot of history between us going into the emphasis she put on that word *business.*

---

*Page 105. Toni Morrison. *Beloved.* New York: Vintage International, 1987-04

Chapter 4

I think Kaki got involved because Lamarr asked her to. I think
Kathryn got involved because Kaki got involved in the beginning. Later I think the both of them stayed involved because
they cared about the well-being of Tahija, Lamarr and their new
family. I also think that they figured that they could help and
Tahija really needed the help and she wasn't getting the help
from anyone else.

from the interview*

"What's she doing now?" Kaki whispered.

"I don't know," I said, "cooking?"

We were on the sofa listening to Tahija back in the kitchen.
She had been in the house a week. I went over to the see-
through between the living room and the dining room and
leaned across Kaki's upright piano to see Tahija come in with a
sandwich on a plate. I ducked back to the couch.

"Looks like turkey on potato bread," I whispered. "No vegetables, not even a pickle. She's eating for four!"

"Shhh!"

---

*In the summer of 2003, Tahija wrote answers to a series of questions from the
author. All quotes described as "from the interview" are from that interview.
See Appendix for the full interview.

I got up again and said through the see-through, "There's fruit."

Tahija looked up at me, blinked. "I saw it, thank you."

For head covering today she wore just the blue kemar, pinned in back, leaving her neck showing. An oversized t-shirt of Lamarr's reached nearly to the knees of her gray sweat pants. Her small feet were bare.

I called from the sofa, "You want to eat dinner with us tonight?"

"Lamarr's bringing me shrimp and broccoli."

Sauce-smothered food from the depressed, elderly Cambodian couple desperate to sell their bullet-riddled take-out place.

"Oh okay," I said.

That night Kaki and I added the information we'd gained that day to out little store: Tahija Ellison liked shrimp, she liked broccoli, she liked the food to come from Lamarr; she got bad headaches; she talked on the phone, a lot; she had to have ice in any drink except milk, and she didn't much like milk, it gave her a stomachache; she took long showers; she hated her hair (she said); she dyed her hair (what color we weren't sure because we hadn't seen it yet); her idea of bed rest was walking rather than running up the stairs; her face brightened when Lamarr came in but she spoke as if she was angry with him, but when she was really angry with him she didn't speak, she breathed shallowly, loudly, ominously.

I'd be the cause of that loud breathing myself soon enough, but in those first weeks Tahija and I got along great. Co-dependent me was falling over myself trying to guess what she needed and get it for her, not yet knowing or going the further way of accepting that most of what she needed I could never get her, like her father out of prison and her mother off the streets, like Lamarr into a good job, like welfare reform rolled back to where you could at least weather a storm with it.

Against these great needs what was a bowl of fresh cherries? Something. Something given with love.

* * *

Tahija had mentioned a liking for cherries. I found them out on the Avenue. The Avenue had everything. On the corner nearest us stood Fine Fare, a four-aisle grocery store owned by a local Palestinian family. It had the basics, with a slant toward Spanish foods. No obnoxious ads over the PA system, no PA system, no scanners, no bored, sullen teenager dragging your stuff over scanners, no superdiscount card to remember to bring, no superdiscounts, no coupons, no double coupons, no parking lot to search for your car in. The checkout clerk was either the sad-eyed only sister of the owning family, tense with worry over her brother and parents trapped in Gaza, or a mother from the neighborhood. A kid you knew bagged for tips, and they delivered.

Past Fine Fare was a dense stretch of shops, most of them as narrow as the row houses, but deep and densely stocked: cards and balloons, baby furniture, pizza, jewelry, meat and poultry, prescriptions, closed youth center with overgrown lot, semi-dead hardware store, dollar store, shoe store, large pawn shop, larger dollar store, thriving hardware store, drug rehab apartments, pawn shop, lot store, Catholic Worker clinic, storefront *Iglesia de Christos,* Chinese takeout, check cashing, fruits and vegetables, tables of sunglasses and watches, tapes and CDs, shirts, hats, belts. And over it all the El tracks, a sort of roof to the corridor made by the storefronts. But you'd never mistake this for a mall. No chains (except Rite-Aid), no climate control, and the sounds, steady as fountain water: rap, Latin brass, cars and car alarms, busses squealing to loud air-braked stops and groaning up through their gears, people shout-talking, and seven times an hour during peak hours the in and outrush of the trains, with their vaguely British female voice warning, "Doors are opening, doors are opening, please step away from the doors" and "Doors are closing, doors are closing, please step away from the doors."

At Miss Suzie's fruit and vegetable stand, in between cassavas and big dirt-pocked yams, I spotted them — a quart of shining red cherries, cherries that remembered summer. I whisked them home, washed and arranged them stems-up in a clean white bowl, and proudly set my display on the end table beside the sofa where Tahija lay reading.

"Found some cherries," I said.

"Nice," she said, not looking up from a Norton Anthology she'd found on our plank and cinderblock bookshelf. She had on a t-shirt that showed a snapped-in-two rifle, and below the rifle, stretched by her belly like newsprint on silly-putty, the words "Stop the Violence."

"Well," I said, "I guess I'll head down to the lot."

"Okay," she said, as I left. "Don't let those kids run over top of you."

The lot was an open stretch of land in the middle of the block where three adjacent row houses had been demolished. The block committee had cleared it of rubble and spread three dump-truck loads of sludgy soil from the sanitation department. In the spring we'd plant grass. I had started a play group that met there. Children three or so to about twelve came and played the old competitive games like kick ball and dodge ball, and the newer cooperative ones like human knot or pass the hula-hoop around the circle, the goal being to fit your whole body through it without letting go of the hands you held.

By the time I said goodbye to Selim, Mariah, Daisy, Samadhi, Shyeena, Robert, Hakim, Porsha, Erica, the King sisters and all the rest it was dark. Tahija had gone up to her room, Lamarr's tape player was in its spot on the end of the bookshelf, and, washed and drying in the dish rack, leaned the bowl that had held the cherries.

When did I start loving Tahija? I'm not sure. I remember to the hour — laughter in the bath, a nap in the sun, a 2 AM bottle — when I started loving each of her children, and when my love for Lamarr became independent of my love for the brother he reminded me of. But with Tahija, love offered was always too much, and never enough. It was a promise you could never keep because it fell directly into a pit of broken promises, melded there in the heat of her anger into the two-edged sword that would cut her and the offerer both. But I don't put it all on her — the difficulty of loving her. I had a hard time knowing when to give and when to pull back, what was her need and what was my need.

I was meeting regularly at that time with a spiritual director named Marcelle Martin. Marcelle was a long-time friend of mine who lived about a mile away, having moved to North Philly at nearly the same time I did, and independently of me. We had been surprised to find that not only were we moving to the same city and the same neighborhood at the same time, but that the respective love interests we were moving in with were Quakers who had in turn known each other for years. This synchronicity made me value all the more the chance to work with Marcelle, who was helping me see the difficulty I had setting healthy boundaries.

I was a sand castle and the kids on the block were waves — rushing, lapping, crashing, persistent, ever-present. Too many of them had only one parent (or grandparent), and that one living either in the extreme want of welfare or in the sometimes less extreme want of low-paid work. Hardly anyone in my neighborhood who worked, it seemed, worked just forty hours. Whether it was cooking, waitressing, lawn service, telemarketing, retail, or the health care industry, the standard work week seemed to be more like sixty hours: six ten-hour days (or nights), with many people working more, and long commutes in the mix. So many adults working from can't-see to can't-see, or depressed, or drugged-out (legally or illegally), or sick, or in prison, and then welfare reform forcing the more stable mothers to work out of the neighborhood — it made a famine for the children.

So many kids needing stimulation, encouragement, tutoring, organized sports, hugs, a safe place to play, computer skills, and me with the white face, the ask-me posture, the she-can't-say-no sign stuck to my back. When Tahija moved in, need that had been a lockable door away was now down the hall brushing her teeth, or sobbing into the phone. It was a dwarf star with the gravity of a thousand suns. How could I come near without being absorbed entirely? How could I ever say no? But if I couldn't say no, what was my yes worth? As with the Soufflé Gran Marnier.

In between the kitchen at the back of the house and the living room in front was the room where we ate most of our meals. We called this the shamrock room, after the spindly shamrock plant that struggled for light on the windowsill. The refrigerator was there, because it wouldn't fit in the kitchen, as well as bookshelves of Kaki's AVP materials. In the corner stood a tall-backed chair — stretched beige fabric on a wooden frame that sort of bounced. This was fast becoming Tahija's chair. She'd sit in it, talking on the phone or to us, one leg folded up under her: her sociable-mood chair.

She sat in it now, bouncing and watching me read.

"I'm bored," she sighed.

I looked over the top of the book. "Umm, want to cook something?"

"We can."

I closed the paperback, got down Kaki's mother's Betty Crocker cookbook, and handed it to Tahija. She commenced to read the table of contents.

"About Custards. Baked or Cup Custard. Caramelized Custard. Caramel Custard. Coffee Chocolate Custard. Chocolate Crème Custard. Rich Custard. Fruit Juice Custard. About Sponge Custards."

Having slogged through custards, we turned to the grandly named Soufflé Gran Marnier. The recipe warned us to study the whole section on dessert soufflés "before attempting," then went on to name ingredients, like cream of tartar and Gran Marnier Liqueur, I just knew the Avenue that had everything was not going to have.

Tahija wrote out a list of ingredients and stuck it on the refrigerator, where it stayed. For months. Because I didn't know what Betty Crocker meant by "arrest the cooking." Because I was a tomgirl who'd been off building tree-forts when my mother was cooking. Because baking was something Tahija did with her grandmother and I hadn't moved all the way into the village yet.

Because I was already within the gravitational field of the dwarf star, saying Yes when I really meant, "Umm, I'd rather read."

Maybe everything I did for Tahija after that, including learning how to say No and stick to a Yes, was all Soufflé Gran Marnier.

"See that truck?" Tahija stood at the front window massaging her lower back. I went and stood beside her. A waterworks truck idled at the nearest corner.

"Working on the sewage system again," I said

"It's been there all day," Tahija said. "That's not a repair truck. They're undercover."

"You been watching too much TV."

"TV been watching these streets! Wait, you'll see. That's drug squad setting up for a raid down at Lupita's or someplace. Or FBI, could be FBI."

"Why would the FBI be worrying about little old Hancock Street?"

"Remember Move?" she said. "The police took out a whole little old street that time, now didn't they?"*

Two workers stood beside the manhole smoking and talking.

"Could be DHS," Tahija said quietly.

DHS — the Department of Human Services, the state agency that investigated claims of child abuse and neglect and sometimes took children into custody. We'd meet DHS soon enough, but in a sense this was my first meeting — through Tahija's eyes.

"You think they're watching us?" I said.

"Watching *some*body."

A man came out of the truck with a wrench and went down into the manhole.

---

*Move is a controversial back-to-nature, political-religious group. A 1978 police attempt to evict them from a West Philadelphia house erupted in gunfire that resulted in one police death. Nine Move members were convicted of murder. In 1985, a police standoff with the group ended when police dropped a bomb from a helicopter. Eleven Move members were killed, including five children. The fire that resulted burned out of control, destroying all sixty-one homes on the block.

"They're not getting these three," she said. "Me and Lamarr, we'll drive straight to Colorado, to my dad's."

"I thought your dad was in prison?"

"My stepdad Gary's the only dad I ever knew growing up; he's in Colorado, an electrician."

I watched the idling truck awhile longer, breathing in the exhaust that reached us through the leaky windows, wondering: was Tahija paranoid, or street smart? Were the two different stages of the same thing? I didn't know. But standing beside her at the window my heart knit itself around a commitment: Whatever this girl felt she had to do to keep her triplets, I was going to help her do it.

I came downstairs to find a bay of bright sails spread out across the living room: Tahija with three Muslim friends sewing new robes, which were called outergarments. Tahija had spread her old black outergarment over a bright length of blue and gold striped cloth and was cutting along its outline, using the old as a pattern for the new.

"This don't look like bed rest," I said.

Her friends looked up nervously, but when she laughed, laughed too.

"This is Taleah," Tahija said.

"Hi."

"And Taheera."

"How you doin'."

"And Latangela."

"Welcome."

"Pinky's in the kitchen."

Except for Pinky, all of these friends were still narrow-hipped and giggly. Maybe that's why I didn't see much of them after the triplets came. They went back to the shallows between girlhood and womanhood while Tahija stroked hard for open ocean.

When Tahija, reaching for a scissors, made a face and held her belly, I ran to her.

"You need some water?" I ran for water without waiting for an answer.

"You forgot the ice," she said, handing me the cup back. I went for ice, causing some serious head shaking and mm-mming among the Ta-La people. Tahija can complain that I tried to spoil her kids, but she can't say I didn't try to spoil her first. And anyway, she was supposed to be on bed rest, not doing calisthenic sewing all over the livingroom floor. She was only six months but where triplets are concerned, we'd soon find out, six months is more like eight, because seven is term.

Those babies were coming and they were coming soon. But not before their every-day-more-crowded womb was draped in vertical stripes of blue and gold.

Chapter 5

"We're together."

Lamarr Stevens

I may not have deserved it, but I got it. Age, race, educated speech (as needed) — these gave me respect and privilege Lamarr and Tahija had no chance at. I could dress in jeans and sweatshirt, no-name sneakers, hair a mop, while they wore their best and spent hours on their heads, and still, at the clinic or the welfare office, in stores, I'd be spoken to first, deferred to, trusted, respected. What could I do with this privilege but try to hold it over them like an umbrella as the rain of disapproval poured down? Unwed mother, unemployed father, teenage parents headed for welfare ... accurate labels, maybe, but looked at another way this all looked, well, another way. I thought of Biblical matriarchs like Sarai and Hagar for whom birth was a miracle; of agrarian societies that worshiped fertility; and of hunting tribes, in which the mother of many sons was greatly honored. In any of those times and places a young mother bearing triplets would have been a cause for celebration. And imagine, in modern America, a middle-class couple trying everything, until one thing, a new fertility drug or a second-mortgage operation works — too well! But how, say the happy parents, can there be a "too well?" Word goes out, congratulations and offers of help pour in. Every visit to the doctor is like a celebrity appearance. Have the names been chosen? Will you add an extension onto the house? Does your husband's company provide paternity leave?

"Tanya Ellison," the receptionist called out.

"Ta-*hee*-ja," Tahija corrected her, going to the window.

"Whatever. Fill these out."

Lamarr, Tahija, and I were sitting in molded plastic chairs in Temple Hospital's high-risk maternity clinic. In front of us was a poster that read "Never, Never, Never Shake a Baby." The *nevers* were in a column, each *never* bigger than the next, and "Shake a Baby" was squiggly, as if *it* had been shaken.

We'd been in the waiting room for several hours. People-watching helped pass the time.

"That's a weave," Tahija whispered, looking up from the forms. "She think people can't see that's a weave? *Come* on now." Then a few minutes later, "Ew, she better not sit her nasty self down here."

A thin woman in a dirty gray raincoat and scuffed, laceless shoes had entered, bringing a smell of the subway stairwells with her. She took the chair nearest the door and gazed straight ahead. I thought of Sally Washington, a friend of mine who'd been strung out on the street, once, and had recovered — both sobriety and dignity. This woman could too.

The receptionist put on a video: uncrowded waiting room, potted ficus tree, Monet water lilies on the wall, thirty-something blonde woman ushered into an examining room where an unhurried doctor answers her questions.

I picked up a pamphlet. North Philadelphia, it read, had one of the highest infant mortality rates in the country, with 16.7 deaths per 1,000 live births in 1991, down from a high of 23.1 in 1989 (when the national rate had been 8.9 deaths per 1000).*The woman on the video told the doctor she was excited, but a little nervous.

---

*From a Temple University School of Medicine grant report, which also points out that at the time of the report, 1991, not one private obstetrician practiced in the area.

What were some of the causes of this high infant mortality rate? There was a bulleted list.

- Chronic hypertension
- Undetected diabetes
- Inadequate prenatal care
- Poor maternal nutrition
- Preterm delivery
- Maternal drug and alcohol addiction
- Fetal drug and alcohol addiction

Except for addictions, Tahija had or soon would have each of these conditions. Her diabetes would be mistaken for gestational diabetes and go dangerously undiagnosed for five years, despite typical symptoms. She also suffered from polycystic ovarian syndrome — a sometimes painful condition that caused hemorrhaging and might interfere with future pregnancies.

"That's some corny shit," said the woman with the alleged weave.

"Right?" Tahija agreed. *Corny,* I'd learned from the kids on the block, meant white, sort of, not white skin per se but a patronizing manner or general lack of style. White people weren't seen as inherently corny, in the way, say, that young black men on the New Jersey Turnpike might be seen as inherently criminal, but the margin of error was very small. I knew from telling stories at the lot that a sentimental plot turn or one "okeydokey" could quash the attention of ten engrossed children. And they *would* let you know.

The video ended and another came on. How to bathe a (pink) baby. Was improper infant bathing on the bulleted list of the causes of high infant mortality in North Philadelphia? It was not.

"Like I haven't washed a baby," Tahija said.

"Maybe you didn't do it co-rec-tally," Lamarr said.

"Shut up," Tahija said.

"You shut up."

"*You* shut up."

"Ya'll *two* shut up," I said, experimenting.

"How you gonna tell us 'shut up'?" Lamarr said.

"Like she just did," Tahija told him.

"Shut up," he said.

"You shut up."

Finally they called us. Like patients everywhere who've graduated to the examining room we assumed the wait was nearly over. Wrong. Tahija sat on the edge of the examining table swinging her legs, the silver stirrups like big question marks.

Did she want me there? Did she miss her mother? Where *was* her mother? Tahija's grandmother, the only family member Kaki and I had met so far, had nothing good to say about this missing mother. Tahija did not defend her or offer details. We knew only that she was somewhere in Philadelphia, and that Tahija, born Shannon, was the oldest of her five children.

Lamarr pulled a pair of latex gloves from a box on the counter. "Me and my brothers used to swipe these all the time." He puckered the wrist of one and blew it up. "Makes a good balloon. Or — " he spun with a flourish and filled it at the sink, "a handy-dandy squirt gun."

"Don't aim that thing at me!" Tahija screeched when he aimed it at her.

Just then the doctor came in. He was a resident, very young, with a smooth baby face and winning smile. I realized that except for cops and the guys who lined up outside the methadone clinic, I hadn't seen a young white man in weeks. How relaxed he was, how self-assured.

Poking out from his hospital blues were red clogs. I caught Tahija's eye and mouthed it. "Corny." Under cover of our laughter, Lamarr decanted his squirt glove.

After a brief examination, the resident upgraded us to the supervising physician down the hall, a fiftyish black man sitting behind a desk. He introduced himself as Dr. Hughes and offered Tahija a chair. Three residents from three different continents stood along the wall observing. Red clogs handed Dr. Hughes a folder. The older man glanced at it before turning a stern gaze on Tahija.

"Have you been following strict bed rest?"

"Trying to," Tahija answered.

He looked me over. "This is your social worker?"

"No," Tahija said, "she's … "

"A friend," I put in. "We live in the same house."

He considered this, studied Lamarr (who squirmed like he was about to get busted for all that filched latex), and then addressed us as if we were before him in a lecture hall.

"The danger of septic poisoning is great. If one of the fetuses should die in utero, the remaining two, although in separate embryonic sacs, would be at great risk. For this reason, the fetal hearts must be monitored around the clock. Which means hospital bed rest, starting at the twenty-fourth week."

"She's already twenty-one weeks!" Lamarr said, his tone reminding me that he had fainted, Tahija told us, passed out cold when the ultrasound showed three.

"Twenty-one and two days," Tahija corrected.

"What happened to nine months?" I asked, feeling a little faint myself.

"We don't speak in terms of *months* at this point," Dr. Hughes told me. "Months, after all, vary in length." He paused to let the gravity of my error sink in. "For triplets, you'll be doing very well, young lady, if you can keep them in the womb twenty-eight weeks. No stress, no exertion, bed rest, and good diet."

I asked him to define "good diet," so I could hear back what I'd been saying all along, thank you.

"And of course you know delivery is likely to be by c-section."

I looked at Tahija. Clearly she had not known it. The little girl who'd started the car and rolled out into traffic was heading fast for the freeway, no turning back.

We were a more somber group riding the elevator down to the lobby. Lamarr stopped at the security desk to sign us out while Tahija and I continued.

"Excuse me," I heard, then more firmly, from behind, "*Excuse me.*"

We turned. It was the security guard, an older man with constellations of pinpoint moles beneath his eyes.

"Sign out please."

"I signed her out already," Lamarr told him. Confused look. "We're together."

We're together. It echoed back from some hillside of intuition within me. It felt, as Quakers say, rightly ordered.

Chapter 6

That year in sixth grade I had a real chip on my shoulder. I had questions for everyone and everything. I remember asking a guy with a Kufi on in the hallway at school a bunch of questions [about Islam] and he answered them, I don't know why. I guess it was God's way of stepping in and just letting me know he was seeing everything and I wasn't alone, but I didn't realize it was a sign until the next year. I was walking up the back hallway and I see my cousin fighting some boys and I thought they were serious and I got into it with one of the guys named Lamarr. A few days later the guy Lamarr asked me if I would be his girlfriend. At first me and my cousin made a pact that I would go with him and she would go with his friend but we never told them that was why we said yes. We got together on October 28th and I remember that because it was exactly two weeks before my birthday, which is November 8th. After awhile my cousin and her boyfriend broke up so without thinking I broke up with Lamarr. I thought it wouldn't matter because I thought we could still be friends but I actually had feelings for him. I thought they would go away but they didn't. A few months later I asked him whatever happened to that guy with the Kufi, and he said, "Are you serious?" I said, "Yes." He said, "That was me." Now you see we were meant to be.

One day Lamarr seen me drinking. He grabbed my drink and threw it away. That same day he seen me smoking and he threw my whole pack of cigarettes in the middle of Broad Street. I was so mad. I bought another pack and I hid them thinking that he wouldn't find them, but he caught me taking it out and threw that pack away and after that I could have easily got another pack, but I didn't, I quit.

My Life as I Know It

After Tahija had been with us about a month, Lamarr's family was evicted. He and his twin brothers moved into their older sister's basement. She lived a short bus ride from us. Lamarr came nearly every day, bringing food for Tahija and lifting her spirits. He was considerate and friendly, often helping with projects around the house, but three things kept us from letting him move in, as he said he wanted to do.

First was the remarkable amount of time he spent in the bathroom, of which there was only one. It became Lamarr's room, as in, "Have you seen my glasses?" "Yeah, up in Lamarr's room." Looming much larger than the bathroom issue was the grandmother issue. Agnes Grealy did not want Lamarr and Tahija "shacking up." She'd have been happiest if he was out of the picture altogether. Not realizing how soon she'd be out of the picture (*sometimey,* Lamarr called her), we respected her wishes.

Finally, we didn't trust him. If you didn't keep your guard up, he'd be — as Kaki had warned me — playing you like a banjo. Job interviews, for example. He kept getting them, kept borrowing money for tokens or a TransPass, but when we asked about the interviews we'd invested in the answers were suspiciously elaborate.

Downtown one day, Kaki and I visited a shoe store where Lamarr was supposed to be working. When we asked to see him, the manager told us he'd quit. Kaki was hotter than fish grease, as Tahija would say.

"Okay, here's what happened," Lamarr started.

We were sitting around the dining room table, reflected in the floor-to-ceiling mirror Kaki always told people had been put in, with the chandelier and security bars, by the previous owners. Tahija was upstairs.

"I went back into the stockroom, to get some size-eight loafers. They're down low, right?, so I sit on a crate, and suddenly, I just fall asleep."

"You just fall asleep," Kaki said. "Let me get this straight." (Always an ominous phrase). "You finally find a full-time job, you're a month away from being the head of a family of five, five — "

"Four weeks away," I said.

Kaki looked at me. "Four weeks *is* a month."

"Not really."

"That's right," Lamarr joined in, spying a hole in the defensive line, "Dr. Hughes, he told us — "

"Whatever!" Kaki said (angry, but not corny). "You fell asleep. *In* the stockroom, *on* your third day of work. Had you been out running the streets with your friends all night?"

"His so-called friends," we heard: Tahija at the top of the stairs with Purrsilla the tricolor cat in her lap.

"He's been here mostly," I said. Kaki looked at me without quite as much love, I must say, as I had grown used to expecting.

"I think my sickle cell's acting up," Lamarr said, hanging his head, eyebrows humble as caterpillars.

Lamarr's mother had told Kaki Lamarr had the sickle-cell anemia trait, not the disease. On the other hand, Kaki had seen his blood in the bathroom, seen how he crashed sometimes, weak and disoriented. Later he'd be diagnosed with adult-onset diabetes, which ran in, or, more aptly, devastated his family. Three stomach ulcers turned up as well.

"So you quit because you fell asleep?"

"No, because these two clerks who found me wanna get smart, calling me lazy. I was about to bust somebody in the mouth."

"And all the AVP workshops you've taken," Kaki said. "I guess you can talk the talk — "

"But he can't walk the walk," Tahija finished it.

"You might as well come on down here, miss bed rest," I called up to her.

"Well if you think I'm buying another Transpass for another job search," Kaki said, keeping us on point, "you've got another think coming, Buster."

"Buster?" I said to her that night, when we were alone in my third-floor room.

"Yes Buster, Missy, and I don't appreciate your undermining me."

We were sitting on an old sofa that faced the room's two windows, which looked out on the apartment building across the street. To the left, across a busy intersection, was the park, and to the right, beyond the flat acres of rooftops, the bright arch of the Ben Franklin Bridge.

I asked her to consider the many mistakes a middle class sixteen-year-old could make and still count on basic support. I told her about working as dorm director at a private college: the vacations, the cars, the electronic toys, aggressive cultivation of any suspected talent. "And if someone stumbles — major resource activation. Those kids are hothouse orchids, Lamarr's a dandelion in a sidewalk crack."

"But those kids aren't necessarily happy."

"Well then that's on them," I said, remembering a few particularly gloaty ones.

"Listen to you," she said, "getting all ghetto."

"But I'll never say 'motherfucker.' "

"You just said 'motherfucker,' " she said.

"So did you."

"You said it first."

"Shut up," I practiced.

She tried, but couldn't say it back. "I was taught it's, well, trashy."

"As in white trash?" I asked.

"I suppose that's what my parents didn't want us to sound like."

I thought about that, about who I wanted to sound like, and not sound like; about where I'd come from and who I was. At the heart of my family was a gigantic shut up: secrets and shame, shame about being poor, being Irish, Scottish, Catholic, being servants; shame about the alcoholism and incest running through the generations like a toxic river, shame that made white privilege and the power it gave us look like a no-money-down-no-interest deal not to be passed up.

By adapting my speech and helping out where I could, I hoped to be accepted, included, made finally to feel worthwhile. But no one can make us feel worthwhile, and if our "help" comes with that expectation it's no help at all. The path outward to a wider cultural perspective and real usefulness goes inward first. For me that path led back to the strengths and weaknesses of my family of origin, and to my working-class roots. The longer I lived in North Philly, the more the Sweet Honey in the Rock lyric, composed by Bernice Johnson Reagon, rang true for me

> We all, every one of us,
> has to go home.
> Some of us were born
> on the bottom.
> We grew up
> from the bottom.
> And then we declared
> we would never return
> to the bottom.
> But we all, every one of us
> has to come home.

By the long or the short route, through the ghetto of the one-time national capital or the ghetto of the heart, we have to go home.

One of Lamarr and Tahija's favorite movies is *Sister Act II*. It became one of mine too after the four of us watched it together in the living room. In *Sister Act I*, a Las Vegas lounge singer played by Whoopie Goldberg hides out from the mob in a convent. Disguised as one of the sisters, she transforms their pitiful choir into a phenomenon, going on in the sequel to lead the school's underdog chorus to a first-place showing in a big competition (meanwhile saving the school and revitalizing the neighborhood). At the finale concert, a mother who had forced her daughter (played by Lauryn Hill) to quit the chorus storms in, only to find the audience in hushed thrall: her daughter's solo.

53

Teachers who inspire, parents who finally wake up to our gifts — isn't that what we all want, what so few, poor or rich, have? In middle school Lamarr had set his sights on the prestigious Philadelphia High School for the Performing Arts. He took the written tests, sang an audition, and was accepted. Only the paperwork remained. It was never turned in.

Kaki believed that his parents' addictions and inability to consistently support him had as much to do with the racist oppression they and their ancestors had endured as with personal failings. It was therefore her responsibility, she believed, to make up for some of what Lamarr lacked. Did she have a need to meet his needs? Did I? And was that okay, a mutual need? The question troubled me. But Lamarr, like a hitchhiker in a hailstorm, wasn't asking questions.

We didn't let him move in. Much of the time he was in the house anyway. His jeans and t-shirts hung from the backyard clothesline, the yellow corn oil bucket he kept used oil in became a fixture on the kitchen windowsill, and his tape player maintained its place on the bookshelf. And now and then, from shower or backyard, drifted a curl of song so sweet, so perfectly pitched, we who heard grew still … to better hear: what might have been, what might yet be.

Lamarr and I were eating fettuccini Alfredo, his favorite of the things I cooked (but there would be a search for concealed vegetables). He was talking about potatoes, about all the ways he had found to cook them when his brothers were left in his care.

"You know potatoes contain all the vitamins and nutrients the body needs," he told me. "You could live on nothing but potatoes for years and be fine."

"To be sure," I said (my grandparents' brogue), "if not fer taties where would we be?"

To be sure, he was winning my heart. Now he might have guessed I was Irish, but Lamarr had no way of knowing that the younger brother he reminded me of more and more every day had himself kissed the Blarney Stone. Joey could rub two facts together and get expertise. To be fair, both of them were genuinely knowledgeable on certain subjects, in Lamarr's case cars, reptiles, films (horror especially) and, as I was about to find out, handguns. We were interrupted by what I took to be the sound of a car backfiring. Lamarr put his fork down and tilted his head. It came again.

"Magnum .44," he said.

"What, you can tell from here?"

"Sure."

I thought he was fronting — trying to impress me with his gangsta' guise.

"How come I hear so much gunfire," I asked him, "but never anyone, you know, scream?"

"Because the sound of a gun firing travels further than a scream. And anyway," he spooled pasta onto his fork, "dude getting shot don't always have time to scream."

I would meet the triplets' two grandmothers, their maternal great-grandmother, and maternal great-great-grandmother. Of their deceased paternal great-grandmother I heard a great deal. But grandfathers and great-grandfathers, except for Tahija's stepfather in Colorado, I did not meet.

In Ireland, when the English took the land, farmers couldn't feed their families. Men couldn't feel they were men. I don't know if the drinking and the sexual predation started then. I suspect they did. I suspect some of the men who couldn't feel they were men became monsters, and the boys who grew up with monsters for fathers or no fathers at all had a harder time becoming good men, and the daughters and wives had a harder time loving them, so that the men had a harder time healing. And so it spiraled, with emigration, especially under the duress of extreme poverty, of famine itself, a shock from which families recovered but slowly.

This was the history I knew and wrestled with. I didn't know all the facts of Lamarr's family history, or Tahija's, but I knew the facts of American history, and had read, listened, and felt enough to begin to understand a little of what it means to be black in these United States. But what it means to be a poor young black man in these United States I have come to understand that no one, unless it is the black woman who loves him, can ever fully understand.

I never got so I could identify the make and caliber of a gun by the sound it made firing, but my hearing did improve to the point where I could hear the scream. I could hear it, as the Irish poet Yeats wrote of waves lapping a distant shore, "In the deep heart's core."

We were playing Pictionary — Tahija and me against Lamarr and Kaki. Lamarr was telling us how he and some friends had been hanging out one summer at a store on the corner of Woodstock and Diamond, not far from where we had dropped them off the day we met Tahija. A drug dealer named Monk came regularly to this corner to collect money and re-supply his sellers, who were all friends or cousins of Lamarr.

"If you lived around here you'd probably know about Monk," Lamarr said.

"We do live around here," Kaki said.

"I mean really lived around here," Lamarr said.

"He means if you grew up around here," Tahija said.

"That's not what I mean," Lamarr said, voice going all high.

"He means we here but we not poor and black here," I said.

"Even if we can talk like it," Kaki said

"Who we? You can't talk like it," I said.

"I can too," she said.

"You may think you can but —"

"All right you two, can it!" said Tahija.

"Can it?" Lamarr said.

"Just tell the story!" Tahija said. "So the dealer pulls up ..."

"One of Monk's sellers, Dave, had been hustling him, so one day Monk showed up to handle the situation. But Dave, man, he had just snorted some angel dust. When Monk asks for his money Dave going to say 'Fuck you,' and laugh. It could be he didn't realize what was happening. That's what some said. I think he just didn't care. What's happening is the dude is getting out the car, walking around to the trunk, and taking out a double-barrel shotgun."

Tahija turned the game's hourglass over and leaned her chin on her stacked fists, watching it.

"Did you and your friends run away?" I asked.

"We ran a little ways and turned around," Lamarr said. "It was a shot gun. By the time he reloaded we would have been on him like white on rice. Anyway, he wanted Dave, Dave was being disrespectful." Though the sand hadn't run out, Tahija turned the glass over. "Monk walked up to Dave, pressed the shotgun muzzle to his belly, and fired twice. Dave's skinny, always was. The blast cuts him in half."

That wasn't the first gun death Lamarr witnessed, nor was it the second, or the third. The first was when he was four. His father came for him in the night, selected him from a bed where he lay sleeping with his brothers and a cousin, and carried him still in his night-clothes out into the night and down a few doors to a bar, where he sat him on a bar stool, walked to a man sitting nearby, drew a handgun and shot the man in the head.

Lamarr didn't tell, when he told me that story, what the gun's bullets did inside the victim. He told me what his father did. What his father did was scoop him up off the bar stool and carry him home.

I imagined Lamarr watching the pavement he played on in the daytime going by under him, voices from the bar receding, no voice, no explanation coming from his father. Maybe the absence of an explanation was the explanation: violence — sudden, meaningless, lethal — surrounds us.

"Can't no Freddy Krueger shit scare me," Lamarr has said. He means the white guy with knives for fingers from the *Nightmare on Elm Street* horror-movie series, and all the other freakish killers: Jason, Chucky, the ghoul mobs in *Night of the Living Dead*. He loves those movies. He loves ideas, intricate plots, and character development too, but sometimes those horror movies just snatch him and he sits in some pit of his psyche staring at a screen, waiting, I think, for the unscreamed screams to break from him at last.

Does Lamarr use the violence he's witnessed and experienced as an excuse? Yes he does. Don't you have your own excuses, evasions, self-deceptions? I do; have been, as Whitman put it, "wayward, vain, greedy, shallow, sly, the wolf, the snake, the hog not wanting in me;

refusals, hates, postponements, meanness, laziness, none of these wanting."* Has the violence he witnessed and experienced damaged him? Yes it has. Beyond repair? That's between him and his God. But I sure don't mean to get in the way by heaping him with blame, for I have seen in myself the ugly habit of scapegoating, and know it is in the psyches of many other whitefolks, and can imagine that, collectively, it might be experienced by the scapegoated as a force of nature. There's a lot of catching up to do, and not everyone can do it on their own. They sure didn't get that far behind on their own. Martin Luther King Jr. put it this way: "It is obvious that if a man is entered at the starting line in a race three hundred years after another man, the first would have to perform some impossible feat in order to catch up with his fellow runner."

Yes Lamarr makes excuses, evades responsibility, maddeningly so, but he's walking into a Chicago winter wind every day, spring, summer and fall. Until you have walked a mile in his shoes ...

When Lamarr tells the triplets about his gangsta' days (may they be over), I hope he doesn't underreport the terror part, like the time when he sat for three days and nights at the top of a staircase waiting for someone to come kill him, his trigger finger so fear-frozen it didn't straighten out for a week. The triplets were almost three then and had moved out some time before. Tahija brought them back for this crisis. They sat beside her on the couch serious as judges, watching with her out the window, listening with her across the city blocks for the shot that would end their father's vigil, one way or the other.

I remember Cosby was on, an episode from when Rudy was little. I remember the super-clean treads on the bottoms of their identical sneakers, and the three versions of mature worry on their faces, each face a variation on the theme Lamarr Stevens.

---

*From "Crossing Brooklyn Ferry" by Walt Whitman

Chapter 7

If you have quadruplets the city gives you a *house,* and they
want to act like my little bit of food stamps is coming out their
own pocket? That doesn't make any sense.

Tahija Ellison, in conversation

We were in the kitchen making dinner. Tahija and Kaki had
just come from one of their visits to the welfare office. Finally
Tahija had gotten into the health care system and been awarded
$248 a month in cash benefits, plus WIC coupons that would pro-
vide formula, milk, cheese, juice, and cereal for the first five years.
She had, however, been refused food stamps because our household income was too high.

"If you have quadruplets the city gives you a *house,* and they
want to act like my little bit of food stamps is coming out their
own pocket? That doesn't make any sense."

"The caseworker, a Mrs. Peterson, very nice woman," Kaki said,
"explained to me that they always count household income in
figuring the food stamp award."

"And if you say it's not shared, they assume you're lying?" I
asked, pushing chopped onion into a pan.

"Or they assume that if there's a real need, it *will* be shared."

And of course people did share, which is what made cuts in any antipoverty program hard on everyone in the community, even those who received no assistance.When they had their own place Lamarr and Tahija would share generously with neighbors in need, too generously Kaki and I sometimes thought, considering how little they had, but that was the way, that was *Ujima,** collective work and responsibility.You didn't say no to the same ones you'd be going to in your own time of need; didn't act so as to earn the label that went so often with white — *greedy.*

For the purposes of applying for benefits, Tahija had to look like an insular, independent household. That night she began a letter-writing campaign to the state capital arguing that we were not family and as such our incomes should not be counted in computing her benefits. If I had an impulse to suggest that we let the household income feed us all, that we take this as an opportunity to venture into becoming some kind of family, I did not express it, partly because the house and most of its income at that point were Kaki's. (Without a master's degree I couldn't teach at the community college in Philly. I'd started the paperwork to get on as a substitute in the public schools, but for the time being all I could find was a holiday season job demonstrating baby grand player pianos.) Even if I had suggested that Tahija forgo welfare and let us support her until Lamarr could, I doubt she would have agreed. The three of us had fun together, and I think she enjoyed our attention — an interlude of adolescence — but Tahija for some time now had been making choices that propelled her into adulthood, and independence.

Of course, she was lining up for dependence on the system, but from the outside it didn't look that bad. She'd heard of people with three children getting as much as a thousand a month (the most she'd ever get was five-hundred). You were called in for a reassessment every six months (under welfare reform it turned out to be every two to three months, with little notice), and if

---

*Ujima is a Swahili word used to designate the third day of Kwanzaa.

you could get into Section 8 housing (ten-year waiting list) you could get by, sort of. And no parents or other nagging adults in your face with, *Have you eaten any fruit today?* and *Maybe if you went to bed earlier* and *Who left this empty mayonnaise jar in the fridge?* Tahija had been acting grown so long there was no calling her back. She was like a pole-vaulter who'd already planted her pole and left the ground.

Or was I just telling myself that? Did she look at us before she leapt, wondering, *Can I trust these two? If I give up control, will they give back unconditional love?* I lie awake nights sometimes wondering if her being refused food stamps was a fork in the road, and where the fork we didn't take might have led us. Did we fail to fully commit?

Tahija didn't explicitly ask for more commitment. Like Lamarr, she accepted what was offered while proceeding along her own path as she saw fit. If the city gave the mothers of quadruplets a house, they were sure going to give this soon-to-be mother of triplets her due. So she kept writing letters, taking as her model the unjustly imprisoned star of her favorite movie, *Shawshank Redemption*. He bombards the state with written requests for library books. Tahija wrote only a few letters (*long* ones), but in the end the state cried uncle. She was awarded almost two-hundred a month in food stamps.

But we wouldn't let her buy a freezer from the used appliance place on the Avenue, which ticked her off and made her all the more eager for her own house, with her own electric bill, which would grow soon enough into an income-devouring monster. But that came later, when she was straight up in the air with her vaulting pole bent like a strung bow under the weight of three three-year-olds — one short of a free house.

Kaki called up the stairs for us all to come down for *Imani*, the last day of Kwanzaa.

I had helped her polish the spiraling hat rack of a candle holder we'd found in the basement, and had shopped on the

Avenue for gifts, but when it came down to it, the gathering felt awkward — like a mandatory house meeting with Faith at the top of the agenda. That's what Imani means in Swahili — Faith "in our people, our parents, our teachers, our leaders and the righteousness of our struggle." So what was I doing lighting the uppermost candle on our makeshift kinara (a real one looks more like a menorah, with the candles abreast)? The same thing I was doing by plugging in the three-foot artificial Christmas tree that sat on the table between the two windows: inviting light into the house at this darkest time of the year.

And we needed it. More uncomfortable every day, Tahija seemed to have crashed emotionally. Lamarr hadn't found a job yet. The Lutheran agency she'd gone to after learning she was pregnant had been trying to place her in a home for unwed mothers. The only one with services for a fifteen-year-old mother of triplets, however, was far outside the city, beyond the reach of mass transportation and, therefore, of Lamarr.

Tahija wasn't having it, and with her blood pressure where it was and Dr. Hughes's warnings in mind, we dared not push her to reconsider. It scared us though: agencies turning her down because they didn't have enough services. What services did we have?

Kaki called again and finally Tahija came slowly down the stairs, supporting her round, high belly with both hands. Without a glance at the Kinara she fell into a chair at the dining room table and dropped her head onto her folded arms.

"Sam did the windows," Kaki said. Sam Harpur had a flare for design. "A little garland, two strings of lights and … voilà!"

"Lock a crackhead in a room with a paper bag and two safety pins," Tahija said hoarsely, not lifting her head, "and he'll come out with something he can sell."

It would take power tools sprouting wings for us to figure it out, but Tahija knew right off Sam was smoking up most of his earnings. She knew a good deal that we didn't, and whether it was the weight of what she knew, or the kicking inside her, or her hormones, she could not seem to lift her head off the table.

Her hair was uncovered tonight, thick reddish braids like so many curved handles on her head, roots glistening in the light of the chandelier.

Kaki sat on the couch and began to read aloud from a library book about Kwanzaa. Tahija groaned, definitely not feeling it. Until Lamarr arrived.

"Hey," she said, lifting her head a little.

What he said next, though, raised her head all the way. He had a job. He'd already worked his first shift. He liked it.

"Doing what?" Kaki said. "Tell us!"

"Telemarketing. Tahija's cousin Mia told me they were hiring and I went this morning, and they were." He set his tape player on the bookshelf and stood in the middle of the small living room, still going coatless I noticed. "But I don't want to give up my music."

"Of course not. It's a day job," I said. "Like me, I'm a writer, but I have a day job."

He smirked at my day job, which wasn't very nice of him, considering I was trying to turn his fifty-cent Tastykake into homemade pie. His pay was $2.33 an hour (don't *ask* about benefits) and three dollars per sale. They gave you a day of training; after that if you didn't make two sales the first hour they sent you home, and better hope you had bus fare because you were way out in the no friendly face, no corner store, big houses behind big lawns suburbs now. Dogs and cops — a bad neighborhood.

But Lamarr had made *four* sales his first hour. He memorized the pitch then adapted it to his audience. Improvisational telemarketing.

"A born salesman," I said. "From this you can move on to appliances, cars, real estate, who knows?"

Kaki was so pleased they went straightaway to the big discount clothes store for Kwanzaa-gift dress shirts so he could meet the dress code. And the next time a telemarketer rang, I couldn't help noticing how young the caller sounded, couldn't help wondering if he was wearing a new shirt.

* * *

We kept remixing the paint, but no matter what we tried, the blue of the trim came out too light, *powder* blue, and the pastel yellow of the walls not pastel at all.

"Schoolbus-yellow," Kaki said, standing with Sam in the middle of the room, which was empty but for an opened stepladder and a few odd pieces of sheetrock.

"Like a child's room," I said.

"Or a *nursery.*"

The room was to be Kaki's new study, refinished with Christmas present money from her mother. Sam Harpur had been hanging new walls and windows, me assisting (which meant handing him stuff, trying to keep up as he strode to the hardware store on the Avenue for materials, making him lunch, and listening to his stories of back in the day).

Kaki walked to the alcove. At the back of the room, this was a loveseat-long space surrounded by windows — the reading nook she'd always wanted. She loved to read, but the light was never just right.

"I know a rug I can sell you," Sam said, "nice Oriental rug, dark — tone that yellow right down."

"I bought the house for this room."

"It's a nice room," I said.

Like the smell of popcorn, an unasked question hung in the air. Tahija was starting her twenty-third week. Any day now at the first hint of labor she'd be going into the hospital, and a month or so after coming out with three babies — three baby boys, the latest ultrasound showed. Where were they going to come out to? Lamarr had received his first paycheck from the telemarketing job but hadn't been able to cash it because he had no ID to show at the check-cashing place. Kaki eventually cashed it at her bank. The need for her help, the amount of the check, and the high rents in our neighborhood did not inspire confidence.

Kaki had confided to me once, in that sweet after-lovemaking time when we search for less physical things to share, the three things she wanted to do yet with her life. One was to cross-country ski from lodge to lodge across Vermont. Another was to hike the Appalachian Trail, Georgia to Maine. A third was to have a daughter. Neither of us had ever had children. She was forty-six and suffered from interstitial cystitis, a chronic, painful condition likely to deteriorate. When I watched her and Tahija laughing about the fabric shop they'd found tucked under an overpass, playing word games or reading *Wind Through the Door* out loud to each other, I wondered: was Tahija her last chance to have a daughter, triplet babies a chance not to be missed?

"We could give it another coat," Sam said, "thin it with some white."

"She's not thinking about the yellow now," I said.

Sam looked at Kaki. He and she were the same height. The first time I visited Hancock Street they were standing on the front steps of the house about to go in, and I'd noticed that: the same height and both broad-shouldered, Sam's back very straight, Kaki's a little stooped. She turned now and went down the hallway to the front bedroom. Sam and I followed.

This room had a dull green rug and a three-foot patch in the ceiling where plaster had fallen. A draft reached us from the old single-pane windows.

"Oh I know," Sam said, "I know Kaki. She's thinking, 'If the babies came home here, which room would they stay in?'"

"Is that what you're thinking?" I asked her.

"No, I'm thinking, 'If they came home here, could I feel okay about keeping the best room to myself?'"

"Sure, why not," said Sam, "it's your house."

"It's your house," I echoed him.

"And this one here already has a carpet," Sam put in.

"A stained carpet," Kaki said.

"There's a ceiling fan," I offered, fearing I might lose my third-floor sanctuary (which I did).

"But it could be a hazard," Kaki said, "if a crib were under it and the baby — "

"Bab*ies*," Sam corrected.

"If one or more of the babies should reach up."

"That wouldn't be a problem until they were bigger," I said, "like toddlers."

We imagined *that* for a minute ... babies becoming toddlers. Here or — we walked back down to the yellow and blue-trim room — here. Or a room in some other house that we might never see, or three rooms in three other houses that Tahija herself might never see. In our hearts, one of the unasked questions was asked and answered. We wanted the boys to come home here. We wanted to meet them.

But what did Tahija want? While Sam and Kaki deliberated about the paint, I visited Tahija in the middle room. A small room, this was more finished than the rest of the house, with a plush pink carpet and pink wallpaper with a brown band going round it like a ribbon on a box. On the band a sequence of scenes repeated: baby bear rubbing tired eyes, baby bear sleeping on folded hands, baby bear rising and shining.

To the left of the door Tahija lay on her single bed with a phone to her ear.

"I'm a call you right back," she said when she saw me.

"Renee?" I asked.

"Renee's mom." She sat up and pulled her sweatshirt over her belly. "See my new outergarment?" She rolled herself into a standing position and walked to the wardrobe. Hanging there was the blue and gold striped outergarment she'd made with her Muslim girlfriends. I crossed the narrow room to admire it.

Beside the wardrobe was a desk where Tweetie Bird sat, schoolbooks stacked between his three-toed feet. Tahija and I had retrieved the books a few days before from the aunt's house where she'd been staying before she went to Renee's. It was a big house in an old, tree-sheltered part of the city, a good place for children, I'd thought, a possible new home. I asked her about it now.

"That's not my aunt really, she's my mom's cousin. Millie raised them both. She don't like Lamarr. Doesn't like him."

"No?"

"Uh-uh. Doesn't like real dark-skinned men. She was mad with me I wouldn't get an abortion, but my mouth was probably what got me put out." She smiled, remembering her comeback when the aunt called Lamarr what she had called him.

"And not first-thing-in-the-morning put out, either," she told me, "but don't-*get*-your-toothbrush one-in-the-morning put out."

"That's when you went to Renee's."

She nodded, hanging the outergarment up.

"Goodness gracious!" she said, her face making me glad I wasn't pregnant.

She sat down on the bed, back against the pink wallpaper, short legs in a diamond before her. She had on a navy blue sweatsuit and gray kemar.

"Seems like ever since we come back here I been getting it from my family. They don't like how I talk, too white; don't like how I act, stuck up; and they didn't like me turning Muslim, though couldn't nobody give me a reason not to."

She looked at me with challenge. I thought of the church women I'd seen shun her, actually turn their backs on her at bus stops, in the welfare office, the clinic. Oppositional as she was, such treatment may have been a motivation. I wasn't going to give her more. And anyway, the best course seemed to be to try to live up to my own highest ideals. To black Americans battered by poverty and racism, Islam brought gifts of pride, discipline, and community, and to young women one thing more: a cloak of purity. Converting to Islam was a choice Tahija, then Shannon, had made with great seriousness and for many reasons. If anything, I wished she and Lamarr were more Muslim — more disciplined, part of a community, studying something.

"If there's one thing my family should know about me by now," she went on, "it's that I'm hardheaded. Come by it honest, from my mom."

"She hardheaded?"

"Yeah."

I waited for more.

"I blame it on us moving back from Colorado, me and my little sister three days on a bus, and some man *stinking!*"

Tahija had a way of saying *stink* that somehow conveyed the smell itself, made it sound like all foul smells rolled into one and, more than that, like the most offensive of crimes: arson, rape, murder and *stinking*.

"Millie was sick, supposed to be dying. But she didn't, and my mom got back in with her old friends."

"Her so-called friends," I said.

"*Exactly.* Smoking that stuff, acting all wild. Left me alone with the baby and the twins so much the twins started calling Lamarr dad." She stopped suddenly. "What're those two doing?"

"Kaki doesn't like how yellow the yellow came out."

We went to see. Kaki and Sam stood in the center of the room.

They turned and looked at us, from my face to Tahija's to Tahija's belly, which was bigger and lower these days.

"Is kinda bright," Tahija said. "Maybe with some blinds ... "

Past the roof of the muffler shop and the higher, vent-dotted roof of the grocery store, the El tracks could be seen. A train pulled in and we heard the vaguely British female voice, "Doors are opening, doors are opening, please step away from the doors." Beyond the El loomed the gigantic rusting milk bottle of a closed bottling plant. I found my way home by it when I was lost.

"I have some plates I can sell you," Sam said, "for behind the light switches? Little choo-choo trains on them."

"Choo-choo trains?" Kaki said, her thin lips set in a peculiar smile.

Sam Harpur didn't sell us those light plates. He gave them to Tahija, for the nursery. And soon it was official: when the triplets came home, barring any unforeseen events, they'd be coming home to Hancock Street.

Chapter 8

It was a calm night. I felt as if I didn't have a worry in the world. I was sitting on my bed reading a book when all of a sudden I began to get sharp pains in the middle of my stomach. I couldn't imagine what was going on and why I had the pain. I waited for about twenty minutes but the pain was still there. It was a constant pain and it made me begin to worry, being as I was five and a half months pregnant I began to not only worry I began to actually panic. I was thinking to myself, why was this happening. It was too early for this to be happening. Was there in fact something wrong. I quickly ran to the bathroom to see if there was any change in my body that I could see, but there was none. I then quickly called the hospital and they said for me to come into the emergency room right away. If I wasn't afraid before I was surely afraid now not knowing what would happen next. The whole way to the hospital I was thinking, is it something wrong with me or is this a normal situation for someone in my shoes. You see I had never been in these shoes before. All of this was new to me so I was very confused and most of all scared.

The panic I was in when we got to the hospital. First they made me wait until the doctor could see me which seemed like forever, but was actually a few moments. I guess when you are afraid you lose track of time. Minutes begin to feel like hours and one hour seems like three. The thought of not knowing what was wrong with my babies began to make me feel sick with fear. All of the emotions that were coming over me were starting to overwhelm me. I had to know what was wrong and why.

My Life as I Know It

One night when Kaki and I were out for the evening Tahija began having pains. Lamarr was with her, and when the pain didn't quit they phoned the emergency room and were told to come in. They took a taxi. It was false labor, but the ER doctor decided to admit her. Hospital bed rest had begun.

When I found her room, Tahija said, not looking up from combing out her hair, "Now what I'm supposed to do in this bed all day, Kathryn?"

"Complain, like you been doing," I said, coming in. She had a single room with a big window looking out on another wing's windows.

"And I can't hardly move without those going off."

She flicked her comb at three fetal heart monitors stacked like stereo equipment beside the bed. Sheets of continuous-feed paper *zeet-zeeted* out the backs and wires ran from the fronts to three belts around her belly. Each monitor beeped steadily, but no two beeped in sync, with the effect of a continuous stream of sound, like an oboe holding a high off-pitch note.

"I don't know how you can sleep," I said.

"I can't, that's just it. Something truly wrong with these people if they think I'm — "

"Hey, you named them."

"They *been* had names," she said.

On each monitor was a strip of masking tape with a name printed across it in black magic marker. Damear, Mahad, Lamarr. I tried pronouncing them.

"Not *Duh*," she corrected me, "*Dah*" — a tired feet hitting hot water type *ah*.

"*Da*mear."

70

"No, Da*mear*."

"Okay, second syllable stressed. So the next is Ma*had*?"

"Close."

She was sitting up on top of the covers, bunched pillows at her back. She had on her Stop the Violence t-shirt, the gray sweatpants, new striped socks. She scooped hair grease from a jar at her side. Her hair reached about six inches out from the top and sides of her head. Braiding it in front of me was either an unavoidable necessity or a show of trust. Of all her passingly Muslim girlfriends, Tahija was the most serious about covering — she occasionally wore even a niqab, or face veil. And here I'd come upon her with her hands up in her hair and she hadn't missed a beat.

"So how do you decide who gets which name?"

"Okay whoever is born first, he's Damear," she said, head to the side, braiding fast along one strand, eyes half closed, "second, he's Mahad, like that."

"You going to call Lamarr Junior?"

"Better not call no son of mine Junior."

If it wasn't himself, walking in with a cheesesteak for two. Lamarr had schmoozed the staff into letting him sleep over in the room the night before, and appeared to be ready to hold vigil until the births, which was a good thing, given Tahija's needle phobia. If any shots were going to happen, Lamarr had to be there.

He set his tape player on the top monitor (Damear) and sat in the one chair. I was glad to see him in a quilted shirt. I'd been wondering just how cold it had to get before a coat of some kind appeared, then I figured it out: the number concerned wasn't in degrees, but dollars.

"How's the telemarketing going?" I asked.

"Going great," he said. "They walked a new client through today checking us out, like we were race horses or something. Credit card insurance. If he signs we'll have full-time for like a month."

I pictured the converted factory Lamarr had described: cafeteria-style tables crowded with back-to-back computers.

Oddly, there were no phones. The computers dialed, moving through databases like mowers through a field. You heard a click in your headset, then a voice, often wary (they'd heard the click too), and in you jumped: icy water all day.

Reaching for her half of the cheesesteak, Tahija set off one of the monitors — a hard-edged *eeee* that brought a nurse running. The nurse moved Damear's sensor around Tahija's belly until the mislaid heartbeat sounded again.

If it had not been a false alarm, if one of the three hearts had stopped, Tahija would have been rushed to the operating room for a dangerously early c-section.

"See, I can't hardly move," Tahija said. "And I sure can't use … that thing."

"The bedpan? Why not?"

"I just can't."

"Look, I'll show you how," I said, moving toward it.

Her laughing caused Mahad's belt to slip, setting the middle monitor off. Lamarr did as the nurse had, then leaned in close to say, "Mahad, get back where you supposed to be!" Sure enough, before the alarm reeled in any staff, it quit. "*Better* mind me," the father-to-be said, pulling Tahija's shirt back down.

"The only one not starting trouble is Junior," Tahija said.

"Don't *call* him Junior," Lamarr said, eyebrows in a Mr. Spock V.

"I'll call him what I want to call him, long as he not big-headed like you."

Thus began the repartee that used to sound to me like bickering, but which I heard now as flirting. A good time for me to leave.

Hearts beating inside their mother, father's voice a sonar through the amnion … as it should be. But other things were not as they should be. Tahija worried her children would be taken by the state as soon as they were born — stork morphed into hawk. For her and Lamarr, as for many poor families, the circling hawk was a fact of life. Because they were so young, fifteen and sixteen, and not in the care of their parents, and because three babies were due, the Department of Human Services had been alerted as soon as Tahija entered the hospital. Soon after, a relative of Lamarr's reported her as a runaway. Inquiries were made. One of her doctors told DHS he hadn't seen any parents visiting and suspected she was homeless. This same doctor maintained that she was too young to handle triplets. (Tahija learned about his efforts through a nurse who had been a teen mother herself and believed, she told Tahija, that she *could* do it.) The hawk was circling.

At twelve, Tahija had become stand-in mother to her two younger sisters and baby twin brothers. From a much earlier age Lamarr had had to scramble to keep utilities on and food in the house as his parents and other family moved from crisis to crisis. Both Tahija and Lamarr had endured evictions, had been without a dollar in the house or an egg in the refrigerator. Both of them more than once had kept DHS from removing siblings as the family life raft took one wave after another. It didn't matter if supplies were so low the survivors were at each other's throats. The raft was better than the frigid deep. The raft was better than the auction block.

The auction block. Had it started there? Was their fear that old, inherited like Tahija's overcrowded bottom teeth and Lamarr's tensile brow from men and women who rarely saw their children grown, who left for the fields before dawn knowing that when they returned after dark one more of their loved ones might have been sold away? Not that their being there could have stopped it, not that strong arms encircling or voices beseeching or hearts breaking could have stopped it.

Though I could look back on my childhood and identify families, some quite close to home, whose children should have been removed by the state, I had not grown up in the shadow of the hawk. My parents and my friends' parents had been presumed competent, even if proven otherwise. Tahija and Lamarr were presumed incompetent, and feared they were not going to be given the chance to prove otherwise.

* * *

Any day I didn't visit the hospital I felt guilty, the more so because I was enjoying the quiet at home. Tahija carried a lot of baggage. For two months she'd been unpacking — stories, fears, habits, needs, attitudes — and with my bags and Kaki's already unpacked (but with backpacks and little carrying cases still popping up all over the place), the house had become noisy with feelings, felt and unfelt, expressed and unexpressed. I was enjoying the reprieve.

Kaki and I did visit, separately and together, bringing food, books, any joke we could find, corny or not, because boredom had become the air Tahija breathed, and she was choking on it.

Life got better when the wonderful nurse who'd become her friend and ally broke hospital rules and delivered a VCR, hooking it up to the hospital TV. I was a little jealous of this nurse. There was something queenly about Tahija ensconced there in the bed, her bright, youthful face, her high energy, her impressive, amply monitored belly. I wanted to be included in her court.

Once when this nurse asked Tahija if she wanted a glass of water, I ventured to inform her that she liked it with ice. The nurse had looked at me like a wad of chewing gum stuck to her best shoe.

Today Kaki was the hero. She'd come with videos from the library.

"You'll like this one," she said, "*The Yearling,* with Gregory Peck."

Tahija looked at the back cover. "Sounds corny."

"It *will* make you cry," I predicted.

"Will not."

"Will too."

It did. But she'd forget she'd ever seen it. Those bed rest weeks were such a blur of tests and needles and interrupted sleep, of the heart monitors waking her up at all hours (the way babies soon would). She'd remember a few things: the dream in which the blood pressure cuff became a man grabbing her; the smart-mouthed doctor who kept telling her she was too young to be a mother; and how she'd held out and not once — *not once* — used the bedpan.

Such were the heights of hardheadedness to which Tahija Ellison could rise. I think hardheadedness alone, forged during those weeks into fierce determination, enabled her to keep her babies inside her as long as she did. Now when contractions started up she called for a shot whether Lamarr was there or not, because the shot stopped them, for a time. And she'd lie perfectly still, breathing for them, eating for them, by sheer concentration of will buying them precious days in which to compose healthy lungs, hearts, brains. They weren't going to be like those preemies hooked up to all type of tubes and machines, not if she could help it. Dr. Hughes had said term for triplets was seven months, and seven months she'd make it.

But time couldn't pass any slower if it tried, and it did appear to be trying.

Chapter 9

I had to endure one hospital room, no walking around and strict bed rest. I had little visitors but I had three regulars, my partner in life the father of my children who never left my side. He had been there from the beginning never missing an appointment, and now that I would have to be in this hospital for awhile he would be subjected to sleeping in a chair or on the floor for the whole six weeks. I know he was probably thinking, how long will I have to be here on this hard floor or cramped chair? You would think that being in a hospital they would have at least a cot or something for emergencies but in my case there was none to be offered. We did what we had to do to survive.

My Life as I Know It

Three days of rain had ended, snow was predicted, in between we had overcast and windy. Philly can do overcast and windy like no city I've seen. I was on the El platform waiting for an off-peak train, trying to keep the wind out of my old down jacket. It was a solid navy blue that showed escaping feathers nicely. I was due for a new one (or some new duct tape), but I still wasn't working, unless you counted the player piano job, which I did not. I felt discouraged. Six months before, I'd been teaching writing and literature courses to community college students, living in the mountains not two hours from most of my nieces and nephews, with time to write and a small, friendly Quaker meeting to be part of. I missed them. I missed their potlucks.

Watching a rat scurry under the tracks, I remembered living in Philly when I was twenty, a Floridian in her first city winter. I remembered wanting to leave.

As I waited, I was spotted by Angelina, a friend of Barbara Parnell's.

"Kathy!" she waved and hurried over. "I was just talking to my good friend Julio there," she blew a kiss to an elderly man. Somewhere between fifty and sixty, Angelina was built like a half-back (gear on), but in her mind's eye must have been as dainty as a daisy. A quarter-moon shaped scar halved her forehead, hairline to the bridge of her nose.

"Kathy, honey, I don't mean to talk, but you know that meeting you and Kaki had at your place?"

"The block-committee meeting." It had been weeks, and Angelina had already reported to me what she seemed bent on reporting again.

"I just don't think it's right yous girls being so nice and all for Barbara's sister to come in, eat up your food like it was going out of style and then turn and say what she did."

Barbara's sister had come to one of our meetings, eaten, used the bathroom, stolen twenty dollars out of Tahija's bedroom, and left. Barbara was embarrassed, Tahija hurt and furious.

"She's messed up," I told Angelina. "It's her addiction talking."

"Well you know what," she leaned closer to me, whispering in her South Philly twang. "It's not what she said it's what Barbara said that really gets my goat."

"It was awhile ago, Angelina. Did you get your application from senior housing yet?" I could see a train pulling in at the next station.

"And after all yous girls done for her."

I didn't know exactly what Kaki and I had done for Barbara, beyond respect her as a human being. I sighed.

"Okay, what did Barbara say?"

Angelina rose to her full height, squared her shoulders, and stepped closer. "She said, to her sister, that lowlife, I was there, she said, she called yous girls, after all you done for her, 'those white bitches.'"

"Did she."

I could imagine Barbara joining in with her sister in talking trash about us. I could believe, too, that her every smile was a mask and that under the smile she hated us, hated all white people for what they had done to her and hers, the hatred deep in her bones. But I also knew that we aren't, any of us, all mask and bones, hurt and hate. We are something more, and that something more in Barbara and in me connected.

"Believe you me Kathy, when I heard it it was all I could do to keep from bashing her up side of the head with my god damn fist." She showed me her big red fist.

Angelina had a short fuse. She'd grown up in tough, treeless South Philly, where the drug trade first took root. I could guess some of the ways in which her fuse had been shortened.

"Angelina Balboa," I said. She didn't laugh. About racial matters Angelina was dead serious. A compulsion to fight seemed to bring her to our neighborhood. Most people could see it was mental illness of some sort and knew not to start with her, but occasionally she'd find a taker. She found a taker in me that day I'm afraid. Not that I wanted to fight her, but that at some level I accepted her paranoid perspective; at some level I believed, feared, expected that everything — Barbara's teasing, Lamarr's stories, Tahija's trust — everything was a mask like the one Paul Laurence Dunbar wrote about, and that under the mask everyone was laughing at the dumb white bitches.

"Here's my train."

"Kathy," she took my arm. I felt little, like the Kathy who'd never gone away to college, never worked to grow beyond her scrappy us/them Queensborough state of mind.

"What?"

"Tell your honey hello for me," she said.

"I will."

"And tell her nothing yous girls do in the privacy of your own home is anyone's god damn business but your own and if they got a problem with it, *fuck* them, and their little dog too."

"Okay Angelina."

"Tell her."

"I will, don't worry, I'll look forward to it. Have a nice day."

"You too, sweetie." She wiggled her fingers goodbye.

I rode the El downtown to City Hall, where I waited for the bus that went up Broad Street and past the hospital. On top of City Hall's wedding-cake layers stood William Penn. He faced west, toward the Delaware River and the much lower statue of Tamanend, the Lenni Lenape chief with whom Penn had made a lasting peace. Beyond City Hall, out of sight but on my mind, stood central Philadelphia's two great meetinghouses. Historic sites, these were also, unlike most of the other historic places in the nation's first capital, still actively living their founding ideals. I had attended these meetings, and others farther out from the city center, all the way to the suburbs, but I had not found one where I felt at home. Always something stood in the way, something to do with money, and attitudes toward money, or wealth, as inherited and invested money is more aptly called. This wealth … I wanted it for my neighborhood, for the library that closed so early and had so few computers, and this in the city with the nation's first public library. Why, I could walk to it, take a tour through it, but I couldn't find more than five books of poetry in my neighborhood's library, and the summer before it had been closed for months — steel shutters rolled down over the doors.

When I went to this one meeting I was often moved to give a message about wealth. I had spoken once about a *New York Times* front-page photo: a crowd of businesspeople, men mostly, white mostly, looking upward in wondrous joy. At what? I had wondered. At the stock market's closing numbers. What did we worship? What closed our ears to the divine will? What bound us most to our self will?

Though I loved the quality of their worship and the aura of the building, folks at that meeting had not seemed overly eager to have me keep coming. Whether it was my stockmarket message, my sneakers, or my lover I wasn't sure, but one in fact asked if I knew, perhaps, about the other meeting, just a few blocks over. I said I did, thank you.

Quakers were doing a good deal for and in the inner city, and had probably done more for justice than any one group, but I didn't know that then. I felt like an outsider. I might have served as a bridge reaching out from my new neighborhood; instead I was becoming more *of* that neighborhood: isolated, unhopeful, easily aggrieved. As a passing sedan sprayed me with cold slush, it seemed to me William Penn faced away from North Philly on purpose.

I found Tahija straining forward to fit a yardstick under the big plastic socks that covered her calves — Ted socks they were called; every few minutes they inflated and deflated, keeping her circulation going. She was in hospital-issue clothes now — a pink gown with red roses. Her face was more broken out, and the circles around her eyes showed darker, wider, with a fine crosshatching of lines running across them.

She looked over at me and kept on scratching. "Hey."

"Hey," I said. "How'd you sleep last night?"

"How can I sleep with these things grabbing me?" She fell back and huffed as if she'd been running, then pointed to a doctor passing in the hallway. "There's that one doctor wanna get smart. Talking some, 'She's too young to keep those babies,' and 'Why isn't her mother or her father visiting?' Real ignorant. They better not send him in here no more."

She tried to fold her arms but an IV port in one wrist got in the way.

"Ow! I'm fit to tear this thing out!"

Tahija was bigger and more miserable every day. No food or movies or conversation alleviated bedsores, constipation, boredom, kicks from within, and monumental frustration. She always lit up when a cousin visited, and again whenever her great-grandmother Millie called, but the fun, if ever there had been any (and I think at the start there had) was over. She'd stood in line to buy a ticket on the Superthriller roller coaster but now her car was stuck at the top with no way down but down — straight through a Caesarian section into a mother lode of motherhood.

I went around and sat in the chair by the window. "Lamarr at work?"

"Supposedly."

"Hear from your mom again?" Her mother had called a few days before.

An agonized groan came from the hallway. Then we heard, "I wish somebody'd take this motherfucking spike outta my motherfucking back!"

On the way in I'd passed a pregnant woman moaning and pacing in the hallway.

"They started the epidural," Tahija explained, "then the doctor said, 'Hold up, it's not time,' but they left the needle in."

"Well why don't somebody come?" I asked.

"They'll come when they ready to come," said Tahija, cynical woman of the world, the world where no one was for you, and anything organized, governmental, or official was set dead against you.

"Maybe they just — "

"Some-bo-dy!" the woman yelled, knocking me a few notches closer to Tahija's cynicism. Just how good was this hospital, sitting as it did smack in the middle of one of the highest infant mortality rates in the world? Was it a cause, or an effect? Were most of the women on the maternity ward poor because the neighborhood was poor or because anyone with the means went elsewhere?

I stared at the three monitors. Paper stuttered out the backs onto foot-high stacks for trained technicians to read. Who was paying for all this? Did Lamarr still have that telemarketing job? Suddenly my head was pounding ... fluorescent lights, moaning woman, beeping monitors ... anger. I felt angry at Tahija. Who did she think she was? Why didn't she know her place? She should be grateful, she should be humble.

Tahija Ellison was about as far from humble and grateful as you can get without leaving the solar system. She was a bane to residents, nurses, and doctors alike. She was an arrogant, selfish, ill-tempered adolescent. To share my house, my money, my time, my best friend and lover with this ornery stranger, this pretentious child, this hurt and angry woman so in need herself of mothering, who carelessly and without means to support them was bringing three innocent lives into the world....

I felt the air pressure shift as before a thunderstorm. Hopelessness. Hopelessness building, coming in to drench everyone — children, parents, me too if I stayed.

Wanting to duck out of the storm, I didn't see how scared Tahija was. I didn't see how her complaining was really a crying out, and how her arrogance, like a tree's branches, mirrored roots as large and complex, deep branching roots of fear and worthlessness. She knew she wasn't paying for all this. She knew she was perilously dependent on a system that left needles in the spines of its patients and did not love her. As I did not. Not in that moment.

After some awkward conversation, I left. The three heart monitors beside the bed went on beeping, beeping without interruption like ... well ... hearts.

Walking up the block as the light began to drain from the cloudy sky, I met Elva, the block captain's wife. Born in Philly of parents from Puerto Rico, Elva did all the cooking at a halfway house for released prisoners. She had a daughter in Job Corps and a son at the community college. She was around forty, with stylishly short hair hennaed red, the most crowded, messed-up mouth of teeth I'd ever seen, and a smile that made you rummage your memory for jokes. She and I had been elected co-secretaries of the block committee.

"Hey Elva," I said, "how you doin'?"

"My feet are *killing* me. Will you look at that?"

Back at the corner I'd just turned, a terrible scene played out. A skeleton of a woman, hardly human, age indeterminate, was making her way on shaking legs toward a robust young man, a crack dealer. He had bleached-blond hair, a thick down coat, the popular orange boots. And he was laughing at her. She fell down.

It was like watching strips of tire tread fly away from a blowout. Somehow she stood, and wobbled toward him.

"Isn't that Angel," I said, "Julia's son-in-law?" Four of Julia's grandchildren came to my playgroup. "Elva, how come so many of the guys named Angel are so *bad?*"

"Right?"

Elva always affirmed pessimism. You could say to her, "Elva, the world is evil and we all have the heart of Hitler," and she'd say, "Right?" in that affirming way. But the last thing I needed just then was to have my sinking spirits affirmed. But it was in the air, like carbon monoxide, and I was not strong enough, not centered enough in hope, to counter it.

The skeletal woman wore a flower-print nylon dress and shoes that had once been high heels. She was white, with straight brown hair to her shoulders. She had probably come over from a nearby stretch of the Avenue where addicts from Fishtown sold sex to men in cars. Kaki would have gone to speak with her. Sometimes when she saw people dealing she approached and just stood there, calm, watching, until they stopped. I didn't think anything short of death was going to stop this woman from buying the five-dollar bliss for which she'd just sold her body, probably for the same price.

When she had her prize, she hurried on those impossibly wobbly legs to a vacant lot and disappeared behind the shell of a car.

"See?" said Elva, "That's why, that grant money we got for the play-lot? It has to go for a fence."

I had been making a case for picnic tables.

"That girl have her babies yet?"

"Tahija? Any day now."

Elva shook her head. "I hope you two know what you're doing. Those young girls, they don't wanna stay home, hear all that crying. And with three, Lord-have-mercy. Well, let me get home." But she didn't move. "I known Angel since he was this big." With her hand she showed a small boy's height.

"Should we go talk with him?"

"Hell no! Soon as I eat I'm a call the precinct, *a*-gain. Let him sit his ass in jail awhile. Say Hi to Kaki, and tell her for me she's getting way too busy."

Kaki *was* getting way too busy. With me around she could do more work, much of it volunteer. But what about my work, my writing? Walking up the street, my jacket wet through at the wrists and collar, hiking boots holding up, I thought about what Elva had said. What if Tahija left us with the babies? What if she neglected them, beat them? Were we prepared? Would we do more harm than good? Were we really helping Tahija and Lamarr, or encouraging dependency? With welfare reform tossing thousands off the lifeboat monthly, neither checking to see who could swim nor keeping count of the drowned, shouldn't this young couple get busy building a boat of their own?

Can you build a boat while treading water?

In the house, I laid myself out on the sofa and thought of the addict. I should go to her, bring her home, feed her. But how much had happened to her that I couldn't undo? If I had more energy, if I were a better person than I was, if I didn't have so much of my own baggage, if I could get off the sofa and go back out into the rain to the vacant lot, into the pain that had fallen in love with the brief bliss of crack, and would not let it go. Unless by some miracle. If I was a miracle worker ... if I was one with the source of all miracles, of all the small healings that compounded over a lifetime constitute the greatest miracle.

But I was not. I was tired, I was forty, I felt like a failure. The tortured gait of that woman as she scrabbled toward the thing that was stealing her soul would not leave me, has never left me. I thought of those zombie movies: *Dawn of the Dead, Return of the Dead, Night of the Living Dead.* ... Didn't we live in a time of the walking dead?

That day on the sofa, the room dark and the cold rain falling and falling over all the houses and vacant lots and streets of the city, over the prisons and the hospitals and William Penn in his broad Quaker hat, I felt it was so, and that I could do no more than the still living in those movies do: run, run like hell.

85

Chapter 10

After about four weeks, Kaki and Kathryn told me that they might want me to leave because they didn't think they could handle me and the boys at their house. I got so stressed and depressed that I would have to find another place again I just gave up with everyone. To top off all the bad things that were happening to me, someone called DHS and said that I was a runaway, and I thought they were going to try to take my children away from me. When I found out, I started contracting too much, and soon the doctors couldn't stop the contractions anymore so I let them go ahead and get me ready for the delivery of the boys.

My Life as I Know It

Years later Tahija would say yes to one of my invitations to a Quaker worship service. Several messages came out of the silence that day. One was a paraphrase of something Martin Luther King Jr. had said: When you choose to work for justice and peace, nobody promised you your blood pressure wasn't going to go up. That day, on the other side of so much, I smiled. But in the darkening living room that cold February I felt too much was being asked of me. I doubted I could handle it —Tahija, Lamarr, babies, babies in this neighborhood. I doubted the light I'd seen in her eyes that first day. I doubted whether I could live up to my own light, whether I could sustain the yes I'd offered so quickly.

Too quickly?

I should have prayed, meditated, walked for as long and as far as it took for fear to turn loose my heart. I didn't. I went up to my third floor room and wrote this in my journal.

I don't feel entirely clear to go ahead with having the babies come home here. My motives are definitely unclear. A friend warned that while I might think I could handle it, I probably can't. She dreamt me walking away from it all and warned that I might do that. She's probably right. It's hard though to let go of the idea.

I still have that file. It's dated February 8, eight days before the triplets were born.

"I want you to be happy here," Kaki said.

At the river, the Delaware, at a spot where it was very wide and boulders lined the shore, water gently rising and falling between them, we sat between a pier and a fenced-in power plant.

"We can help them whether they live with us or not," Kaki went on. "They'll need plenty. Rides, baby-sitting, furniture. We can even loan them money for move-in costs, from what's left of what my mom sent for Christmas."

"That's for new windows in the living room."

"The windows can wait," she said.

"They're drafty."

"Not too."

"Hang a wind chime there and see," I said, then, "She can't get welfare if she's living on her own." It was a new rule of welfare reform, meant, I supposed, to keep teens from using pregnancy to get away from parents. But what if the parents had themselves gotten away?

"She won't be living on her own," Kaki said, "she'll be living with Lamarr."

"Look, Kaki, there's a minute left on the clock and he's down ten points, deep in his own territory."

Her father and mine had been big football fans (Packers and Dolphins, respectively).

"How many time-outs left?" she asked.

"No time-outs left," I said.

"I want you to be happy," she said. "I want you to stay."

A barge passed slowly, trailed by gulls. I thought of Amy Denver, another character from Toni Morrison's memorable cast. She's a white girl, a runaway indentured servant. In woods just south of the Ohio River she comes upon Sethe, running from enslavement, very pregnant and too weak to go on. Patronizing and self-absorbed, Amy nevertheless gives the help human decency demands, doctoring Sethe's mangled feet and helping her deliver the baby. Then she's off for Boston, where, she has heard, they have velvet (she loves velvet). It takes a black man and his sturdy boat to get Sethe and the newborn across the river into freedom. This seems fitting, but I always wished the white girl had talked less and helped more. I always thought I would have done better.

"I want you to stay," Kaki said again.

The next day Kaki took Lamarr to lunch and told him that we still wanted to help, but we had changed our minds about Tahija coming home to our house with the boys. I called Tahija's grandmother Agnes Grealy and told her the same thing. She said we'd done more than most would have, we should feel okay.

I didn't feel okay. I dreaded facing Tahija. I found her propped on pillows between the stacked monitors and a pushed-aside food tray, eyes closed, a palm on her forehead. A grayness had come to her face, like a film of dust on mahogany. I thought of the girl I'd seen walking toward me across the parking lot that first day, Tweetie Bird in her arms, a bounce in her step. She looked so much more than three months older.

"Hey," she said when she saw me, opening her eyes briefly. "You want this pudding?"

I looked into the cup. "Nasty."

"Right?"

I told her how much we liked her, how interested we were in her life and well-being, how willing we were to continue helping.

"You're putting me out," she said. One AM, and don't *get* your toothbrush.

"We can help with first and last, security deposit, all that, and if you need baby-sitters — "

"They're not going to let me live on my own, Kath-a-ryn."

"Who 'they'?"

"DHS!" She spoke in a stream: "If I don't have verifiable income — verifiable income, not *help* — they going to declare me unfit, an unfit parent. I told you minors can't get welfare now unless they living with an adult, so how I'm going to show verifiable income if I'm not getting a check and then I'm an unfit parent, see? They'll be waiting in the delivery room, take them *right out* the doctor's hands."

She looked me in the eye until I saw — the underside of the hawk, the splayed talons, the greedy beak.

A nurse entered, prepared a syringe.

"Are you her social worker?"

"No," I said.

"Family?"

I shook my head no.

"Then I'll have to ask you to leave."

I left.

Chapter 11

On the fine day of February 19, 1998. My joy had finally come but it wasn't the right time. I mean it was the first time Lamarr had ever left my side. This day would be the first day that I would be alone at the hospital. He had to meet with Kaki for breakfast and this particular day I honestly felt bad. I mean my head hurt my back hurt I knew it was time. Everyone around me said they didn't think it was time [. . .] but I knew. I never felt like this until today and about one minute after Lamarr left my water broke. I rang my emergency buzzer and by the time the nurse had came he had already got out the hospital. I didn't think it could get any worse than this.

My Life as I Know It

It was kind of crazy in the delivery room because I had to have the c-section and I was trying to wait for Lamarr to come back and I was all by myself. I had to call my cousin to be there with me because I didn't think Lamarr would make it back in time to see the boys born, then I also had a lot of doctors and nurses in the room because every child had their own team of doctors and nurses in case of any complications.

from the interview

It was the start of her twenty-eighth week. Tahija was an Olympic marathoner approaching the stadium, a pilgrim nearing Mecca, a mother carrying children to term, or as close to term as anyone can carry three.

The night before the morning she went into labor she told Lamarr she felt sick. As he had most every other night of her long confinement, he slept on folded blankets on the floor. In the morning she felt the same, and told him he should cancel his breakfast appointment with Kaki. He didn't though, and minutes after he left the room her water broke. She told the nurses to run after him, but he was gone. And so she was alone when the hospital social worker came with her briefcase and informed her, after verifying that she was the one expecting triplets, that an anonymous caller had reported her a runaway. DHS was opening a case.

Soon after the social worker left, around noon, the contractions began, and this time the shot that had been stopping them or at least slowing them down didn't do anything. She paged Lamarr, but he didn't call back. He always called her back. Lamarr calling her back was the one thing she could count on. She punched in the code that meant *emergency*. Still no call, and no Lamarr all big and smiling in the doorway.

She called his friends and told them page him, go find him, tell him come straight to the hospital. Then she called her cousin Mia, who lived close by, and told her, "Get yourself over here quick because I'm about to have these babies."

Temples throbbing, womb clutching and unclutching as it had been doing now for days, she lay with eyes closed remembering scenes, images from her life … Lamarr in the hallway at school, his smile, Lamarr throwing her cigarettes into the street, the feeling he gave her … the ocean at Wildwood, how light she felt with him, the waves lifting and settling them, lifting and settling, the music of the boardwalk, close yet far, the double ferris wheel tipping … and then farther back in time, turning the corner of her street and seeing — what? — some pick-up truck angled like an accident across the sidewalk, three strange men changing the locks on her house. Not even asking them, not having to ask what they were doing, knowing every last thing in the house would be forfeited for back rent, and no mother arriving all loud to rescue her oldest girl's school clothes, her pictures, her journal, her video collection, the stuffed animals arranged just so on her bed. Homeless since then, now again. Though herself a home for three.

Lamarr was eating a ham and egg sandwich. Unaccountably, his faithful pager wasn't working. Kaki sat across from him asking questions that she hoped would lead him toward more clarity about his future. Because it was his future, gosh darn it, and when was he going to wake up and smell the roses?

"Roses?"

"Appreciate life."

"I appreciate it."

"Do you appreciate the fact that you are about to become the father of three?"

"Yes."

"Well what are your plans for the future?"

Lamarr's future was a favored topic of Kaki's. Her own father's work ethic waited like bunched bulbs to be separated and shared. He had been a successful advertising executive. He'd raised two boys and two girls who'd gone to college and become successful in their own right — an engineer, a head nurse, a high-profile missionary, and Kaki, former middle-management executive with a 401(k) and some very nice suit sets to show for it. Kaki wanted Lamarr to be able to provide for his family, and long serious talks over food were somehow part of that. They talked about community college, about trade schools and training programs, about The Streets, as in — was he still running them, gambling with his life now that he was about to be a father?

Lamarr reminded her about his best friend Dimitri. Dimitri had been shot at close range, in the head. He spent most of a very long night dying.

"I sat with him," Lamarr said.

"I know you did."

"Sat with his mom after. I'm not about putting my mom through that."

"I'm glad to hear it."

She couldn't hold them off any longer. As a nurse swabbed her belly purple she paged Lamarr one last time. Then they lifted her onto a gurney and the room that had grown smaller and smaller over the last weeks was suddenly behind her forever.

Down the corridor, past the room where the moaning woman had been, past the nurse's station — "Good luck sweetie." "You go girl." "At last!" — then through another contraction to surgery and down a long, long hall, fast toward the *No Admittance* doors and through, into the bright lights of the operating theatre.

Mia appeared, out of breath, and received her instructions.

"Don't look away, not once. You hear me?"

Mia nodded as a nurse fit a surgical gown over her arms.

"And make sure they're taking pictures. Is somebody taking pictures?"

Somebody was.

"I want pictures of all this because if something goes wrong … Mia, you make sure they don't leave nothing in me, like they did my mom. All right? Mia, you listening?"

Mia looked like she was going to faint. And there hadn't even been any cutting yet.

As they were getting into her car, Kaki noticed that the month of cheesesteaks and cheesefries from the deli across from the hospital had put some weight on Lamarr. Was he still working out? she asked. He wasn't, he said, hadn't had time. She suggested he start again soon. He said he thought he might.

Three female obstetricians prepped for surgery. One was from Turkey, one from China, one from New Jersey. Behind and beside the three female obstetricians stood three assisting nurses, and behind the three assisting nurses one three-person emergency post-natal team for each baby. That made fifteen doctors, nurses, and technicians — all women, as Tahija had requested.

Only the anesthesiologist was a man. And he was useless anyway.

Scrubbed and prepped and ready to enter was the male doctor who had been saying for six weeks that she was too young to handle three. Well she was *about* to handle three, and he was about to miss his big chance to witness triplets being born — the first ever at Temple University Hospital — because she refused him admittance.

Mr. Useless gave her an epidural, which did not work. Might as well have been aspirin. She felt everything. Just like at the dentist, and did the dentist listen to her? No, he did not listen to her, either. Nobody paid her any mind, not even Lamarr. She should page him one more time because he always ... and now ... but ...

Lamarr Stevens strolled down the maternity ward hallway and turned into the room he'd been all but living in for six weeks. Then he bounced out like a handball and tore off down the hall.

"Straight down and left!" a nurse called after him. "She's — "

She heard a doctor say, "I have the first one."

At 1:55 PM, with Lamarr in full sprint, the name that had been on the top heart monitor settled like a butterfly onto the forehead of a healthy three-pound eight-ounce boy. Damear, the oldest, though little Lamarr had made it nearly all the way down the birth canal and was crowning.

A nurse placed Damear beneath a heating lamp. Gloved hands reached in and lifted out Mahad, the smallest at three pounds four ounces. Meanwhile Lamarr, about to become big Lamarr, let them put a surgical gown on him and pushed through the crowd in time to see his namesake being pulled back from the birth canal and lifted out through a doorway he hadn't even known was there. Little Lamarr, the big guy at three pounds nine ounces.

Of the births, Tahija wrote, "The happiest memory I have of being a mother is the first time I heard them cry, because the doctor told me that they might not cry because they were real premature and their lungs might not be developed enough. The second was when I held them in my arms at the same time. I knew they loved me just as much as I loved them from the little smirk they had on their face, like *Joy I finally see who I was kicking all that time.*"

Part Two

Yes

Chapter 12

Why cosmetics?

It seemed to me a kind of purgatory, to have to stand all day beside the dark puddle of the baby grand with nothing to look at on one side but banks of lipsticks and eye shadows and on the other racks of $9.99 earrings, with handbags and perfume sets on the farther horizon, and me like a before shot of a makeover case.

At least the young woman at the Estée Lauder counter had started talking to me. A laid-off bank clerk, she was as bored as I was, and just as tired of the baby grand's limited repertoire (or more tired, since someone replaced me when my shift ended). Holidays it had been Christmas lite and Christmas holy, then the guy from the showroom brought Disney Favorites.

"Bear Necessities" was tinking away now, keys doing their ghost thing, just like the old-time player pianos, except the baby grand had the sound of a baby grand, and the felt-tipped hammers inside the raised lid were a wonder to watch. For a while anyway.

The triplets had been born. We'd heard through Lamarr that they were doing well, with only one, Mahad, needing an incubator. Tahija was doing well too. When he told us about the malfunctioning pager and how a cousin had been called to the hospital, I felt a wave of remorse. I might have been the one called.

A middle-aged white couple with two children approached the piano. The younger child, a girl, sat down without asking and spread her hands over the keys. I interrupted "Bear Necessities" so she could play a short recital piece that ended with a happy glide into the upper register. We applauded.

"Very *good* dear, excellent," said the mother. "Now you, Jason."

Jason took the bench and played a longer, more difficult piece, a march. More applause and praise.

The live music had attracted a small crowd. I noticed a very short, elderly woman looking on with great intensity from the edge.

"Do you play?" I asked her.

She shook her head no, then pushed a boy beside her forward. "But he do."

His hands came up and rested on side of the the piano, so that I saw them reflected in the raised leaf. A boy of eleven or twelve in a striped button-down shirt.

"Would you like to?" I said. "It's a beautiful piano." And it was, I realized, seeing it through his eyes ... a priceless thing.

He walked past the two who had just performed and sat before the keyboard. I just knew there was no piano in this boy's home, and in his school maybe a tired once-a-week music teacher. Then how — you guessed it — how had he learned to play as well as he played?

"Mommy, he's bending his wrists."

Oh he bent his wrists. He bent his whole self, and that piano too. The salesclerks came from behind their counters and stood close, as did clerks from other departments and shoppers from as far away as men's clothing.

How did it sound? As with an amazing wine, you remember of something like that only the fact of your amazement. It was improvised, with gospel flourishes and a jazz velocity. It was something his grandmother had prayed over; it was a lifetime of prayer manifested in music.

I wanted to give him the piano. I wanted to take down their address and work like a dog until one day when I had earned enough — he finished. You hadn't expected it until the last few notes, but then clearly, definitively, yes, it was done.

"You must be proud," the father of the two children who'd played first said.

"Oh," the woman answered, backing away, her reflection receding in the raised leaf, "He's a good child."

With that they walked off, back toward the place where soul was, where all of us white people who'd heard longed to go. So long as we didn't have to be poor there. So long as we didn't have to be black.

The second dazzling pianist to grace the baby grand was a very thin, light-complexioned woman of about thirty-five who flitted through cosmetics handing out flyers, the bell of a red bullhorn poking out from under an arm.

"TJU discriminates," she cried, "TJU discriminates. Read this, it's all here, racial discrimination at TJU. I was fired because I was black."

As seemed to happen often to me at that job, because I was stationary I guess, and open to listening (*Disney Favorites* had worn quite a groove by now), I was privileged to hear some of her story. It was a confusing one, recited breathlessly as her flyer hand flicked in and out fast as a pinball flapper.

She'd been a lab technician at Thomas Jefferson University. She trained someone younger and white who was promoted over her and then that someone took a disliking to her because she was black and then something else happened and she was laid off, but they never called her back in.

"That's a shame," I said. "How long have you been laid off?"

"Eight years two months. But if I can get on *Nightline,* they'd have to — flyer for you."

"Have to ... ?"

"Rehire me. Of course I'd need a court order. But I have to raise money for the appeal first."

Before the lab technician job, I learned, she'd studied piano at Philadelphia's own Curtis Institute, one of the most prestigious

101

music conservatories in the world. I asked if she would play. She said she hadn't in years, her campaign took all her time.

"Just anything," I said. "Even scales. It attracts people, you'd be helping me out."

She handed me the flyers, set the bullhorn on the piano bench and sat down, flapping out the back of her teal-colored raincoat as if it were the tail of a tuxedo.

Her playing drew a crowd too. The piece was modern, cacophonous, and very long, full of battles, Baltic cities under siege, rags on bleeding feet.

When the last chord had disappeared around a curve of Eastern Europe's long rutted road, she sprang up, and before I could ask what it was she had played she snatched the flyers from me and saying something about rush hour commuters, headed off at a near run, bullhorn swinging, for the street entrance.

"What *was* that?" I called after her.

"Rachmaninoff," she said over her shoulder

"Come play again, will you?"

She waved without turning, but never came again. I saw her on street corners a few times after, shouting through the bullhorn, her talent, I feared, as wasted as the flyers littering nearby gutters.

It was hard to forget her, and the other people I met at Strawbridge and Clothier, the other stories I heard. One man who must have been near eighty told me how he'd tried to apply for a job as a clerk when he first came back from the war. Though he'd been decorated all they'd consider him for was janitor. That wasn't the worst of it, though; the worst of it was the toilet. White only.

"So now," he told me, tugging the lapel of a suit coat, a stately man with a thin moustache, "I stop by from time to time and make use of the facilities."

I laughed, sharing some of his satisfaction. Yet at the same time I felt ashamed, and wondered why he was telling me this. Was telling me part of the payback? I wasn't sure. But I knew I was becoming more white somehow — more conscious of racism and white privilege — and also less white — more open to other perspectives.

Unsettling. The TJU woman, for example. Was her cause legitimate? Or her mental state unbalanced? Or could it be both? And the woman I saw from time to time in the supermarket who'd come up to me and show me her arm — "I'm so white," she'd say, "do you see how white I am?" Had wanting to be white driven her insane, or was that just one form her insanity took? Was it the always wondering if a slight, an insult, a missed promotion or lost job was racial that sent blood pressure up and self-confidence down, and drove the more vulnerable off an edge?

And it sure couldn't help matters much that right where you shopped for that perfume you gave your Aunt Elita every year some fool had put a piano that cost more than your house *and* your Aunt Elita's house combined.

Now *come* on, I thought, thinking in Tahija's tone, giving it the octave jump she did when extreme ignorance was involved, *That don't make no sense.* It was living with her those months, I realized, that must have left this fork in the tree of my perspective.

But what had I left her with? Anything she could use? Anything more than a story she could tell when she was an old woman, if she made it to be an old woman, about whitefolks. How they pull out just when you need them.

"Excuse me?"

I had made the mistake of revealing the player piano's price. The salesman in the showroom had told me to say just, "There's a range." But people asked.

"That's right," I leaned on the piano, "but it doubles as a dining room table."

"Wouldn't fit in my dining room," said the middle-aged black woman who had stopped to watch the felt-tipped hammers make their way through a song. She called her friend over from the earring racks and told her the price and the friend shook her head.

They walked away still shaking their heads, as if this forty-thousand-dollar piano was just one more piece of evidence of whitefolks being some kind of way.

"I'll take a check," I called, a lame joke that worked sometimes. If I could get people to laugh they might fill out an interest card, and filled-out interest cards were the only proof that I'd shown up for work. But people weren't laughing. Time for a break.

I walked through handbags to *The Boar,* a life-sized bronze pig standing in a fountain formed by water trickling out over its tongue. The fountain was in a sort of foyer between facing pairs of elevators, and tired shoppers would sit on its low wall. I sat with them a bit. I liked the sound of the falling water and the sparkle of copper and silver on the bottom of the pool. From the fountain I trolled the department store's bulk candy section. Safely past that (quarter pound minimum) I surveyed the gourmet salads and spreads, ending up at the ice cream counter, where I ordered a hot chocolate.

"With whipped cream?"

"With whipped cream."

With whipped cream and me climbed up to the balcony (which at the price they charged they better have) and took a table near the edge. Sipping, looking out over the store, I realized why the piano had been placed where it was. Cosmetics sat in between the street entrance and the outlet to the mall. It was a sort of thoroughfare where, as I watched, a winding dragon of winter-bundled children wove, bunching and then opening again accordian-like at the piano, outlining the boar's fountain, and continuing on through gourmet foods.

A preschool class, it looked like, about fifteen of them sashaying as they walked, trying to face ahead while reaching forward and back for their classmates' hands. A teacher held on at each end. They and all the students, I noticed, were black, except one student. He was a sandy-haired boy walking second from the rear, with a delicate little girl in a blue wool coat in front of him and

104

a round-faced boy in a red Phillies jacket behind. He had on a green ski jacket.

They wound through tables to the ice cream counter beneath me. The children closed together, dropping their arms but keeping hold of one another's hands. The teacher in front said something to the teen-ager behind the counter. I slid my chair closer to the rail and leaned over.

How quietly and patiently the children stood.

"Just a plastic cup?"

"Yes, how much per cup?" said the front teacher. Her long coat was draped over one arm, a loaded backpack sliding off the shoulder of the other. She turned loose the hand of the first child in line to slide this pack back up. The little girl grasped the tail of her blouse instead, and watched.

"I don't know. A quarter?"

"That's too much," called the teacher at the back of the line, "let's try the food court." The lead teacher extended her hand, the lead child took it, and the line U-turned away from the counter. I guessed that the teachers had juice and crackers, but had forgotten cups. I looked down into the paper cone of my hot chocolate. It had cost more than cups enough for all of them.

When the rear of the line passed beneath the balcony the white child looked up, straight at me. Then he smiled. It was a smile that seemed to underline what his body language had already said, "I am one with this line, content with the others to wait for our snack."

That smile stayed with me. I saw it in the bottom of my cup, and in the windows of the subway I rode home. Late that night, on the third floor, as I sat writing in my journal, it came back to me … the peaceful smile, his oneness with the line. I turned off the light and pulled my chair up to the window. In the park, lamplight lay like frost on the branches of the bare trees. From a telephone wire near the window a pair of white leather sneakers hung by their laces, the lower one turning slowly, the upper still, as if poised mid-step. A pigeon perched on the wire and began to groom itself, setting the sneakers swaying. They lulled me like a hypnotist's pendulum and I found myself remembering a Quaker meeting in New Paltz, New York. Twenty or so silent people on plain wooden benches facing the unornamented center of a plain room. The silence ran unbroken for a time, and then deepened suddenly, as a stream opening into a deep pool.

Sitting within this silence, I seemed to drift into a sort of movie, more conceptual than visual, but I felt I could see the concepts, in a way. They were outlined against a patina of sadness, a sadness that seemed to be around me but not in me, at first. What I saw was American history as a series of missed opportunities to right the wrong of slavery. Noble ideals yet glowing red and gold from the forge of revolution bent so soon with hypocrisy. Indentured servitude, by self-serving law changed to slavery (for the African servants only), and that becoming uniquely North American chattel slavery. Not following even slow England's lead and ending slavery, but importing more and more people, breeding them like animals. The Abolitionists, yes, and service on the Underground Railroad, but the back bench too. Proclaim LIBERTY throughout all the Land unto all the Inhabitants thereof. The Civil War, a nation wrenched apart, and when freedom was bought at such a ghastly price to let it slip away, Reconstruction not the caricature but an amazing oasis, democracy proven, tried and proven and … betrayed, into the hands of the insurrectionists. If Lincoln hadn't been killed … if forty acres and a mule had been given … if slave pensions had become a reality … if land grants had been granted to the freedmen too, as Sojourner Truth dreamed … if Jim Crow terror hadn't been allowed to run on so long … generations with no vote, no schools, hunger, flight … if the cities fled to had opened their arms or given at least the grudging welcome the cheap-labor immigrants were given … if the labor unions hadn't slammed their doors … if the nation had respected the black vets come home from Europe … had given pensions and home loans and farm loans fairly … if the schools had been desegregated when the court of the land decreed them desegregated … 381 days walking to get a seat on the bus … thirty-nine years old! Hoover hiding death threats, police cars circling a hotel in Memphis … Marian Anderson on the steps of the Lincoln Memorial, "Sweet Land of Liberty," if only King, if only Malcolm … Rodney King on every television, and so many prime-time times a night men of color in cuffs, men and teenagers with their faces to the sidewalk, the chain as through shackled ankles running back through every era of America's making.

Quaking, I rose to speak about what I'd seen in the silence. Only a fragment, it was enough; when I sat the quaking stopped and my breath was given back to me.

Sitting, eyes closed, I had prayed then as one washed ashore. Let me do something, let no new harm be done, let the wounds be healed, let us not miss the next opportunity, let me not miss *my* opportunity. Use me. Change me. Use me. If the Underground Railroad was shut down too soon ... if this nation, conceived in liberty (what love I felt then for my country!) and dedicated, *dedicated* to the proposition.... In the silence that day, sitting on the hard bench beside a white woman who'd moved her small children into Mississippi's Freedom Summer and a man who tried to live the Sermon on the Mount, I was blessed with a clear perception, and responded with a clear prayer, to which that boy looking up was an answer.

Miss not your opportunity.

In Philadelphia, I opened my eyes. The pigeon was gone. The sneakers were turning like a wind vane in the wind. *Walk with her,* I heard (a gentle voice). *Walk with her.*

But would she ever want to walk with me again?

I didn't know. Kaki was at a meeting. I didn't wait for her to come home. I knew she'd be glad I had changed my mind, and it seemed to me Tahija was the first person I should tell. So I threw on boots, coat, and hat and headed for the El. I wanted to knock at every door and announce it: They've been born, the triplets have been born, they're fine, they're coming home, here.

Unless I've blown it.

Had I blown it? I felt like Scrooge after his three-ghost night. If I got another chance, I sure wasn't going to blow it again.

Chapter 13

Now it was my chance to put myself in my mother's shoes and try not to make the same mistakes that she did, not because I didn't want to be like her but because I saw what she went through and I learned from it and I wanted to change the cycle before it started. I knew that their lives hadn't begun and I wanted them to at least start out right even if it might not last forever.

My Life as I Know It

Adversity, responsibility, adult pressures — these had given Tahija Ellison a maturity beyond her years. It was a maturity she would pay a high price for, in stress, and the physical breakdown prolonged stress brings. She was not a superwoman, and carrying super burdens wasn't going to turn her into one, it was only going to wear her out. But when I saw her in her new hospital room sitting up in a flowered shirt and black nylon headscarf, telling her one cousin about how the other one had almost fainted in the delivery room, she did seem to me remarkably strong, with the strength of one who's come through fire. "And I say there is nothing greater than the mother of men."*

---

*From Walt Whitman's *Leaves of Grass*

We had talked the day before. I had told her I'd said yes too soon, had then said no too soon, and that I hoped — and I knew Kaki hoped too — that she would let me go back to a yes: an attained yes, a yes with commitment. I asked her forgiveness for having taken away what security she had as she went into the delivery. She gave it freely, generously, gave it with an unearned bonus — her description of the births, which now the cousin was hearing.

"So you didn't let him in?" Crystal asked. She was a wiry, athletic girl Tahija's age.

"You talking about the doctor who kept saying you were too young?" I asked.

"Right," Tahija saw me.

She looked good. The dusting of gray had gone from her face and there was some color in her cheeks again.

Lamarr came, Kaki soon after, and we heard all about the births one more time. Kaki was as happy as a Liberal Lutheran in the front row of *A Prairie Home Companion*. I knew it when she announced (she who hadn't bought anything that cost more than a hundred dollars since the Carter administration) that she and Tahija were going shopping for a sewing machine.

"As soon as you get out."

"They told me three days," said Tahija, "but watch me blow this candy factory in two."

And she did.

"Turn it off. Okay turn it back on. No turn it off!"

Sam Harpur shouted instructions from the bathroom down to Kaki in the basement. We'd had a phone call from the DHS social worker assigned to Tahija's case. They were coming to inspect. Our very house would be a perch for the hawk, with the hope that it might fly on.

I was sweeping plaster dust from the hallway carpet.

"What we need to do is fix that ceiling," I told Sam. The lath showed behind the crumbling plaster.

"No time," said Sam. He was kneeling beside the sink tightening a pipe fitting with his bare hands. "Besides, they're not worrying about all that. They want the utilities cut on and working is all." Sam Harpur knew the child welfare system, a hard-won knowledge he was willing to share.

Okay!" he called, letting go of the pipe. "Turn it on! See? All it needed was a new washer." He stood up. "What else?"

"Garbage disposal."

"They're not worrying about —"

"Just in case," I said.

While Sam worked in the kitchen I vacuumed and Kaki washed windows, finishing with the big mirror. She wore the light gray sweat pants that she often wore at home, and a blue-green plaid shirt over a white turtleneck. As she stretched and bent she seemed to be cleaning her own image. She was energized. She had people in her life — teenagers, babies, neighbors, me — and a sense of purpose, a sense of serving a higher purpose. The anti-gay rhetoric of the Christian right hurt her deeply. Sometimes I worried her service to the poor grew from a desire to prove herself an upstanding Christian. Having been raised Catholic I thought I knew the old original-sin shell game when I saw it. But it's hard to walk away from the games we're born into.

When the house was cleaned, Kaki and I sat on the sofa waiting. Sam went out for a cigarette and we heard him talking to Miss Tina about the triplets coming. She said she'd already heard it from Miss Ruth. Miss Ruth had been in for tea, and I'd told her. Miss Ruth promised to pray for the boys and their grandmom. I had said I'd pray for the grandson she was raising, and his mother. Now I heard Miss Tina tell Sam she would pray for him. We were a praying block, Hancock Street. Had to be.

The face of the hawk was not the face we had expected. It was female, black, and young. It was tired.

Miss Williams had many forms for us to fill out. These she pulled from a boxy briefcase where file folders were packed tight as cards in a deck. Background check, criminal record check, child abuse clearance, employment history, residence history. We were writing for a good half hour, then she interviewed us and filled out other forms. Finally she stood to inspect the house, clipboard in hand.

We visited the nursery first. She switched on the choo-choo light and checked off a box on the form. There was no box for *sun streaming through windows,* or *tree,* or *buds portending leaves.* In the bathroom, she flushed, tried the hot and cold faucets in the sink and bathtub, and checked off more boxes. Down in the kitchen she opened the refrigerator — check; tried the faucets — check; and the stove's four burners — check.

"The oven only goes on for Kaki and Tahija," I explained. Kaki turned her back to the oven and gave it a kick in the broiler. We waited for the whoosh. Check.

"Canned food?" she asked.

"We eat mostly fresh," I said.

"I need to see some canned vegetables."

Behind soba noodles and bow-tie pasta I found two cans of corn and a small can of mushrooms. Check.

Four walls and a door, gas and electric, running water, plumbing, canned food — the minimal requirements needed to ward off the hawk. And yet, for many, these requirements were too much.

Miss Williams closed her briefcase, put on her coat, and went to the door. She told us her supervisor would be in contact, but things appeared to be in order. As long as Tahija and the babies came home here, the case would be closed.

When she had gone, Sam Harpur opened the door and leaned his head in.

"She ask about the hallway ceiling?"

"No," I admitted.

"She try the garbage disposal?"

"No."

"Told you."

* * *

The nursery is the happiest place in a hospital. Evenly spaced cribs stand by the window like mounds in a vegetable garden, each a miracle and a promise of miracles to come. Kaki and I went down the row reading names. No Damear, Mahad or Lamarr. Kaki slid her big glasses to the end of her nose.

"They're so tiny. With my family, I'm used to seven, eight, even nine pound babies."

"Big Swede," I said. But indeed these newborns seemed very small. I remembered my sister's three; they'd all been big babies carried to term, or a little over. Inner-city babies and African American babies in general tended toward premature birth and all the attendant problems, including low birth weight. I had read that preemies catch up by the age of seven. What did it mean though to be born having to catch up?

A nurse wheeled a crib to the end of the line and returned with another. We knew immediately which chess set this pair of pawns belonged to. Except for their mother's big almond-shaped eyes, both faces were Lamarr's in miniature.

"Dang," I said, "no DNA test needed here. He couldn't deny being the father if he wanted to."

"And apparently he has no intention of denying it. Far from it." Kaki pointed to a name tag on one of the cribs.

"Damear Donovan Stevens," I read, "Lamarr Lamont Stevens. Not Ellison. Wow. How many sixteen-year-old fathers step up and sign the birth certificate?"

"Certifi*cates,*" she corrected.

They might weigh less than four pounds, they might be in for a fight, but they had a father, and his name.

Mahad, still in an incubator, wasn't brought out.

"What a shock it must be," Kaki whispered, "the mother's heartbeat suddenly gone, and the two closer ones too."

"Seems like they should be together."

"Maybe they're enjoying all the room."

And indeed, the crowding had caused Damear's facial bones to form asymmetrically, one eye and cheek bone set slightly deeper than the other (temporary, the doctors said). They slept, and slept, then Damear opened his eyes. His walnut-sized fist found his mouth.

I couldn't get over how small they were. "They're like babies in those photographs, you know, snuggled into a man's big hand."

"Multiple births are almost always low birth weight," Kaki reminded me. "Three and a half pounds is good. She did good bringing them this far."

"She did great. Do you hear that?" I tapped the glass. "Your mom did great."

"You probably shouldn't tap the glass."

"They're not fish," I said.

She laughed, the laugh lingering in a smile, and I guessed she was very eager to hold one (or more). And I guessed too, knowing her, knowing how her heart went always to the underdog, that though she had not even seen him yet she already favored three-pound-four-ounce Mahad. Mahad Dante.

"And to think we almost missed this," Kaki said.

Her first reproach, if reproach it was. I looked at her as she studied the newborns. She had not been angry with me when I changed my mind, neither the first time nor the second. Had something shifted between us, or had we simply learned more about each other — that I was unpredictable, she more solid?

She felt my gaze and returned it. I slid her glasses back up her nose. She glanced at the other baby watchers, one or two of whom were looking at us now. I stepped closer and reached for the band holding her hair in a ponytail, pulling it down and off.

"Hey," she said.

I doubled it on my wrist. It was a thing I did. To have the pleasure of returning it to her later, in a moment when we needed her long hair out of the way.

On the day before Damear was scheduled to come home Kaki and I visited my sister's in New York. When we came back three days later the house was quiet. We stood in the living room listening: a new quiet, a different quiet, quiet with a sleeping baby at its core.

We climbed the stairs and stood in the hallway listening. The nursery door was open, and through it we saw an empty crib flush against the far wall, in the alcove of windows that was to have been Kaki's reading nook. Curtains had been hung.

"It was good we went away," Kaki said.

The door of Tahija's room was also open. Inside, beside the bed she would soon move into the nursery, stood a white wicker bassinet, the open end toward us, so that if we stood in the doorway, if we leaned in just a little, but didn't *go* in ...

Inside the bassinet, asleep beneath a blue blanket, was the center of the new silence, Damear. He lay on his back, head to the side, facing us, one perfect ear showing. He had on a white elastic headband with a blue rose at the front.

"So were you the one with the craving for cherries?" I said. "Or were you the shrimp and broccoli guy?" I felt like I knew him, and his brothers, hands fitted now into the gloves of their bodies.

We jumped back at a crackling noise. Baby monitor on the desk, Lamarr's voice coming from it.

"Not there, put it here."

"They're in the backyard," I whispered.

"We should go tell them we're home," Kaki whispered back. "Let them show him to us."

"Maybe they have," I said, "leaving the door open like this."

So often, later, the door would be closed. Reluctantly we pulled ourselves away and went downstairs.

When I first moved to the house on Hancock Street the backyard had seemed ridiculously small. Why bother, I'd thought; why not just have a bigger kitchen? But those twelve feet, going back, and twenty from side to side, with a locust tree in the corner and a collar of soil within a cinder-block wall, seemed bigger as time went on. And when the midday sun reached the opening between the house and the back wall of the muffler shop, as now, it was a backyard you could love.

There on the sunlit pavement stones Tahija and Lamarr worked, Tahija holding the headboard of a crib while Lamarr moved a can of powder-blue spray paint over it.

"Ya'll should have coats on," I said, opening the door.

"Oh we had a time with that first crib," said the unsurprisable Tahija. "That one side doesn't wanna go up."

"Missing a piece," Lamarr explained, moving the can in slow passes.

I sensed Kaki's urge to run for her toolbox and try to repair the side in question, but their smiling faces, their joint confidence, the noontime winter sun made a tableau and a triumph of the moment: young parents nest building. We ought to leave them to it. Our challenge was to be a resource without undermining their own resourcefulness. So, although we worried about the spray paint they were using on the crib, we said nothing.

Later, though, I went around furtively cracking nursery windows, wondering, as I would many times in the coming months, just what my responsibility was to the babies in the house, and how I might meet it while remaining an ally to the parents.

Chapter 14

My childhood was easy until I got back to Philly and then it got
super hard. The boys' childhood is nothing like mine because I
will never let it get super hard for them, I don't care what I have
to do.

from the interview

On my way to the third floor that night I peeked into Tahija's
open door to see Lamarr in the overstuffed orange chair, a floor
lamp shining down on him and his son.

"He still asleep?" I asked.

"Been woke and gone back."

Damear's face rested on his father's strong forearm, his
lighter complexion highlighted, his little stockinged feet in his
dad's big hand.

"He looks like you," I said.

"Pumpkin head."

"Why you call him that?" I asked.

"Haven't you noticed what a big head I have?"

"No," I said, telling the truth.

"Fat head on a stubby little neck."

"Don't you call my baby fathead,"Tahija said, coming in.

"I didn't call him fathead," Lamarr answered. "I called him pumpkin head. Kathryn says he looks like me."

"He looks like me,"Tahija said."Mahad looks like you."

"Then who's little Lamarr look like?" I asked.

"My mom,"Tahija said."Has her same light-green eyes."

"How you gonna call them *light?*" Lamarr asked."His are dark green.Your mom's are way light, freaky light."

Damear woke and worked an arm out of the blanket, as if he meant for his eyes and no others to be the focus of conversation. Damear's eyes.They were the black of black agate marbles, lamplight reflected as bright in them as planets in a deep desert night. You didn't see his pupils until he looked directly at you, and then you saw deeply into them — twin wells fed by one underground stream.What buckets he'd lift from those depths I couldn't know. I hoped I'd be around to find out.

Damear was born with two teeth — small off-white teeth set at an angle in his bottom gum.

"Those aren't teeth," the doctor said.

"*Look* like teeth."

"Babies are not born with teeth."

"Then what are they?"

"Calcium spurs.They will dissolve of their own accord.They are not teeth."

Tahija said they were teeth, milk teeth, that milk teeth ran in her family and they would not dissolve of their own or anyone else's accord.

She was right. Those two teeth, the not-teeth, made themselves known during breast-feeding and held their place as baby teeth came in, like the baby himself holding his place as his brothers came home.

First from the womb, first from the hospital, the only one with teeth and the only to be breast-fed — Damear, Mear, Mearmear, Meana.

118

* * *

When the day came for little Lamarr to be released his great-grandmother Agnes Grealy appeared, to escort his parents to the hospital and deliver him home. Seeing the bassinet in Tahija's small middle room, she assumed all three were to be crowded in there and proceeded to tell us what she thought of that plan.

"Why when I ran a day care center each crib had to have at least eighteen inches on either side, and furthermore, the temperature must be kept at at least — "

With a flourish, I opened the nursery door.

Matching blue flounces fell from the made-up mattresses of the three cribs (Tahija's work); morning sunlight picked out what color remained in the old carpet Sam had sold us; and a new space heater had the room close to eighty degrees.

"Well, this'll do," said the grandmother.

Lamarr walked in with Damear in his arms and was told, "*Put that baby down, you'll spoil him.*"

My heart sank as Lamarr lowered his son into the crib. From my perspective, the growing bond between them was a tender shoot to be watered, not pruned. But these boys were not going to be raised from my perspective, and if I had accepted that then and there I'd have saved myself a good deal of heartache.

Kaki came in, swooned at the temperature, and went straight to the space heater. To her way of thinking electrical appliances came with two settings only: off and low.

"Tahija says can you watch Damear while we're going for Lamarr," big Lamarr said to Kaki.

"I can," I said to her, "if you have work."

Kaki looked at me — *yeah right.* We'd both helped with him a little, but his time so far in our arms could be measured in minutes. Kaki was as eager as I was for an uninterrupted stretch of baby.

"Oh, I think I can make the time," she said, fronting majorly.

"But don't pick him up," the grandmother said. "That baby should never be picked up unless he's sick."

119

Lamarr arched his left eyebrow. He knew we'd have that baby out the crib the moment they left. Did he approve though? Was this no-holding rule one he and Tahija intended to follow?

"All right now, come on ya'll," Tahija said.

"Like it's you been waiting for us," Lamarr said.

Twenty Damears could have fit width-wise in the crib — he was so small. He wore a baby blue onesie. Tahija had just bathed him and rubbed baby oil into his skin and in the bit of hair on the very top of his head. Did he sense that soon one of his brothers would be near again? They hadn't touched since their adventure in the delivery room, when he beat Lamarr into the bright light simply by lying still and waiting. Had it been a vaginal birth he would likely have been last and been given the last name, Lamarr.

"Now he ate, he doesn't need to eat again," Tahija said as they went down the stairs. "And don't pick him up, it'll — "

"I know," I said, "spoil him."

With parents and grandmother gone Kaki and I walked Damear around the room, showing him the bare branches of the tree outside and the patterns sunlight laid on its smooth gray trunk. Although we would love to have shown him Purrsilla the cat (who would not by any means be persuaded to enter the nursery), and the downstairs, and the backyard, we did not take Damear anywhere that day, except into our hearts.

I had held plenty of babies, but holding Damear then, when he was so tiny, just over four pounds, and so profoundly present, I felt something in me rising to the surface, something I hadn't known was there. When I laid him back down in his crib I could not put that feeling down, and never have.

In the movie *Sankofa* by the Ethiopian director Haile Gerima, an African American model on a shoot in Africa visits Cape Coast Castle, the infamous citadel where captured Africans were held before being carried off to death during the Middle Passage or short terrible lives in the so-called "new" world. The tour turns nightmare when the model is suddenly wrenched backward in time to a life of enslavement.

She survives the Middle Passage and is sold to a plantation. There, she looks on as a woman far along in pregnancy is whipped to death. The white overseers stand guard, guns ready, forcing the Africans to watch. When the woman breathes her last a midwife steps forward. The others encircle her, facing outward, defying guns and dogs, determined to save the unborn one. From within the circle the cry of a baby sounds out and the newborn is raised up — life taken from death.

Lifting the newborn to heaven this way is an African tradition. Within the cauldron of North American slavery it became a radical act of defiance. We will survive. And this one may be the one to lead us out of Pharaoh's land.

She was not there in Temple's operating room to do it, but back home in the nursery, as Damear slept, Agnes Grealy unwrapped little Lamarr from his receiving blanket and held him in both hands high over her head, smiling as Lamarr took pictures.

Kaki and I were honored to witness this. And I was aware — could not let myself be unaware — that if an ancestor of mine ever had witnessed it they might well have done so from behind a gun, or through the iron grating in the deck of a slave ship.

Little Lamarr had gotten used to the bottle and couldn't be persuaded. So along with breast-feeding Damear (he of the precocious teeth), expressing milk to be frozen and delivered to Mahad, who was struggling to reach four pounds (the hospital benchmark for release), Tahija now had the added chore of bottle-feeding little Lamarr.

At five pounds, Lamarr the baby did in just a few hours what big Lamarr hadn't been able to do in six weeks of sleeping on the floor of Tahija's hospital room: win over the grandmother. She favored little Lamarr shamelessly. He was the only one raised up to the ancestors that way, and when she went with us to a doctor's appointment it was little Lamarr she wanted to hold.

He was a handsome baby, to be sure. Of the three, his eyes were the most striking: green, and as lavishly lashed as his mother's, larger even than hers. His features were pleasingly proportioned, his forehead high and shining. He too was a joy to hold, and the first one I saw laugh. Though Damear would lead the three developmentally for a time, Lamarr was the most active. You could see how it was he'd found the birth canal first. Before long the windows on three sides of his crib showed handprints and footprints, and the blinds that hung there would not stay hung long. He was tender headed and had an awful time teething. He cried so much he was nicknamed Wah-wah (*a* as in *at*), which was shortened sometimes to Wah.

The one who had managed to be both the first and the last, with the "bad" hair, the "good" eyes, the long lashes, all three of his father's names, his great-grandmother's favor, the only one to suck his thumb — little Lamarr, Mar-mar, Mar, Wah-wah, Wah, on the bed beside Damear.

Mahad was breathing well enough on his own but still couldn't seem to maintain his body temperature. More life-threatening, though, was that fact that he wasn't sucking efficiently. They searched out tiny veins and fed him intravenously. The veins spasmed and collapsed. They had been about to try a vein in his head when Tahija walked in on them and forbade it.

She of the needle phobia said he was too tiny for all that sticking, they'd stick him to death. He gained two ounces, then lost three. He was a brush fire on a rainy day, not quite catching. He was the question no one wanted to ask: Is this nature saying two is enough?

"Why isn't she bringing milk in? Why isn't she visiting?" It was the head nurse from the hospital nursery calling. Mahad still hadn't gained enough weight to leave, and with two home Tahija's visits had dropped off.

"The other two take all her time," I explained. There was a pause. "The other two *triplets.*"

"Well doesn't she want this one?"

I knew enough about the system by then to know that this was no casual question, and that a flip answer, or an in-depth honest one, could cause problems. So I didn't say, "I'm not sure what she wants or if she knows herself what she wants; she's fifteen, poor, and in the middle of a series of traumas that'll take her years to begin to recover from." Nor did I ask the nurse if she'd read in the papers about the Albanian refugee mother of triplets who right in our neighborhood had killed herself just the week before, herself *and* the three babies.

I just said, "We'll be there shortly, and thanks so much for calling."

To enter the nursery, you had to wash and put on a paper gown and mask. Then you waited like a diner to be shown to your table. This time, we waited near an older baby. He was a very dark-complexioned boy in a crib off in the corner, wearing only a diaper. And he was *screaming*. I noticed a pacifier beside his mouth and leaned over to put it in.

A nurse rushed up. "You're not supposed to be touching the babies."

"He was crying."

"I know he was crying," she said.

"For awhile."

She glared at me. When a pinkish little girl's crying brought two nurses fast I felt, as Tahija would say, some kind of way. Was Mahad getting less care because he was dark? Was it starting already? I didn't know the whole story; you never know the whole story. Maybe the older baby had been crying for days and they'd tried everything. Maybe he was a crack baby, and inconsolable.

But I remembered another black boy, also dark and big for his age. I had been volunteering at a public-sector day care center. In one class they sent me to was a boy who had obviously earned villain status. The only black male in the mostly white class, he was punished often. When I knelt to comfort him after a scolding he fell into my arms and sobbed convulsively: pain that had been building for more than one hard day.

I told the two teenaged white girls in charge that I thought he was being punished too much. They said I didn't know him, that he was very bad. He was four, and as far as I could see a quiet, well-behaved child. Outside later, when a girl playing near this boy began crying, one of the caregivers swooped down without investigation and yanked him up, carrying him by the armpits to the open window of the classroom and tossing him through like a sack of laundry. The boy screamed through it all.

The center's director refused to fire those two girls. She could pay only six an hour, she explained, and six an hour didn't buy you much.

Standing in the nursery waiting to see Mahad, remembering that boy's shaking sobs, and other children, other cruelty and injustice I'd witnessed or heard tell of, I did not reach out to touch the off-limits baby a second time. But I made him a promise. I promised that in so far as it was in my power I would favor the one in the corner, the one singled out to receive the poison of racial hatred. Unfairly, unconditionally, over the sweetest, most innocent white child, even should that child be of my own blood, I would favor and prefer him.

Well aware that no one action or series of actions on my part could begin to balance the scales, I nevertheless made my covenant: I became — before I even knew the word — a Reparationist.

When we were let to go to Mahad at last, we found him awake, eyes staring blankly at the ceiling, fists clenched beneath his chin. A kind nurse brought a rocking chair over and Tahija sat to accept the tiny bundle. Mahad wore a white stocking cap, his wee chin and nose crowding up close to a little bow of a mouth. She held the bottle of breast milk she'd brought to his lips. He appeared to suck but when she held the bottle to the light we saw how little had gone in.

She kept trying, and eventually accomplished a full ounce, then surprised me by asking if I wanted to try.

I sat down and felt his almost weightless weight in the crook of my arm.

"He's so tense," I said.

"It's all that *sticking* him, I told you," Tahija said.

His eyes, smaller than Damear's and Lamarr's, were medium brown, and focused unblinkingly at the fluorescent lights overhead.

"See what's happening is," Tahija explained, "he's holding his tongue against the roof of his mouth. "Try holding his tongue down with your pinky."

I did, and it seemed to be working, but when I pulled the bottle out we noticed the diaper tucked under his chin was soaked. I gave him back to his mother. She tried it with his head lower, the bottle higher, her pinky in his mouth; she tried nuzzling his neck so he'd laugh and unloose his tongue. The third-shift nurses came and the second shift left. Finally Tahija raised an empty bottle.

"Four ounces!"

"Four ounces," echoed a nurse.

"She got four in," called another.

"Good job."

She burped him. More praise. When the time came to leave, we didn't want to. He looked so small and alone in the crib, hands fisted, eyes glazed, mouth open, as if in shocked surprise.

"Guinea-pigging him is what they're doing," Tahija said as we walked between snow banks to the car. "Going to try and put a needle in his head!"

"It's awful."

"I told them 'I didn't sign for that!' Now you know me Kathryn, do I look like I'm about to sign for them to stick a big long needle into my baby's head?"

"No."

"Guinea-pigging him to death."

This sounded paranoid to me, until I thought of the Tuskegee Syphilis Experiment, and of the ads in subway cars for people to "take part" in clinical trials. "A Hundred Dollars a Day. Big Completion Bonus." You never saw such ads on the freeways heading out to the suburbs.

"You've got to get him home," I said. "Get his weight up, get him home."

And she did. At six weeks old, Mahad, or Mahddy as he was often called (rhymes with *body*), lay between his brothers for the first time since Damear had been lifted from the womb.

It was a wonderful sight. Though their faces were quite similar, and people would often confuse them, they differed in many ways: Damear, Mear-Mear, was relatively stocky, with a round face, head still mostly bald, just a bit of hair on top, the black agate eyes; Lamarr, Marr, Wah, was longer, with the high forehead and thinner face, a full head of tight hair, and green-sometimes-brown eyes; and Mahad, Mahddy, Mahd, thin and short, the darkest, with chipmunk cheeks and brown, widely spaced eyes, his hair somewhere between Damear's and Lamarr's, his hairline straight and low.

Tahija combed a glistening curl so it dropped handsomely over Mahd's forehead and took their picture. Marr caught hold of Mahd's diaper. Mear found his arm, and all seemed to agree that it was good to be together again. It was the way it should be.

Chapter 15

Mahad was said to be failure-to-thrive only because he wasn't the same weight as the other two. He was a small child then he's a small child now and if I could I would sue them for discrimination of age because like the doctor said he wouldn't have given me a hard way to go if I would have been older, but I know I have always acted older than my age, and I am real responsible.

from the interview

A tutor from the school district's homebound program came for a few hours each day, and some evenings Tahija and I met on the third floor to discuss poems and stories I'd given her to read. She liked Poe's "The Tell-Tale Heart," Alice Walker's "Everyday Use" (though the use of dialect made her uncomfortable), but Shirley Jackson's "The Lottery" was just too sneaky. She was a good reader and a tough critic. I looked forward to seeing the English books she'd bring home once she went back to school.

As we talked, one or more of the triplets might be crying downstairs. And even if not, I had a sense, a weight, like a dragging anchor, of their needs waiting to be met; Mahad especially, but Damear and Lamarr too, needing to be held, talked to, stimulated. Tahija bathed and dressed them every morning. Their cribs and the nursery were tidy, sheets and blankets laundered, bottles washed, formula ready. She was efficient, and had spurts of manic energy from which the whole house benefited. But she didn't hold them, didn't seem to like holding them.

Had I supposed she would? I guess I hadn't thought that far ahead. But now that they were in the house my maternal-instinct tricorder was beeping wildly — such a density of infantile need so near. And there in front of me, not quite fifteen-and-a-half years old, was their mother with all *her* needs, some born of her stage in life and of the role she found herself in now, some remaining from her past.

Tahija's needs felt to me like a maze I must wind through in order to reach the boys, whose present, raw, very meetable needs called out. Why, though, did I feel they called out *to me?* They had a mother and a father. I was not even family. Now and then Tahija called Kaki mom, as she did her friend Renee's mother. It seemed an affirmation of their connection, a freestyle extending of family. But I was just Kathryn, a friend, available for baby-sitting, not a meeter of needs.

And yet I felt them, wanted to meet them, or through them to meet my own unmet infantile needs. Which we can never do, really. Accepting that, mourning the past, moving on — that's maturity, isn't it? In that sense, though I was forty (and-a-half), I was not very mature. Maybe that's why Tahija never called me mom. Maybe that's why I kicked and screamed like a baby myself.

Mahad was so detached. His eyes didn't focus, and when you picked him up his whole body stiffened, as if touch stung. A nurse came weekly to weigh them and over his first few weeks home Mahad actually lost a few ounces. Kaki and I offered to help feed them, were eager to help. Tahija said no, thanks, they were all right, she was all right. She'd ask if she needed it.

But Mahad couldn't ask. I longed to hold him, to wear a baby sack and carry him with me everywhere, to bathe him slowly, gently, the warm water an invitation to relax, live a little, *live*. A nurse friend told us about ICU trauma, a condition of premature babies caused by too much exposure to hospital lights and noise. For Mahad, life so far had been hunger and pain, needles and glare. Why stay?

Tahija was down in the living room with her tutor. I stood at the top of the stairs listening: algebra still; history next. I went into the nursery. Damear lay on his side playing with an activity board. Lamarr slept. Mahad, because he overheated easily, had on only a diaper. I laid my hand on his chest, my thumb and pinkie touching mattress on either side. I felt his heart flutter like a moth in a jar. I thought of a dream I'd had ... two babies playing while a third tried to climb up a narrow set of stairs.

"Mahd," I said, "Mahddy."

Tahija's feeding method was to lay the baby on his side and prop his bottle on a folded blanket. I didn't think Mahad was getting enough that way. Often his blankets were wet. I'd coax her to, but whenever she tried to hold him he arched his back convulsively and made unpleasant snuffling noises — a side effect of being premature, the doctor had said, and probably temporary. Mucus bubbled from his nose. Tahija couldn't put up with this. She had about as much patience as, well, a fifteen year old. Mahad would have been a hard baby to care for even had he been the only one.

I held him. His spine arched. I massaged his back and walked him around the room, visiting Lamarr, who slept on his belly, bottom in the air, and then Damear, who lay playing with his toes now.

"Damear wants you to stay, right Mear-mear?"

I laid Mahad beside Damear and did "The Itsy-bitsy Spider" for them. Mear laughed when the sun came out "and dried up all the rain" (I made a rainbow with my arms), but Mahad just gazed at that spot on the ceiling that he'd been gazing at all along. I walked him more, hummed, rubbed his back. When he finally untensed a little I wanted to rush him downstairs to his mother so she could hold his softened body and tell him she wanted him to stay too. But I dared not. I held him until I heard the tutor leaving. Then I laid him back down and brushed his cheek ... as wind would, and leaves, soft cloth and lovers' hands, if only he stayed.

When I left him his little fists were tight to his chest, as if reining in a team of horses only he could see.

Mid-April and the cherry trees in the park were in full bloom, but it wasn't until you left the city that you realized the whole hemisphere was in bloom. I had driven with Marcelle to her Quaker meeting in the suburbs, and was standing on the porch of the old stone meetinghouse when I heard persistent chirping close by. A tiny bird no bigger than my thumb hopped along the wall, sideways from stone to stone. I watched awhile then went in.

There were only about ten of us in worship, but the silence was good, drawing me down through physical tension and mental static to the depth where I could better open to the Light within. I was not moved to stand and give a message, but about halfway through a message seemed to come to me, for me alone, in the form of an image: the bird hopping from stone to stone. I realized it had been trying to climb upward. To what? It must have fallen from a nest and been struggling, was probably struggling even as I sat there, to get back to it, and live. And Mahad — wasn't he, even as I sat there, struggling like the tiny bird to survive? I had to do more.

When I came out, the bird was gone. When I got home, I talked to Tahija about the bottle propping and asked if there wasn't more I could do. At that time, she was weaning Damear from the breast and he was having a hard time with it, crying a lot and earning the label spoiled and greedy. Little Lamarr was very active, demanding much attention. Poor Tahija was exhausted and stressed. When Lamarr came to watch them she caught up on her sleep, sleeping once for twenty-four hours straight. I don't know if she could have done more if she wanted to. And not wanting me to do more than I was doing (the WIC shopping, a share of the laundry, baby-sitting when asked), she dug in.

The visiting nurse declared Mahad failure-to-thrive. A nurse friend told me the only hope was to hold him nonstop. I didn't know what to do but I felt I had to do something.

That night I tiptoed down to the second floor and stood listening outside the nursery door. Was she asleep, or listening too? I inched the door open and passed into the baby powder scented warmth. Two steps brought me to Mahad's crib. In the dark I could see Tahija on her stomach on top of the covers, one arm flung out. Mahad was awake. I picked him up. Three steps and we were out in the hallway. Carefully I pulled the door closed and went into her other room. If I got caught at least I wouldn't have taken him out of her space. I had a bottle of formula waiting on the armrest of the orange chair, the chair where I'd seen Lamarr holding Damear that first day. Where was he now? Running the streets, Tahija liked to say, out running the streets with no coat on. But what did that mean? And had we freed him to do it by taking his family in, or would he be doing it anyway?

I didn't know. I only knew this baby was slipping away, and that knowing it I had to do what I could. I sat down and turned on a dim light. I talked softly to him and caressed his cheeks as I fed him the bottle, letting him go as slowly as he liked. When he finished, I held him against my chest, talking to him, rubbing his back, rocking a little from side to side. He fell asleep in my arms.

When I laid him back down, the crib creaked. I heard Tahija breathing. It was not the breathing of sleep.

In the morning, cleaning bottles at the kitchen sink, Tahija held one up for me to see, "Mahad played me."

The bottle had an ounce in it. "What do you mean?"

"Trying to act like he was all hungry, but he wasn't."

"Oh," I said. I didn't admit what I'd done; she didn't confront me. It was a kind of compromise, I guess, and the best we could manage.

But that "oh" haunted me. *Was* it a compromise, or cowardice? Had I lost all sense of boundaries — to be sneaking around in the night? Should I have called DHS? Did bottle propping warrant calling in the very thing Tahija most feared? She had three, after all, I told myself. And three helpers — Kaki, Lamarr and me — that she wasn't using enough. But she had a firm idea of how much was enough. And if it didn't seem enough to me? Was this the infant in me talking, worrying, whining for more? Or a witness called to speak truth to power, even if that power felt herself to be powerless?

"We'll have to draw blood from an artery," the doctor said.

They were testing Mahad to see why he wasn't gaining weight. The doctor, an older man we liked, had tried already to draw blood from veins in Mahd's arm, his leg, his foot even; each time the vein had spasmed.

"You'll have to sign a release," he told us, and left to get the form.

Tahija and I waited. Mahd lay listless on the table, too drained even to make the paper under him crackle.

"I wish we could just dress him and get out of here."

"Without letting them do the tests? They'd be after me. You've got to keep up with shots, all that. I haven't missed an appointment."

"I know."

"And I save every piece of paper they give me."

She did too. Her purse was a veritable filing cabinet.

The doctor came back. Tahija signed the release. The doctor prepared the needle.

"You want to wait in the hall?" I said.

She shook her head no. "You want to?"

"I'll stay."

The targeted artery was high on the inside of Mahad's thigh. Tahija held his hips and legs while the doctor worked. Mahad's head fell to the side, eyes locked on mine. In them I saw an elemental human plea: *Make this stop!* Maybe the procedure didn't last as long as I remember, but that look with which he met my eyes will last forever. Because I could have made it stop; could have told the doctor he wasn't gaining weight because we weren't feeding him enough, plain and simple.

Finally the doctor had his vial of blood. I noticed sweat at his temples. As Tahija dressed Mahad, like putting clothes on clothes, the doctor looked at me. They didn't generally look at you.

"You're her caseworker?"

"No. We live in the same house."

"You going to stick with her?"

I said I was. Weren't we joined by Mahddy's blood? If she had failed in any way I had failed in the same way, and one way more: I had failed to persuade her to give more to the snuffling, rigid one who came after the other two had staked their claims. It was left to Mahad to persuade her.

The blood tests revealed no condition that might be interfering with Mahad's growth. At the next visit, therefore, the doctor refused to send Mahad home with Tahija and Lamarr. He ordered that he be kept in the hospital for forty-eight hours. Tahija was to feed him under supervision every four hours. If Mahad gained weight during that time it would be taken as evidence that he was not being fed adequately at home and DHS would immediately assume custody.

"Of all three, or just Mahad?" I asked when Kaki told me the news. Tahija had called from the hospital, asking for us to watch the other two and for a ride home at the end of the forty-eight hours.

"I presume just Mahad," she said, going immediately to her address book and her network of friends, which included social workers, city administrators, and a councilman's staffer — people we could ask help from if … we didn't like to think about *if.*

"It's probably a ploy," I said, walking Lamarr as she rocked Damear. "To scare her."

"Well she's scared," Kaki said. She had visited the first day and reported that Tahija was holding Mahad constantly, with Lamarr spelling her for bathroom breaks.

"She's not even complaining. She's just holding him, feeding him."

"Well there'll be some complaining if they take him, I'll tell you that. Complaining won't be the half of it."

I think I was afraid of Tahija. She had a temper, she'd go off on you. But I realized too, thinking of her there in the hospital, nurses and social workers watching her — a whole flock of hawks! — how very defenseless she must have felt; incendiary language, a well-advertised temper, and the threat of violence were all she had. Plus Lamarr. But what power did Lamarr have in that world? Would he hurt someone who tried to take Mahad? Would Tahija? What then would happen to Damear and Lamarr?

At the end of the forty-eight hours Kaki drove to the hospital at the appointed time and waited in the pick-up zone for the three of them to come out. She described it to me later, how she waited an hour before deciding to go up. In the room, she found a DHS worker she'd never met before standing, briefcase in hand, with the apparent intention of leaving with Mahad Dante Stevens.

Kaki demanded to be told what was going on.

"Are you family?" the social worker asked.

"Most certainly, and I most certainly expect to be told what's going on here."

Some people sprinkle their speech with "like" and "actually" or "you know." Kaki prefers "most certainly." She says it the way her English teacher-former marine lieutenant mother says it, and whatever she says she employs the diction she and her siblings were drilled in nightly at the dinner table.

Whether it was that diction (thank you Dona Nelsen), her confidence, or how she gave her pinky to Mahddy to hold, the caseworker relented. A new case would have to be opened; they'd be around to the house again, and Tahija would have to accept in-home services, but Mahad could remain in his mother's custody. He would come home a second time, to stay.

All that week Tahija sat in her chair in the shamrock room and held Mahad. She held him while she poured formula for the others. She held him while he drank his formula. She held him while she read and while she talked on the phone. As she had bonded with Damear during breast-feeding, she bonded now with struggling Mahad. He stopped tensing his body and arching his back when she held him. He came home to his body.

Soon came the day when a visiting nurse announced the boys' weights like a perfect report card. They were gaining. Mahad was gaining. He would make it.

We're climbing the hill behind the country place where I've been living as a caretaker. The boys are five. Tahija and Lamarr are back at the house making dinner. I have the three in front of me. Little Lamarr leads the way, a bundle of sticks in his arms for the campfire, with Damear, carrying one stick, a few yards behind. Mahad's beside me. They have on matching faded denim jeans, matching blue winter coats (though it's sixty-something), and those orange-colored boots from the famous boot company supposedly owned, as his dad had told me, by the KKK.

Damear tries to walk across a flat mossy boulder and slips, landing in the ferns. I help him up and call a halt to the march.

"Okay you guys. See this green moss? Please don't walk on rocks that have moss. If you walk on them, you might slip and get hurt, all right?"

"Arright," says Damear, and goes on, Lamarr beside him. Mahddy just stands beside the rock in question, giving it the once-over.

"Watch me walk on the moss rock and not slip, Kath-a-ryn."

"I don't want you to Mahddy because you might get hurt."

"Watch me not get hurt."

"Alright go on."

I walk alongside, but he makes it fine, turning to give me his sly smile as he jumps, running before his feet have even hit the ground to catch up with his brothers.

Middle born, last home, first to bust his head open and have to be rushed to the emergency room (five stitches) — Mahad, Mahd, Mahddy, Mahd-man. Thriving, with distinction.

Chapter 16

DHS never helped me and I wish there wasn't such a thing
because they made me miserable and they didn't help me one
bit. If I could go back I would sue them for harassment. I was a
fit parent they just couldn't get past the age. I was in a stable
home but they still couldn't get past the age. They need to start
judging a person by the person, not the age.

from the interview

DHS caseworkers came around to the house soon after the
scare over Mahad. This time, along with young Miss Williams,
came her supervisor Mrs. Chissom, a no-nonsense woman who
shook our hands briskly, gave the furnishings and our attire a
sharp look, and got down to business. Accompanying them but
clearly apart — her clothes neat but not professional, only a
purse in her hands — was a fiercely silent, gray-haired woman
who took the rocker in the corner and proceeded to examine
the books on our bookshelf. This was Mrs. Hayes, a home aide
who would be coming to the house three days a week to provide
as yet unspecified services.

Everyone declined tea. Mrs. Chissom would take water.
"With ice?"

With ice. She and Miss Williams sat on the sofa, their brief-cases weighing a deep V into the cushion between them. Kaki and I carried chairs over from the dining room table while Tahija sat at its head watching the proceedings in the floor-to-ceiling mirror. She wasn't tempting fire, but neither was she feeling very cooperative, because this was a fire she'd passed through already. Lamarr had not been invited. Though his name was on the birth certificates, he never seemed to show up in the system's paperwork. The post-welfare reform TANF program removed some disincentives to marriage and active participation of fathers, but many remained, as did a three-decades deep pattern that was itself part of a larger, much older family-break-ing pattern.*

Mear, Mahd and Marr were upstairs. I would have liked to have them with us, maybe get a smile out of Miss Hayes. It was a shame, so many perfectly good laps going empty.

They were opening a new case, Mrs. Chissom explained, but their goal was not to take the children into custody. I could see Tahija in the mirror. She had an arm on the chair back and her head resting on that, looking at the floor. Their goal, Mrs. Chissom went on, was to ensure good care, which was why they were rec-ommending the Lighthouse, a day care program in a community center about a mile from us.

Besides her cash allotment, Tahija had been awarded $480 per month for child care expenses. Though the boys were three months old, none of that had been used.

"The Lighthouse provides developmentally appropriate activ-ities," Miss Williams said, "and snacks."

"I don't want my boys eating pork."

"Excuse me?" said Mrs. Chissom.

---

*TANF (Temporary Assistance for Needy Families) replaced AFDC (Aid to Families with Dependent Children) after welfare reform in 1996. Based on income eligibility and designed to support single mothers and their children, AFDC had built-in disincentives to marriage and even cohabitation of parents.

"They don't eat pork, they're Muslim. Almost every kind of snack, you read the ingredients, you'll see: made with pork, pork products, gelatin."

"Even marshmallows contain pork," I informed the group.

"My boys won't ever eat a marshmallow unless it's *Halal*,"* Tahija announced.

Mrs. Chissom sighed and looked at her watch.

The presence in the rocker spoke: "Plenty worse things in this world than pork."

I looked at Kaki. Did she mean teens having sex, or us? Was lesbianism worse than pork? We had discussed coming out to DHS. Kaki was inclined to, coming out being a sort of hobby of hers — the larger and more conservative the audience the better. I feared coming out might hurt Tahija's cause; and, too, it seemed presumptuous, as if we assumed being white trumped being gay. The first time around with DHS we had settled on a don't ask, don't tell policy, though our answers to certain questions probably had given it away.

"You don't have to leave them there all day," Miss Williams said. "You could pick them up on your way home from school." (Tahija would be going half days once she started back.)

Tahija wasn't having it. Besides pork snacks, she told us, day care meant germs: cold germs, flu germs, mumps, measles, pinkeye, ringworm, strep. And what did they pay the people who worked in the Lighthouse? The caseworker and her supervisor didn't know the precise figure. Tahija did. It was $6.50 an hour, and $6.50 an hour wasn't enough for them to hire anybody she cared to leave her babies with. Didn't we see that news show where a hidden camera caught day-care workers molesting the children?

Well then who, Miss Williams asked, would watch them while she was at school?

"Why do I have to go to school!"

She didn't have to go to school, Mrs. Chissom explained, massaging her temples, but if she wasn't in school or working or in

*Free of pork and blessed by an imam

a work-related training program she was not getting a check. WIC would continue, and health care, but no cash.

Mrs. Hayes intoned, "State not paying no more for people want to sit around making babies."

From Tahija came the labored breathing I had seen send even Lamarr running for cover.

Kaki rushed in with, "Now I don't think that's fair. She's taking the Depo-Provera."*

"Only sure way is abstinence," Mrs. Hayes announced.

"So," Mrs. Chissom pressed on, "who is going to watch them while you're at school?"

"Lamarr needs work," Kaki said.

"Lamarr?"

"The father," I said. And why wasn't his birth control method or the lack thereof under discussion?

"The childcare allotment cannot be paid to the father," Mrs. Chissom said. Neither was he eligible for job-training or placement programs, though if he found above-the-table work the state would be happy to garnish part of his wages to "recover" TANF payments Tahija had received — a double disincentive.

"Other family members are, however, eligible," Miss Williams said.

Tahija looked out the window toward Barbara's apartment across the street. Not Barbara, I thought. Then she looked at me. Not me, I thought. Then everyone, including Sister Abstinence, was looking at me.

"Have the criminal record checks been done on these ladies?" Mrs. Chissom asked the caseworker.

"Yes ma'am, previously."

Oh no.

"Easy commute," Kaki said.

I did need a job. I had worked as a nanny years before, in a much wealthier part of the city (one child, twice the pay). And

---

*Depo-Provera is a form of birth control given by a shot every three months. The side effects include weight gain, which, combined with high blood pressure and diabetes, could be life-threatening.

my heart started pounding, actually pounding, at the thought of having them to myself all day.

All day all week? Was I out of my mind?

"I'll help when I'm here," Kaki said. She'd recently become co-director of the Philadelphia branch of the American Friends Service Committee, a three-fifths time position that let her work at home.

Four-eighty a month came to one-twenty a week. Before or after taxes? I thought of the generations of black women who had cared for white children for no pay during slavery, for very low pay later. I met Tahija's eyes. Had she noticed the serendipity of my moving to the city in the very same month the triplets were conceived? It was like I'd gone deep for a pass, and the pass was just then spiraling downward. Whether it was to get these people off her back, please Kaki and me, keep the childcare money in the house, or because she thought it was in the boys' best interest — I didn't know, but when her words, "Kathryn's *been* helping with them," were seconded by the look in her eyes, I felt the ball meet my fingertips.

The next morning I stood in the second floor hallway wondering: Was the nursery door partway open, or partway closed? Hard to tell. With the frame out of plumb the door never fully shut. Tahija had another week yet before going back to school, but, emboldened by my status as nanny-elect, I poked my head in.

"Hey," I said, "hope I didn't scare you."

"I heard you coming down the stairs."

Unflappable. She was sitting on the floor, back against the bed, legs folded. Before her was a lime green plastic basin, and naked on a towel beside that Damear, Mahad, and Lamarr.

"You're letting the heat out."

I butted the door shut behind me and sat on the end of the bed. Lamarr had one of his feet up close to his face, and Mahd, in the middle, reached for it. Damear was intent on his mother as she lifted him into the bathwater.

141

Holding him in one hand, she washed him rapidly with the other, working up a lather in his bit of hair. Then she rinsed him with hand-cupped water and laid him to her left on a fresh towel, drying him with it. The same with Mahad, who looked surprised, and Lamarr, who wailed at the first touch of the water.

"Maybe it's too cold for him," I suggested.

"He's all right," she said, sounding angry to me. Or maybe she was just tired? She rubbed oil over everyone, head to toe, put fresh diapers on and brushed their hair. Then she laid them across her lap — one at a time, same order — to suction out their nostrils: left, right. They did not like it.

"You wanna look all nasty, snot nose?"

She seemed angrier still. At them and the little daubs of their noses? At big Lamarr for not being there? At me for having come uninvited into the room? At my European nose, whose narrow slits didn't display what all was in them? I should have asked her why she was angry, but I was, I guess, afraid. She reminded me of the girls bussed in the year my junior high desegregated; not the skinny, honey-colored ones who went out for cheerleading and picked their Angela Davis afros to stunning circumference, but the hot-ironed, night-colored, spark plug shaped girls who moved like storm clouds through the halls. Did they act threatening because they felt threatened? Did Tahija feel threatened?

"You don't mind I came in, do you?" I asked when the three were back in their cribs.

"No."

A no without eye contact. She was cleaning up: putting bottles of body wash, baby powder, baby shampoo, baby oil in their places.

"So when you start school, you want me to wash them that same way?"

"I'll wash them and dress them before I leave."

"Oh okay."

"And I'll feed them too, first thing, again when I get home." She paused to look straight at me. "Don't you feed them."

"All right."

142

"They're on a schedule."

"I got it. I'll have an easy job."

And it was an easy job, at first, and a joy. Unless she was at a meeting or facilitating a workshop, Kaki was home and very willing to hold a baby while she worked at her desk or to watch all three so I could take a break. Lamarr came nearly every day, more in the late afternoon and evenings, when I was off. If he came during my shift I might watch them with him for awhile, or leave them to him, though I was wary of that because Lamarr Stevens wouldn't change a diaper if you hid a winning lottery ticket in it. (*That* changed.)

Every two weeks until school let out and I was again unemployed, Tahija took her state-issued Access card to the bank machine on the Avenue and came back with a business-size envelope fat with folded twenties. Two-hundred-forty dollars. This she'd hand me with a flourish, like she knew I needed it, which I did; like it was payback for sticking with her; like we were together in a new way — bound by the unspoken agreement that windfall for one was windfall for both. I think the money balanced, somewhat, the power differential between us, and made it easier for her to give up some control over the boys. I wasn't a helper anymore, I was hired help. Big difference. I could be given instructions, reprimanded; I could be fired.

And I would be. But there were some wonderful times first.

Chapter 17

we need new words
for what this is, this hunger entering our
loneliness like birds, stunning our eyes into rays
of hope.

— from "Blake," by Lucille Clifton

There is a lake in the mountains, near where I used to live. Once, I brought Kaki there. We'd hiked two miles in, and as the day was hot and the water crystal clear we decided to go swimming. Floating on her back among the water lilies, long hair radiating outward, Kaki said, "Always remember me like this."

I said I would, and I will, but there is another image my memory holds even more dear. It is Kaki on the sofa in the diffuse light of dawn giving the triplets their 6:00 AM bottle, which she did for a time to give Tahija a little more sleep.

She holds Damear against her chest with her left arm, the wrist of that hand at a sharp angle, positioning the bottle for him. Mahad lies across her lap, drinking from the bottle in her right hand. And little Lamarr lies on the sofa to her left, alongside her thigh, his head near her knee and drinking from the bottle propped there. Sometimes she grips the bottle in her left hand between her shoulder and chin, so as to free that hand to hold the bottle of the baby alongside her leg. This way everyone gets human contact, and whoever is slowest, usually Mahd-man, gets two arms at the end.

Service, nurture, love — clear mountain lakes. It's good when we come to one to linger, float, make memories.

Monday morning and I hadn't held a baby since Friday afternoon. Tahija was downstairs getting ready for school, so technically I wasn't on duty yet, but I couldn't wait. I cracked the nursery door and poked my head in.

Damear was holding onto the rail of his crib and flexing his knees. They were six months old and standing was all that. Mahad in the crib opposite was studying Damear's technique. Lamarr was in the wind-up swing. I picked him up and with him in my arms kissed the foreheads of the other two, talking as I went. Tahija had already fed, bathed, and dressed them, with Mahad and Lamarr in two styles of smartly angled new braids. (Damear didn't yet have quite enough hair for braiding.) Lamarr's hair was longest, his braids ending in inch-long tails now. Unbraided, his hair rose five or six inches off his head. Bush baby, his parents called him. I liked seeing it natural because I knew, or heard, what he went through getting it braided. He was tender headed, Tahija said, and best get over it.

"I'm about to go down and say goodbye to your mom," I told them, putting Lamarr in his crib, "but I'll be right back, okay?"

"Aya-a-a," Damear said, smiling and bouncing, but as soon as I turned, two-thirds of them started crying. I left Mahad with a cracker and took Damear and Lamarr down.

Leaving the nursery was a risk. Tahija oversaw all room transfers. No babies on the first floor unless she said so. But her kemar was on and her book bag packed. I figured my shift had begun.

In the shamrock room Kaki was sitting at the small round table eating toast and cereal. The spindly shamrock plant sat on the windowsill behind her auditioning for *A Raisin in the Sun*.

Tahija was in the kitchen filling her water bottle. When she came out and saw me with some of the same kids she'd been tending since dawn, she scowled, but went on in conversation with Kaki.

"How's he going to say I'm not a real Muslim anyway?"

"Is *he* one?" Kaki asked.

"He's Fruit of Islam, you know, bean pies and Elijah Muhammad."

"And you're plain Muslim, not F.O.I.?" I asked, slipping into the chair opposite Kaki. "Right. And they like to take some kind a attitude, always in somebody's business. But he better not mess with me, not today, because — " she chucked Damear's chin — "I'm" — and then Lamarr's — "not playing."

They loved it. Their heads turned to follow her every move.

"Maybe you could engage him in conversation," Kaki suggested, "explain your point of view."

"Come on now, Kaki, conflict resolution at Dobbins High School?"

"That's just the sort of place where it's needed."

We heard the El. "That was yours," I said, checking the clock.

"Another one coming," Tahija said, heading for the door.

Damear and Lamarr and I leaned forward watching her open it. "Bye," I called.

"Bu bu... *bay*," Lamarr added.

She turned, outlined by the open door's glare. "Bye, be good."

"Mahddy's up there with nothing but a cracker," I told Kaki, taking a piece of toast from her plate to split between Damear and Lamarr. "And you know that's gone."

Kaki was halfway up the stairs when he started crying. The crying stopped, and she reappeared with him pressed to her.

Often during the failure-to-thrive time Kaki had held Mahddy. She became a fast one-armed typist, Mahad in her other arm. It can only have helped her community work, I thought, to be holding the future as she planned nonviolence trainings and networked with people of influence.

Mahddy sat contentedly on her lap now, head back against her red sweater, cracker crumbs freckling his chipmunk cheeks.

"Hey, who ate my toast?" she said.

"Make some more," I suggested.

She did, under Mahddy's watchful eye, and we helped eat that, too.

Was I just meeting his need, watering spindly roots, or did I have a need to bond with Damear? Better to ask someone who's parachuted out of an airplane whether they have a need to land. It happened that fast. I remember the day the glue set. The other two were asleep, Tahija at school. I rested on my side on the edge of her bed, my body a guardrail as Damear crawled about on the expanse of wine-red bedspread, discovering its braided tassels and the curiosities on the windowsill: a bonky plastic cup, the squishy nose-suctioning bulb, a hard red comb. Soon the exploring wore him out and I laid him on my chest to sleep.

I have always loved that place between waking and sleep. It's a crowded shoreline, an intertidal zone rich in imaginative life … images, symbols, dreams, memories, insight. Damear lingered there, raising his head now and again to look into my eyes, questioning, opening, going deeper, coming back to look into me again before he submitted completely to sleep's warm depth. I followed soon after, and when I woke found that there had been a blending, there in sleep, or in sleep a journey to some place where we are all of us blended. Waking, I simply remembered that place, that oneness; I think Damear did too.

I bonded that deeply with the boy I cared for the first time I was a nanny, with one of my sister's three, with my brother Joseph, and with Damear.

Kaki still had her bedroom-office on the second floor at the front of the house. She lived with traffic noise on one side and, with Tahija's bedroom next door and the nursery down the hall, teen and baby noise on the other. I couldn't blame her for wanting to turn the unused room on the third floor into a bedroom. Our bedroom.

When I first moved in we had felt we ought to forgo sex, for a time, until some green light of higher direction told us move ahead. The problem with that, living in the same house, was that all manner of other green lights kept going off. She was just too wonderful and, well, there. Soon we were forced to lower the bar: separate beds in separate rooms. But now, with so much activity on the second floor, all rendezvous of a romantic nature tended to happen on the third. Why not just put the bedroom there? It did make a kind of sense, as if our sacrifice of space and privacy brought with it a little bonus: an unselfish reason to lower the bar still more.

Or put it right on the floor and just step over it, as if it were ... well ... a broomstick. Neither marriage nor civil unions between same-sex partners was legal at that time, any place (in the U.S. anyway). In some Quaker meetings — Kaki's included (with my old meeting beginning to deliberate the question) — gays and lesbians were being married or, using some other term, joined "under the care" of the meeting. Still, growing up when and as I had, marriage was not really within my conception of what my life could be. In a sense though, as we walked together with this young family, Kaki and I made marriage-like commitments. Circumstances seemed to push us into it, but I wonder — did we feel we had to earn a right so many others took for granted?

So, sharing a bedroom was a symbol. This particular symbol, however, was not a very pretty one. The room measured ten by ten. Clammy plaster crumbled from the walls, which the previous owners' son, a troubled teen, neighbors had told us, had painted dark purple. Spills of this purple, and older colors, lay like growths on the bare floorboards. The barred window looked out on the same alley Tahija's window did, with views into the rooming house next door.

"It needs a lot of work," I said.

"Lamarr's younger brothers could do it," Kaki said. The twins, Donovan and Dante, visited from time to time. I liked them because they liked to hold their nephews.

For the work it afforded two young men, and the step deeper into commitment it gave two women too long alone, the purple room became a bedroom (not, however, a master bedroom), and the stage for one of my most treasured memories of Lamarr.

Donovan and Dante, with Lamarr, did do much of the work, framing the walls and hanging Sheetrock, but first the old plaster had to be sledgehammered off. Somehow one Saturday this job fell to Lamarr and me.

Within minutes we were two white-haired, dust-covered people, and by the end of the day the floor was buried under half a foot of rubble.

"That was the easy part," said Lamarr, lowering his dust mask. "Hard part's getting it out the house."

Someone told us later we might simply have Sheetrocked over the old plaster. That's not what we did. What we did was lower it from the roof using a rope-pulley we bolted there. Because the third floor had only two rooms to the other floors' three, its hallway window opened on the flat, tarred roof of the nursery, a kind of terrace. We shoveled rubble into Spackle buckets that we then passed out through the window and carried to the edge of this roof. Then I went down through the house to the backyard and looked up at Lamarr on his belly on the roof, shoulders and arms over the edge, ready to lower the first bucket. His hair, half an inch or so long then and worn natural, was framed by the pale-green leaves of our tree, with behind the leaves blue sky. He'd inch a bucket down. I'd reach up to steady it, bearing some of the weight as he eased it the last few feet to the ground.

In this way over and over I trusted him not to lose his grip and let a bucket drop onto my head, and as many times he trusted me not to let go too soon and let one yank him over the edge.

When Sheetrocking began, I'd bring the triplets up one at a time to see their dad and uncles at work. One day through the whirr of the drill I thought I heard a radio. Then the song stopped and started over at the beginning.

I put Mear and Mahd together in a crib and went up with little Lamarr to investigate.

The twins were identical and so I can't be sure, but I think it was Donovan holding a length of Sheetrock steady as Dante drilled screws through it while Lamarr measured for the next cut, all of them singing Al Green's R&B hit "Cupid." They were good.

They saw Marr and me in the doorway and quit.

"Don't stop," I said, "that was great."

"Aaay!" Marr added, slapping the doorframe.

"They suck," Lamarr said, "I can't get them to practice."

"*You* suck," said one of the twins.

"Yeah well your breath stinks."

"*Your* breath stinks."

"Your breath stinks so bad ..."

The twins were two years younger than Lamarr, thinner and shorter and a lot more stylish: pretty boys, he called them. They wore their unbraided hair in a shaped inch, like an aura around their heads. Little Lamarr would take after them.

"So where'd you guys learn to sing like that?" What I really wanted was for them to sing some more.

"Just did," said one of the twins.

"Our dad decided he might as well make some money," Lamarr said, "started coaching us."

"Not anymore?" They hadn't lived with their father for several years.

"See this?" Lamarr picked up a five or so foot length of two-by-four. The twins dropped their arms and looked at him. "He'd beat me with one of these. Made me go get the electric drill first." Lamarr took the drill from his brother and held it to the board. "Then he'd drill a hole in it, making sure I watched."

I tried to picture him little, watching his father drill the hole, as his son was watching him now. "How old were you?"

"When it started? Five ... six. He never beat the twins. Just me." He handed the drill back to his brother. "Want to know what the hole was for?"

I didn't want to know what the hole was for. "What was it for?" "Simple," he said, dropping the two-by-four and turning back to the Sheetrock, "cut down on wind resistance."

I was on the floor, back against the sofa, letting Mahddy finish his bottle while the other two played. Damear had gotten hold of a teakwood bowl about two inches across and as deep. He quickly discovered, banging the lid onto the bowl's round rim, a new sound. *Clack.* A small, round, pleasing sound. *Clack clack clack.*

Lamarr reached for the sound, took the bowl from Damear as if from his own hand and moved it to that center of the universe — his mouth. Ah, wood against teething gums. Protesting not at all, Damear just stared — a Jedi thing, big Lamarr called it. When Lamarr's attention wandered, Damear leaned, took aim, and got the bowl back. *Clack! Clack clack clack.*

Then he tried the lid against a book (so-so), the rug (no good), a block (score!), Lamarr's head (an unsatisfying thunk). But what the wood loved most was itself. What a joy when, later, after losing the bowl to Mahad, Damear found it in one of his hands, its reliable lid in the other, and in himself the knowledge of what to do with the two.

Clack clack clack clack clack!

Chapter 18

The only problem I had was I didn't want them held all day because I knew I wouldn't be able to get anything done if they were too spoiled. Kathryn felt that they should be held more but if she sat and held them all day she would need a maid to cook and clean and she would need a nanny to watch the baby for herself to get washed. It was three of them not one which is totally different you can't even compare the two situations. I think we had a difference of opinion.

from the interview

I overheard two crossing guards at a corner talking. They were neighborhood women, forty-something, dressed in uniform blue, patent-leather billed caps. They were talking about a woman who was pushing a baby stroller across the street.

"That baby's too young to be outdoors," said one crossing guard, an African American woman.

"No, he's not," said the other crossing guard, an Italian-American woman.

"Sure he is."

"But he's six months old, if he's a day."

"That's right," said the other, "too young to be out in this pneumonia weather."

They were not arguing, merely stating what each took to be commonly accepted facts.

It's healthy for babies to get out into the fresh air, the colder the better, toughens them up. It's unhealthy for babies to be out in the air, especially cold air.

Put that baby down, you'll spoil him! You can't hold a baby too much!

Don't you cut your eyes at me. *Look* at me when I'm talking to you.

You don't have to call me "miss," just call me by my name. *Child,* did I hear you call that lady by her name? Didn't I teach you better?

Child-rearing "facts" and philosophies vary greatly by culture and class. I knew that, in my head; now my heart was about to find it out.

By mid-summer Damear and Lamarr were crawling quite a lot, and fast — up on their toes, Lamarr preferring reverse. Mahad would get in position and watch them, rocking, revving the engine. I felt they needed to crawl and explore their world, and that that world needed to become gradually larger. Pots and pans from the kitchen cabinets, books from the bookshelf, Mommy's stuffed animals (Tweetie Bird presided over a whole menagerie now), phones, the interesting space beneath Kaki's desk, and every little thing that was too big to fit into a mouth — all these should be their domain, I felt … the whole (baby-proofed) house, with a good stretch every day in the park, also their domain, as was the whole natural world, the sky especially, the wind and the sun. I wanted them to know how rich they were.

There were cultural differences here, to be sure. But Tahija and I were by temperament on opposite ends of the range of those differences: me way down at one end with *Meet every need;* she at the other end with *They don't have needs I don't say they have.* She said *spoil* as if it were a disease, and me a carrier. I learned that not everyone considered spoiling as awful as did Tahija. I learned this from our neighbor Miss Tina. Miss Tina worked days and watched her granddaughter Kayla evenings. Sometimes she sat on her stoop with the four-year-old in her lap, and I'd sit on mine (usually babyless). One day I asked her if she wasn't worried about, you know, spoiling the girl.

Miss Tina laughed and rocked backward, hands in the air. "Oh I spoil her something terrible, I admit it, I'm to blame."

A woman after my own heart. I laughed with her, relieved. But grandmothers have rights caregivers don't, and how did the girl's mother feel? Was she just putting up with the spoiling until she could get her own place and move out? Was Tahija?

"I blame it on Dr. Spock."

Kaki and I were walking around the park. It was late March and already the cherry trees at two of its corners showed fat pink buds. Four times around was a mile.

"What do you mean?" Kaki said.

"My mother told me she wanted to pick me up, she was burning to pick me up, but Dr. Spock was God then and Dr. Spock said to keep to the schedule. My father's mother picked me up, she spoiled me. My mother moved us away from her."

"So you didn't get enough nurturance?" She put an arm around me, then removed it: hard to power walk that way.

"And I can't stand it, seeing the boys not get enough."

"The doctors' son," Kaki said, "the one you took care of the second time you lived in Philly, did he get enough nurturance, in your opinion?" she asked.

"No. I was his third nanny. And as for meals, it was Thai takeout every night."

"You're exaggerating."

"I'm telling you, sometimes that fridge had nothing in it but seltzer water and pager batteries."

"Well if that was his parents' lifestyle ..."

"*Lifestyle?* Fruit and vegetable isn't about lifestyle it's about — wait, are you saying it's me? I'm seeing things?"

"You're a perfectionist. Granted a somewhat lazy one, but you're very hard on yourself, and others. They'll be all right. We help when asked. We support the parents, give them love, and they'll be better able to give to the boys."

"Ah, the trickle-down theory," I said.

We'd done our four times around and were walking more slowly through the park, taking one of its two diagonal walkways. At their center, a dozen or so kids played on the colorful new gym, the two swingsets going strong.

"Look," Kaki said, "there's Hakim with an unmet need to have his swing pushed."

Five-year-old Hakim was one of four cousins who came to my after-school play group. Pushing him "higher-no-higher!" I forgot for awhile about the babies in the house, and the baby in me.

"But you'll fly right over the top."

"No, I won't! Higher!"

Hakim flung his head back and shut his eyes, his sneakers bumping the clouds.

Tahija paced the length of the living room reading from the book in her hands. After a convention-defying daredevil dive, Jonathan Livingston Seagull had just woken up to find himself in an academy for spiritually minded gulls.

"Is he dead or what?" Tahija asked.

"Keep reading," Kaki said. She sat cross-legged on the chair, happy, with the autumn chill, to be back in her flannel shirts. She was also happy to have us together in the living room reading aloud. In her world it's what families did, and what she wanted more than anything, I think, was to be part of a family. She would have liked Lamarr to be sitting there with us, as when we watched movies together, but lately he'd been needed to take care of his nieces while his sister worked.

Tahija read on. Jonathan, it turned out, had gone from rebel to sage. He taught gulls to fly like they'd never flown before. He taught them that flying was less about height and speed than faith and fearlessness.

Upstairs, Damear started crying. He'd been weaned for some time, but still seemed not quite to have given up. Tahija stopped her pacing at the foot of the stairs.

"*Da*-mear!"

Louder crying.

"Maybe he needs something," Kaki suggested.

"I fed them, changed them. What's he got to be all falling out about? He's playing me." She read on over his crying then finally marched up the stairs, coming down a moment later with Damear wrapped and quiet in a blanket.

"See?" she said. "Soon as I picked him up, he stopped crying. Means he's spoiled. He didn't need a thing, not one thing."

"Maybe he needed to be held," I suggested, "and now that he has it — "

"He stopped crying," Kaki finished.

Tahija got comfortable in the rocker. His eyes reflecting the lamplight, Damear gazed out at us from the billows of his mother's t-shirt, not the least interested in Kaki *or* me.

"Got her all to yourself now, don't ya?" I said. He smiled, the tears of a moment before still wet on his cheeks.

"Spoiled rot-ten," Tahija said gently. Finding her page, she went on reading and read straight through to the end of the book, stopping only to threaten to write the author and complain about a plot turn that simply made no sense.

Fighting sleep as long as he could, Damear listened to her voice as if to the music of the spheres.

Big Lamarr taught me something about spoiling. He and I had little Lamarr and Damear in for their check-up, the first that Tahija had let them go to without her. We were sitting in the waiting room practicing the waiting yoga, when time for the 2:00 PM bottle came around. Tahija had packed bottles in the diaper bag. Big Lamarr removed one and held it where little Lamarr, in my lap, could see it. Damear was asleep in his lap.

Little Lamarr began to whine and reach for the bottle.

"That won't work," Lamarr said to him. "So you might as well stop."

Uh-oh, I thought, here comes major crying and everyone looking at us. But we didn't have crying. Little Lamarr just sat very straight in my lap concentrating on the bottle as big Lamarr read a car magazine.

"Saturn's getting to be a good buy," he said.

"Yeah?" I was concentrating on the bottle too.

"Engine's made by Toyota."

"I didn't know that."

I thought it extraordinary. Babies in my family would have been screaming bloody murder by then. But little Lamarr just sat looking at the bottle, glancing from time to time at his dad's face. When he started to let out a little whine Lamarr said "Ah-ah-ah," and he stopped.

The spoiled baby in me was scream-thinking, "Oh give it to him for God's sake!"

In a few minutes, he did. Little Lamarr accepted the bottle, examined it, then leaned back against me with a sigh and drank.

"See?" said dad. "Waiting works, crying doesn't."

One night Mahddy wakes with a nightmare. Damear wakes too and stands up in his crib, watching as both parents calm and comfort Mahddy.

"Usually Mear would cry," Tahija said, telling me about it the next morning.

"Being spoiled," I said. I was at the sink doing dishes, Tahija leaning chin in her hands on the countertop.

"Right. He'd cry, or start that laughing like he does, you know. Trying to play you, get you to pick him up. But last night he just stands there in the crib, and stares."

"He knows Mahd needs you more."

"Yeah. Mahd wouldn't stop screaming, not until I held him against my heart — right here."

She showed me, though I knew where her heart was. Hadn't I seen it enlarging daily?

"And Lamarr's going to say he's spoilt," she continued. "But that's not spoilt."

"No. You comforted him."

"He needed it," she said.

"And when he got it — "

"He stopped crying."

How lovely the mixing bowl in my hands seemed then as I went around it with a sponge. Lamarr and Tahija's ways, my ways, methods passed to us along questionable routes, through landscapes twisted by hardship and oppression, were mixing in this house, in talks in the kitchen, under the backyard clothesline, in the nursery. We were changing each other, and it was good.

Chapter 19

whoever walks a furlong without sympathy walks to his own funeral,
dressed in his shroud

— from *Leaves of Grass,* by Walt Whitman

Tahija worked very hard. Though I had never had a child
myself, I'd seen what the first months are like for a new mother.
It's wonder upon wonder, and overwhelming. There can be a ter-
rifying sense of losing oneself to the demands of the newborn.
Depression is common and often unaddressed, with more than a
quarter of teen mothers suffering from it.* Imagine three babies!
Tahija was determined not to let them "run over top of her." And

---

*According to a 1990 article in the *Journal of Abnormal Psychology* (99(1):
69-78), postpartum depression affects 26%-32% of teen mothers, with the rates
increasing for multiple births.

indeed they must have felt sometimes like a stampeding herd, or a tidal wave. Added to these pressures was the omnitheater of watching adults, any one of whom might with a phone call set the bureaucratic ball rolling to take the boys away. There were the home nurse and the DHS home aides mandated by DHS (the indomitable Mrs. Abstinence not, as it turned out, among them). Then there was Kaki and me. It must have been like having two live-in mothers-in-law from another culture. It's a wonder poor Tahija didn't fall apart or snap out. She did go off once on big Lamarr, but it was only a butter knife from the kitchen drawer, and he *had* taken little Lamarr to the house of the very aunt she had expressly forbidden him to take any of her babies to.

She was under a lot of stress. Containment made sense to her and control worked. But when the stretch-limo stroller arrived, I thought sure Mear, Mahd and Marr were going to make the acquaintance of the park at last.

They were six months old when the Lutheran services agency that had given Tahija pro-life counseling when she was pregnant gave her a triplet stroller. Inside the huge box it came in were six wheels; dozens of pieces; scores of nuts, bolts and screws; and twelve pages of instructions. In French. Tahija threw the instructions aside and in one of her manic bursts put it together with two screwdrivers and a wrench.

When I came back from shopping, there it was, as long as the sofa — a twelve-point buck of an assembly job.

"You must be some kind of mechanical genius."

"It was easy."

The seats went front to back, with hoods above and sturdy wire baskets beneath. The cloth was a heavy-duty navy blue patterned in small white dots. I suggested we give it a test drive, with riders.

It was a sunny afternoon, the park alive with people: two half-court basketball games going, lovers under the grape arbor, parents and seniors on the low wall circling around the playground, and children working every inch of the equipment. The infant swings beckoned. I couldn't remember the last time Tahija had gone outside for anything other than a doctor's appointment or a quick trip to the grocery store around the corner.

She came to the door I'd opened and peered out, left and right, focusing not on the green oasis of the park but on the strangers in the crosswalk, the car speeding past, the disheveled man weaving up the sidewalk.

Tahija drew back.

"It's too cold."

"It's almost June!"

"Pneumonia weather."

She parked the stroller in the shamrock room, and there it stayed.

"Those boys won't leave this house until they're four years old," Lamarr declared. I didn't believe him. It was so in his own childhood, he said, and would be so in theirs. But they needed to grow, to explore, to be stimulated by new sights and sounds, I argued. No, they needed to be kept safe, away from dirt and germs, freaky people, and gunfire.

The stretch-limo stroller was in danger of becoming a conversation piece. But I kept asking, and then one warm day as she was leaving for school Tahija said yes.

"Just to the park and back."

"Okay."

"And coats on, zipped up, and hats."

"Right."

"You can dress them in the blue onesies, second drawer, left side."

"Second drawer left."

Tahija dressing her boys was fast and efficient — a gift-wrapper in December. I was not. Getting the third fully dressed before the first got overheated took athletic focus. And then getting them outside! I developed two techniques: Babies in the stroller and then out, or stroller out and then babies in.

In-then-out went like this. After I had them dressed, I'd bring two down, one to a hip, and put them in their places in the stroller. (I felt compelled to place them in the order Tahija always did: Damear, Mahad, Lamarr.) Then I'd run up for the third, who was most likely crying by then. I'd bring him down and put him in his seat. Then I'd buckle everyone in and wheel the stroller into the short, narrow hallway.

The heavy security door wouldn't stay open on its own, so I used the footrest of the first seat, while holding the inner door with my free hand. Then I'd push the stroller forward until the two front wheels projected out from the stoop, with poor Damear (who was quite brave) in mid-air. Then — *boing* (really excellent suspension) — I'd bounce the middle wheels, beneath Mahad, down onto the upper step, then tip back, with Damear pointing skyward now, and bounce the rear wheels onto the step. Then I'd slowly lower Damear, taking it on faith that the sidewalk was down there somewhere.

Once I had us horizontal and facing parkward, I'd go down the line checking everybody. Only little Lamarr, who had a fear of heights, seemed to question, with contracted brow, my nannying abilities.

Out-and-then-in was easier, but only worked if a trusted neighbor was outside to help. What I'd do is bounce the stroller down the steps empty and get it facing park-ward then run back in for one of them, strap him in, and run back for the other two. Usually by then Rosa and her Chihuahua were watching from the window of her third-floor apartment, a grandmotherly smile making her eye patch look downright cheerful.

"*Tres bonito bambinos,*" she'd call.

"*Si, gracias.*"

When we finally reached the park that first day we walked the full length of all four of its walkways, then strolled the shady perimeter, stopped often by folks from the nearby senior center. The boys were so good. Mahad fell asleep and woke up. Lamarr began to cry but shifted to laughter at the sight of squirrels scampering over the roots of a great old oak.

We stopped beneath the tree and were soon surrounded by second graders on recess, Porsha, the youngest King sister, among them. She deigned to act as spokesperson for us, informing the other children that she knew me, I lived on her block, and *no,* I was not their mother, *ob*viously, I only watched them while their mother, Tahija, was in school. And sometimes she, Porsha, helped me.

The second graders absorbed this important information, stared a moment longer, then whirled away like leaves in a gust to decorate the playground with their happy cries.

When I took the boys out after lunch we'd sit on the low wall that bordered the park and watch for Tahija to come up the block from school. Sometimes she'd sit with us and if she was in the mood field the questions that inevitably came. She granted any polite asker up to three, so long as the first question wasn't too ignorant. "How *ever* do you take care of all three?" would be your first and only question.

Some questions brought down her scorn and the questioners were memorialized forever after, as in, "Remember Lamarr's cousin, at that party? Going to ask, 'Do they think alike?' How am I supposed to know do they think alike? Do I look like a mind reader? Or that lady at the seaquarium — 'Are they twins?' *Come on now.*"

One day a girl poling by on a single old-style skate stopped and bent over to see Damear, in the stroller, up close. Then she looked at the other two, in my lap and Tahija's.

"Which one is the baby?"

"Him," Tahija kissed Marr's forehead. They were eight months, and still very small.

"Which one's oldest?"

"He is," Tahija pointed to Damear.

"By about two minutes," I added.

As if she knew she had been granted just the three questions, the girl paused and considered, skating her foot back and forth. She looked from me to Tahija and back at me.

"Do all ya'll live in the same house?"

"We do." I pointed across the intersection. "Third door in."

She looked that way, then back at us. "That's all right."

* * *

It was the lone comment of the woman in Rite-Aid that stuck with me. Like a tick it stuck, like a sliver of glass.

We were out on the Avenue in the stretch limo. Things were going well. Mahad had fallen asleep, as he often did in moving vehicles, and the other two were so busy staring up at the rattling tracks of the El they didn't think of complaining. Tahija had one of her headaches, but she was in a good mood, even answered a few questions when we were mobbed in front of the grocery store. She enjoyed the attention, to a point, as long as people got it that they were triplets and not the results of three separate pregnancies. She was only sixteen, and sensitive to the stigma attached to teenage pregnancy.

We stopped in Rite-Aid. Tahija liked Rite-Aid. Her mother had worked in one once and she bought most of her many skin and hair care products there. We were having a good outing, until that woman said what she did. She was white, around sixty, and already walking away from us when the words hit — five words, one for each of us:

"Well I hope she's done."

I heard Tahija take in a deep breath, steady herself, and set her mind (or did I just imagine/fear it?) to never bring the boys outside the house again.

The woman was gone before I could respond. That undelivered response swelled within me, to come out months later as a letter, and the start of this book.

"These boys are a blessing," I wrote her. "I don't believe you'd shake your head in disgust at the sight of three matched white faces. I believe you value the lives of black boys but little and believe that no good can come through them into your world. Your prejudice is a curtain drawn before your eyes, and your fear and clinging to privilege would draw that curtain over their future. Through the curtain you don't see the bright lights of their eyes — black, brown, green; you don't see the sacredness of the number three: moon, earth and sun; heaven, earth and humanity; angles in a triangle; the holy trinity. What could the universe have meant by such abundance if not a blessing, and a challenge, and a promise: that if we meet the challenge we shall have the blessing.

"Already for me it has been so. What challenge have you not accepted, stranger, woman with skin and hair like mine, about the age of my mother, born in the Depression, knowing the hardship these boys' parents know, though the 90s are not Depression years? Perhaps your challenge today was to smile, and say to the mother what most women of color say, *God bless you.*

"Oh I wish you had stopped and spoken kindly. I wish we had enjoyed the talk so much that Tahija took down your address and promised to drop you a line now and then and let you know how the boys were. Then you would see, the curtain would fall away and you would see not potential criminals, not threats, but children with all the light of childhood in them: perhaps one someday to lead a town or city, or even the nation; perhaps one to create a song or a painting that opens the eyes of your grandchild, walking alone and depressed one day, to the beauty of life; perhaps one to live in great pain and to succumb, to understand the addictions of his grandparents and forgive — them, his parents, himself, and perhaps in there somewhere in his thirties or forties you, the stranger who did not bless him, whose blessing might have meant something. Who can say what it might have meant?"

Chapter 20

Now don't get me wrong I was loved by many, but I don't think that anyone understood me the way that my mother did and at this hard time in my life I couldn't count on her the way I needed and wanted to. I know it sounds selfish and I put myself in the situation I was in however I still believe that I needed her more than ever before at that point and time in my life. I know that at that time in my mother's life she probably needed me too, but I didn't know how to help her. You see for so long I was able to count on her and only her because she was the only one that was constant in my life besides my little sister. Neither of us knew how to help her this was something bigger than us this was about her. It was hard to deal with but we had no other choice but to deal with it because this was our life too.

My Life as I Know It

One day when the boys are five and Tahija and Lamarr have a house of their own, I call to say hello and see what's new. What's new is the boys' bedroom has just been painted.

"My mom brought us two gallons. I tried to get her to stay awhile, but she flew in and flew out. You know how she is." Tahija laughs at her mom's ways. It's an easy laugh, a secure laugh, a laugh with a future in it.

In February of 1997, soon after her daughter entered Temple University Hospital for her six weeks of bed rest, Laura Ellison admitted herself into an ODAT (One Day at a Time) drug rehabilitation program. For the first ninety days she was on blackout. Blackout meant no going outdoors, no visitors, and no phone calls — the aim being to prevent relapse. If new residents must leave, for a doctor's appointment for example, they are accompanied by a resident who's been clean (sober) for some time, or by staff (often former residents with years of sobriety). Breaking blackout rules means expulsion, and given the dearth of drug rehabilitation programs, expulsion usually meant the street, and the street's colder, harder rules.

During her blackout Laura managed to get two phone calls through to Tahija in the hospital, but visits were impossible. The program was her lifeline, and she dared not let go. Later, when she was able to renew regular contact with her oldest daughter, she had no home to offer her. One thing she did have, however, was legal custody, and the power to give it up.

Although Mahad was doing all right and Tahija was cooperating, for the most part, with required services, DHS had not closed its case. In order for the case to be closed Tahija had to be residing with a parent or legal guardian. Since her mother didn't have a place for her and the boys to live, Tahija asked her to give up legal custody to us. Laura agreed because it was what her daughter wanted. And besides, as she told me later when I asked her about it, we were already acting as guardians. Why not make it official?

Making it official meant family court.

Laura Ellison was not what I had expected. What had I expected? Serious, scary, withdrawn, angry, haggard. She was none of these. What you noticed first was a girlish face and eyes so green they actually sparkled. From the corner of one a small tear-like scar hung. At thirty-four, she was lighter and thinner than Tahija — same facial features in a narrower face. She talked in a fast, funny, mocking way that was saved from cynicism by something soft, a soft depth that she seemed to have decided to let a little closer to the surface. She didn't talk about her time on the street or the program she was still in. She made her daughter laugh, good deep laughter that sloughed off months of stress. For this and for her spirit, I liked her. She'd dug herself a hole and now she was climbing out, one day at a time.

Laura had converted to Islam soon after Tahija. On our day in family court she arrived in a silken beige outergarment and kemar, and brown leather boots. We'd met at the DHS offices, and today she treated us like old friends. Tahija's face shone when she looked at her mother, and soon they were teasing each other, Lamarr nearby basking in reflected light.

Family Court was like Penn Station at rush hour, except without the rush: no trains arriving, none departing. You just sat; sat and waited in the crowded, cavernous room, and now and then from one of the many doors evenly spaced in the four surrounding walls — pale wood walls with ornate molding — a bailiff emerged and boomed out a name.

We'd been told to come at 9:00 AM, and we had. Now it was near noon and we were hungry, but we dared not leave, because if the bailiff called your name and you missed it, they just passed you by, we'd seen it happen, and who knew when your name would come around again?

"We should have packed a lunch," I said.

"Right?" said Laura, in that affirming way I'd gotten used to Tahija saying it. "Why do they tell you come at nine when they can't handle but a few families at a time?"

"Don't make no sense," I agreed.

Tahija leaned forward and looked past Lamarr to our end of the line. "Can ya'll two stop complaining, please?"

"All I'm *saying*," I said, "is don't they see we have three babies here?"

"And we arrived well after some of the people they've already called," Kaki said.

"Thank you," said Laura.

"They not worrying about us."

We sat in attached plastic chairs facing a long row of people in attached plastic chairs. It was me, Kaki, Laura with little Lamarr in her lap, big Lamarr with Damear, and Tahija with Mahad. And not a sneaker or pair of jeans among the eight of us. We were going before a judge, *some* time today. Tahija wore a suit-blue outergarment and kemar, new pants showing beneath, and square-heeled shoes. She had gained a good deal more weight but carried it well. It made her look older, though. Not much past sixteen, she could have passed for twenty-five.

Kaki had on a dark gray suit set with a lacy, light-gray blouse, from her Penn Mutual incarnation. She had gathered her hair in the back with a wooden barrette. Only her Birkenstock sandals distinguished her from the lawyers in the room, and the fact that she stayed in one place. Lamarr had on telemarketing-job clothes: dark pants and shoes, dress white shirt, striped tie. He wore his hair natural, about a half inch all around. I had on a dress, a blue flower-print thing with a wide velvet waist and actual darts.

The boys were dressed identically in green corduroy overalls, thin-stripe turtlenecks, and white oxfords. They had a handful of syllables, da-da and ma-ma leading among them. The asymmetry in Damear's face was nearly gone, Mahad had stopped snuffling, and all their noses were developing a little character, a firmness that served to distinguish them more, one from another.

"Hey," a girl walking past skidded to a stop on the wooden floor, "are they twins?"

That's one question, I thought, and not a very good one.

"Now do you see two," Tahija said, "or three?"

"Triplets! Ew, Yvonne, come look. Triplets."

A younger girl came and stared. "All girls?" she asked.

"Boys," said big Lamarr, mercifully.

"Can I hold one?" pleaded the younger girl.

"I don't allow them to be held by strangers," Tahija said.

The two girls gazed awhile longer, and left.

"These people acting retarded," Tahija said in her headache-coming-on voice. She was getting them more and more, a symptom of her continuing high blood pressure.

One of the three doors in the wall to our left swung open, and a bailiff emerged. "Cabbot," he boomed out, "Cabbot."

"I sure as heck hope they're not going in alphabetical order," Kaki said.

They weren't, but what order they were going in wasn't clear. We waited through lunch time and into the afternoon. Everyone had the opportunity to change a diaper. Kaki got to hold Mahad and teach him some Minnesotan. At some point I was handed little Lamarr.

"What do you think of all this, Mr. Stevens?"

He gave me his thoughts in a few wet syllables. I hoped I'd be able to talk to him about it when he was at liberty to say more.

The big doors swung open and the bailiff with the South Philly accent boomed out, "Jefferson and Berrisford."

"Now I'm really getting irritated," Kaki said.

Lamarr, still with Damear on his lap, said evenly, "Might as well not. They'll call us when they ready to call us."

"If I'd known, I would have brought something to read, crying out loud."

"Now stop that cussing," I told her. "You know whenever we go someplace with Tahija we wait."

"It's the truth," Tahija said.

Kaki yawned and got up to stretch her legs.

"That's not a lawyer," I heard someone say. "She's with those triplets."

It was in question because all of those waiting were African American or Latino, while most of the legal-aid people, and all of the guards and bailiffs, were white.

At the other end of our group, to Tahija's left, sat a woman in her early thirties. A lawyer came to speak with her, and we could not help overhearing the conversation. He told her nothing could be done. Today it would be made official. She was losing custody of her son. She broke down. Such grief as I have never

173

seen except at a funeral. But twelve-year-old boys need chastising, she sobbed. She was grateful to her boyfriend for being the man of the house. Didn't a boy need a man in the house? The lawyer nodded, checked his watch, and left.

The woman sat crying, waiting for her name to be called. No one sat with her, unless you counted the eight of us, caught by accident under the bell jar of her misery. Whatever mistakes she might have made in the past, her anguish now was terrible. We suffered with her, even the boys, gazing as one as she hid her face in her hands and shook with sobs; maybe especially the boys, for they saw without preconception, as adults cannot.

In a poem written on the eve of World War II and quoted widely after the September 11 attacks, W.H. Auden wrote, "Those to whom evil is done, do evil in return." Of course a parent who abuses a child is personally responsible, but isn't it disingenuous to pretend racist violence stops with the victim? The violence of four and a half centuries of enslavement, and the near-century of Jim Crow that followed, reverberates still. The African American parent hauled into court for administering the whippings her parents and grandparents administered to her is like the last person in a bucket brigade, except what's passed down the line is not a bucket of water but a punch in the face. When the second-to-last in line punches the last, the weakest, the child, she alone is singled out for public censure.

Where is the court system to try the enslavers who bull-whipped the ancestors, who then whipped *their* children, who whipped their children, and on down to the lone mother in the lobby of family court waiting for her name to be called?

And where did that name originate? With a landowner the U.S. government had given the legal right to own, kill, breed and rape her ancestors. But neither that man nor his descendents nor the government whose capital buildings were built with stolen labor stood up when her name was called. She stood up alone, and alone went to face the judge.

*   *   *

A thirty-something white man with brown hair in a short boyish cut, the judge smiled broadly when he saw us arrayed before him, me on one end and big Lamarr at the other (nearest the exit).

"Why, are they triplets?" he asked.

That's one question, I thought, hoping Tahija would refrain from responding. To my relief he didn't try for a second but went on to the business at hand.

Did Tahija — Shannon Ellison — desire to be remanded into our custody? She said yes, she did. Had the child advocate assigned to Tahija ascertained this to be in the girl's best interest? The child advocate said yes. Did the child advocate assigned to the babies believe it was in their best interest? Yes. Did Laura Ellison agree to relinquish legal custody of said Shannon Ellison? Laura said yes. Did Kaki Nelsen agree to take on the responsibilities of serving as Shannon Ellison's legal guardian until she reached the age of eighteen? Yes she did. Did I? I did.

No questions for Lamarr, though it had been his question to Kaki, if Tahija could move in, that had started us all on our way to this garland of Yes's.

Tourist brochures call it "a medallion in the parkway's necklace of gems." People who grew up in Philly remember playing in it as children. Within sight of City Hall, the Free Library, the Franklin Institute and the Academy of Natural Sciences, Swann Fountain was a flower-lined circle of dancing water.

After leaving the boys with their dad, we women had gone out to eat, stopping at the fountain on the way home.

Laura joked about the fountain's reclining nudes being big bone-ded.

"I'm big bone-ded," Tahija said, "they fat."

Laura found a golf ball in the grass. Someone had the idea that we write our names on it. After we squeezed our names into the bumpy surface with a pen Tahija dug from her purse, someone had the idea that we should get up onto the lip of marble surrounding the fountain.

"One time around for each of us," Tahija suggested.

"Laura in the lead," Kaki said, "because if not for Laura, there would have been no Tahija."

"Ya'll are crazy," Laura said, but hopped up nevertheless onto the wall and waited like an engine for the rest of us to form a line behind her.

Passing drivers must have thought we *were* crazy: two black women in long Muslim robes, one thin, one big bone-ded, leading two white women in office clothes, one tall, one short, around the fountain, squealing like schoolgirls when the wind dashed spray across their path.

For a long time after, that golf ball sat on the piano behind a framed photo of the boys at six months. It was a small thing, but it reminded us of the circles we had made together around the fountain's rising-falling water on the day when we waited all day to stand before a judge and say yes.

Chapter 21

The same year I had to go back to school and when I went it seemed like it was nothing like when I had left before I had the boys. Everyone seemed to be so immature. I had to get out of there so Kaki and Kathryn took me to take the test to get into Community College of Philadelphia and January of 1999 I started classes.

My Life as I Know It

"At what temperature does your breath do this?" I asked Tahija, puffing out smoke as we climbed the stairs to her typing class. We'd been to a doctor's appointment and I was dropping her off late at school.

"The temperature we're at," she said.

Copies of paintings by the European masters hung in the main hallway of Dobbins High School, but there was no heat. It was early December.

Tahija's high school was a great disappointment. She went half days: gym, lunch, English, and typing. Gym was jumping jacks then basketball, with most of the girls watching. Lunch she didn't eat because of the pork threat. English was worksheets: grammar and punctuation — none of the fiction, poetry, and drama that would have developed her already good ear for language and broadened her perspective. And typing — we'd reached the classroom — appeared to be a study hall.

"That the one going to write 'Leave me alone today?' on the board?" I asked, looking in.

"That's her. Counting the hours till retirement."

"Well, try to learn something."

"She gives me work I'll do it."

"I know you will," I hugged her goodbye.

In junior high Tahija had won an essay contest. The prize was a weekend in Atlanta visiting Morehouse and Spelman colleges. Only to graduate to no heat, no challenge. TANF gave her an incentive to stay in school, and she was trying to make it work, but that effort was beginning to seem an empty exercise in compliance.

Driving home I mulled it over. What was my responsibility as her legal guardian? At the very least, I should know a lot more about the public schools. In Philly, they were effectively segregated, thanks to white flight to the suburbs and to the private schools that sprouted like mushrooms after court-ordered desegregation. And because the public schools were funded by local property taxes, and not, like everything else important, by state and federal revenues, they were also broke. There were magnet schools, and soon the state would sanction charter schools. But the first had long waiting lists and the second was yet to come. Tahija seemed stuck. No options — a good definition of dire poverty. But Kaki and I weren't poor. What options did we have that we could extend to her?

There's not much I can claim to have talked Tahija into over the years, but I did manage to get her to attend an open house at the Community College of Philadelphia. She liked it: the high-ceilinged library, the sunny hallways, the small, engaged classes, the diversity. Before long we found ourselves standing in line to register for spring term courses. In front of us three guys went on and on about their amazing and bizarre psychology professor, while two girls behind us quizzed each other for an anatomy test. Purposefulness was in the air, and that air was *heated*.

In January of 1999, two months into her sixteenth year, when the boys were almost a year old, Tahija enrolled full time at the Community College of Philadelphia, which folks called just Community. Her math and English courses were pre-college level, but if she passed with a C or higher she'd advance to the freshman curriculum.

It seemed a good move. Under welfare reform the first twenty-four months of a sixty-month lifetime entitlement could be used for education and job training. We'd already used ten months on the second half of tenth grade, the first half of eleventh, and the summer between. That left fourteen months — time enough, if she went four semesters straight, to earn an AA degree. With that, and maybe a work-study job on her resumé, she'd enter the job market as something more than a nail head under the hammer of minimum wage.

Along with job readiness, I hoped college would give her a wider perspective on life. I knew her well enough by then to know she was hauling considerable baggage. When it came time to start opening those suitcases I wanted her to know that others had been through what she'd been through, and more, and had *come* through, and left a record.

It was a record she had a right to know about. It was her inheritance as a human being.

"So I think, 'When is he gonna check the homework?' Because sometimes he does and sometimes he doesn't, right?"

We were in the shamrock room eating our favorite meal of grilled salmon, mashed potatoes, garlic bread and broccoli. Lamarr was upstairs watching TV with the boys.

"This is the one wears the same shirt every day?" Kaki asked.

"The English teacher, yeah. And I think, dang, here I stayed up till 3:00 AM doing it and he's not even going to check it. But just as everybody's filing out, he comes up to my desk, and he says, 'Let me see your homework.' Like that, like some mafia guy."

179

"He doesn't ask anybody else?" I said.

"No, just me."

"And you have it."

"I have it. I flip open my notebook, and there it is. Done."

"Ha!" Kaki said, dolloping mashed potatoes onto her plate. "He asked the wrong person."

Or the right one, I thought, grateful, knowing how little he earned (two to three thousand a course and no benefits, if he was an adjunct).

This teacher of the limited wardrobe challenged and inspired Tahija. One day years later, when she holds cut-off notices from the water department and the gas company both, when college is a dream deferred, she'll meet him on the Avenue. She won't recognize him at first, but he'll recognize her.

"I can see it in your eyes," he'll say. "You're not making anything of your life." Then he'll remind her what he used to tell her back when she was the youngest student in his class, probably in the whole college: "I know you have something wonderful to contribute to this world."

She felt good all the rest of the day, she told me. "Like somebody gave me money."

Rashakea, Porsha, and Tashi King, three skinny sisters who might have passed for triplets themselves, came by after school and tried to talk me into bringing the boys down to the lot.

"I'll pull them in the red wagon," Porsha offered.

I rarely took them outdoors without permission, instructions, and designated clothes. But it was fun to picture Porsha pulling them down the block — until the image collided with Tahija coming up the block. Porsha pulled them instead in circles around the dining room table. They loved it. Then Barbara Parnell popped in, with a loud "Kath-a-ryn" for a knock. She sat her big self on the sofa, wheezing a little from the walk across the street.

"Don't hand me no baby," she said when I handed her Mahad. Yet she cuddled him and let him explore her moonless midnight face, with its scar rising from her upper lip like an icicle that had fallen and stuck there.

"Got this scar over a dollar," she told Mahad. "Now ain't that a shame?"

Tahija came home in a good mood, revved from an Islamic club meeting.

"Sandra talking some, 'If I had money up front for the cupcakes.' How is it a fund raiser if we paying for the ingredients? Tell me that? Everybody's chipping in."

"She trying to get over," I said.

"Trying to play ya'll," Barbara added.

"Exactly," Tahija said.

Damear was standing, holding onto the bookshelf, head turned to his mom, mouth open (to better hear, big Lamarr said). Little Lamarr sat at the piano helping Porsha make it give up *all* its notes.

"She's working my last nerve, I tell you." Tahija slung her book bag onto the sofa. "And what're ya'll three doing downstairs? Huh? Tearin' up?"

Damear and Mahad answered with an exuberant potpourri of syllables we had to laugh with. Then Kaki came home with the smile I still loved to see.

"Here's Kakino," said Tahija, her own smile punctured at the sight of Mahad reaching for Kaki.

"Where's the sweatshirt you left in?" I asked Kaki.

"Somebody in the workshop talked me out of it, said she was cold."

"Cold my eye," said Tahija.

"Eye-ah!" said Mear, bouncing where he stood, looking up at his mom.

Elva showed up then and fell into a chair to remind us the next day was block party day. We'd close off the street, carry out the trampoline one family had and any pools people were willing to share, cook up lots of food, play games, dance, and enjoy ourselves all day, with not one car polluting the place and imperiling children and pets.

"*Muchachos malo,*" Elva said, smiling at little Lamarr. "How old they now?"

I looked at Tahija. "Fourteen months," she said.

"Fourteen months. Lordy lordy. You need some car seats? I got a car seat from when my grandbaby was little."

Tahija looked at me. "Go on and show her," she said.

"You want to see the nursery, Elva?"

"I can't pull them steps, not after no eight hours."

But she managed, and stood in the middle of the nursery marveling. Beneath each crib stood a row of car seats, nine in all. Some came from the same agency that had given us the stretch limo, some from Kaki's Quaker meeting, some from people in the neighborhood.

"Three infant, three toddler, three whatever," I said.

"Da-amn," said Elva.

"You have three kids all at once people be donating stuff to you too."

"Shit, I have three kids all at once they have to donate me a coffin."

Elva trudged home to start cooking for the block party. The King sisters followed Kaki into the kitchen to help with dinner. They were in there peeling and chopping when Lamarr arrived.

Dinner was chicken baked by Kaki, macaroni and cheese Lamarr had made the day before, boiled potatoes peeled and cut by the three sisters, broccoli chopped by them, salad and garlic bread by me, and chocolate sheet cake by Tahija. We had to put the leaf into the dining room table Kaki's mother had given us. Sam Harpur came by, making it an even dozen.

When Kaki bowed her head to say grace, beginning "Oh great spirit," I felt irritated. Alone we always said a silent grace, speaking out of it if moved to. This blessing, as it went on, reminded me of her missionary brother, who sat squarely at the head of the family table when we visited and intoned a fathergod-filled blessing that made some matriarchal bone deep within me shudder. Why not ask first if anyone else felt moved to say grace? I added this to the list of things to be talked about later, under the category Distribution of Power. Her way in her house, it was more and more seeming. Kaki's father had died not long before I met her, but I felt like I was getting to know him nevertheless.

She ended grace with a Native American "Ho!" that sent the King sisters snickering, and we all joined Mahad, who had already commenced eating. He sat in the one high chair at a corner of the table next to Kaki. Little Lamarr sat in big Lamarr's lap, until some suspected diaper action prompted a transfer to Mom. Damear got lucky me.

As we were passing plates, talking and eating, Rashakea, the middle King sister, looked up at the three-tiered chandelier over our heads. She was an athlete who raced barefoot in the street, and usually won; she was also blunt.

"I could kill ya'll for that chandelier," she said, then quickly added, "psych" — meaning *just kidding;* but she had not as the words came from her been kidding.

"Previous owners put it in," I said — Kaki's line/Kaki's defensiveness mine now. "The mirror too."

We looked at ourselves in the floor-to-ceiling mirror: Kaki and Sam, a head taller than the rest of us, flanking one corner, Mahad between them; then Barbara Parnell, with her air of great feminine beauty; then the King sisters, skinny and braided, Tashi starting to tip into adolescence, Porsha so dark, like good soil I'd told her, or a night sky you can see the stars in; then me, my hair a pale frame to a freckled face; beside me Tahija in her cobalt blue outergarment and black kemar; and Lamarr at the end with his back to the mirror, head turned toward it. The light fell on us all, and yet it was the two white ones who claimed ownership of the chandelier it fell from, the mirror that reflected it, and the house that contained it.

Did I want to own something that elicited a murderous jealousy? Should I get rid of the thing, confront the jealousy, run from it? Were there other options?

I looked from the reflection to Kaki, on my left. She was handing Mahad a piece of potato. He bounced in the high chair — his food dance. He didn't know yet who owned the chandelier, the mirror, the house. Would he feel as Rashakea did? Would his house be like hers: empty of ornament, a cousin just out of prison, disenfranchised, ineligible even for food stamps, effectively unemployable, staring day and night at whatever violence network TV offered up? No wealth had been passed down to the children sitting around this table, no stocks, no bonds, no cash, no land, no house, no car, no tools.

Kaki looked at me, back at Mahad, and up. We could give the chandelier away, and did (to Rashakea on her next birthday, Sam Harpur doing the wiring), but the questions it raised could not so easily be given away.

Chapter 22

as if I have not reached
across our history to touch,
to soothe on more than one
occasion
and will again ...

— from "note to my self," by Lucille Clifton

The last spring of the millennium was a good time.

Laura Ellison completed her recovery program, got a full-time job with Head Start as a teacher's aide, and set a date to marry her long-time partner, a native of Philadelphia who had worked as a prep cook for many years at a downtown jazz club. Kaki and I were invited to the reception. Tahija was doing well in her courses. At the prompting of her tough-guy English teacher she had begun writing her life story, which she titled *My Life as I Know It*. She was active in the Islamic club and studying Arabic with a woman from Dubai. She had her nose pierced, with*out* the consent of her legal guardians. We had to admit, however, that the tiny diamond looked pretty good. At fifteen months, both Damear and Lamarr were walking, with Mahad close behind. The doctor considered this good progress, given that they'd been two months premature, and triplets.

Good progress all around. But the best news of all came from Lamarr. He had been accepted by Phame, a very competitive trade school with a reputation for placing its students in good jobs. In a little over a year he could be a trained machinist earning twenty dollars an hour. I thought his talents lay in more creative and people-oriented fields, but Lamarr loved working with machines too, and he had a family to support. The acceptance filled him with a confidence that was wonderful to see. He'd just turned nineteen. My eyes teared up to think of Joey reaching nineteen and finding opportunity opening to him. And I knew my brother would have relished, as did Lamarr, the strict dress code.

It was dress white shirt, suit and tie, every day. The teachers, most of them men, wore suits and ties too and didn't take any bull. Everything was state-of-the-art: computers, software, library. Classes ran from 7:30 to 5:30, half days on Saturday. For telemarketing and Labor Ready jobs Lamarr had been unable to consistently get up in the morning. For Phame, however, he went to bed early, ate better, and rose at 5:00 AM.

In our neighborhood's heyday a good job could be found, it was said, just by walking down American Street and asking. If by some miracle the factories were to re-open, if the heaped bricks of the Schlitz brewery flew upward into walls and the great rusting vats suddenly filled, the jobs would be taken the next day. But we didn't need every closed factory to re-open. We just needed one to stay open, and to hire one man, Lamarr Stevens.

Along with the very good news of Lamarr's acceptance came DHS's decision to close its case on the boys. The hawk had gone.

The morning of Laura's wedding I went up to the nursery to see if I could help. I was assigned shoes. Tahija was wearing a blue outergarment patterned with silver diamonds and a solid blue kemar. She looked lovely. Her face had cleared up, and a warm, orange-red showed in her cheeks. The boys were in dark dress pants, red shirts and white silk vests, with white Kufis on their heads. They sat on the edge of her bed in their usual order, with Mahad, in the middle, holding a jack-in-the-box as Lamarr wound it and Damear looked on, waiting. A tape was playing, one Tahija had sent away for that taught numbers in Arabic and told animal stories. I was getting to like the sugary tenor of the male singer, and his, "Aaa-llah Akbar, Aaaa-llah Akbar." You just had to sing along.

We heard honking and summoned Kaki from her office so we could get them all into their car seats and down the stairs to the impatient groom. He stood at the door in a Kufi and elegant, calf-length silk robe — handsome, eager, and nervous.

"See you at the reception," I called as they drove away.

The wedding reception was to be held at the house of the boys' great-great-grandmother Miss Mary Millicent Ellison, who had raised Laura and cared for Tahija for several years after the move back from Colorado. We felt honored to have been invited. We'd been to the house once before, to show Millie, as everyone called her, the triplets, but this occasion was very different.

The house was packed. Few of the guests were Muslim. I heard big Lamarr's voice but couldn't see him. The bride and groom seemed not to have arrived yet. There was the aunt I'd met once, but she was talking to someone. As we stood awkwardly in the living room, sort of watching the Phillies game while keeping an eye out for Tahija or her mom or somebody who knew us, Millie spotted us and called us over.

She offered her cheek to be kissed and scooted her niece out of the chair beside her.

"I don't need to sit," I said, and Kaki said the same, but sit we were going to. She sent her son for another chair and two beers and told us how glad she was to see us.

"You girls have been so good, I can't say. I tell everyone at my church what you did for Tahija, and they just can't believe it."

"It seemed like the Christian thing to do," I said.

"God is good."

"All the time," her niece added.

We sipped the beers and conversed. Millie's living room reminded me of my mother's, with its antique-red walls, photo-crowded shelves and rabbit-ear topped TV tuned to sports. Cards stood open on nearly every surface, for Mary Millicent Ellison was the matriarch of a large, respectful family.

She had come north from South Carolina as a young woman, part of the Great Migration, and the South hovered like hickory smoke in her deep voice. I loved hearing it, but couldn't help feel the chill of the niece I'd dislodged.

I remembered something Millie had said the day Tahija and I brought the triplets over. She had said, "Hand me the light one." I was shocked and confused, not knowing how she meant it exactly. Though many people favored little Lamarr, with his big, light eyes and long, handsome face, she had meant Damear, who was, to my eyes, the barest, hardly noticeable shade lighter. To my eyes.

Millie had naturally straight hair nearly to her shoulders and a complexion lighter than anyone's in the room except mine (Kaki tanned walnut brown in the summer). Was her warmth toward Kaki and me some kind of ingrained favoring of the lightest, or was it fear? Though she still watched a few grandbabies (everybody was a grandbaby, even the great- and great-greats), Millie Ellison was eighty-four. She had been born in 1914, forty-nine years after the ostensible end of slavery, and about as many before the Civil Rights movement. What she must have seen.

When the daughter who lived with her, the boys' great-grand-mother, took sick a few years later, Millie wouldn't make use of the visiting nurse service because some of the nurses were white, and she couldn't abide a white person in her home. She abided us, though. It was an honor and a responsibility. I wasn't sure quite how to act — the less said the better, I thought — but I did get the sense that sitting so long in the chair of honor was undiplomatic.

The food arriving gave us a way out, but in the end led to more confusion. I was filling my plate when Damear saw me and toddled across the room.

"Hey Mear-mear!" I picked him up.

Before long Kaki ended up with Mahddy. I made room for them beside Mear and me on a sofa, and we were happily sharing our food when the glacier arrived. The others on the sofa left, and people nearby looked at us, shook their heads, and gave us their backs. It wasn't everyone, but seemed so. I didn't understand. We were helping, weren't we? Why would people be bothered, or even, as it seemed, angered?

I had been thinking of my care for the boys as a kind of payback for the care given to generations of white children, the heartfelt nature of it made clear to me by accounts I'd heard from those children grown up, my peers, and by allusions to it in literature, like Lucille Clifton's poem "note to myself":

> as if I am not scarred,
> as if my family enemy
> does not look like them,
> as if I have not reached
> across our history to touch,
> to soothe on more than one
> occasion
> and will again . . . *

Of course I was being paid — that envelope fat with seven twenties that Tahija handed me with such empowered pleasure every two weeks — but often that went right back into running the house, and I gave more than I was paid for; I gave my love, and supposed, perhaps wrongly, sentimentally, that my love was paying down ever so little, if not on the principle then at least on the interest accrued from that old old debt.

---

*From Lucille Clifton's *The Book of Light:* Copper Canyon Press, 1993.

Wasn't it appropriate and fitting that I should "reach across our history"? Wasn't I taking some of the burden off of Millie's shoulders? Although retired now, she'd worked all her life, raised four children of her own and then some of her children's children. She had said she was grateful to us; she said she prayed for us.

Some people did not seem to think we deserved Millie's prayers. Could it be that I was somehow actually adding to the debt, taking rather than giving?

Taking what? What other historical parallel might the sight of Kaki and me holding (spoiling?) and feeding (stealing?) the boys bring to mind? DHS at the door, with cops; white couples adopting poverty's foundlings; weeping children gazing backward from the slave dealer's cart?

Shaken by these questions and by the fear that whatever I did only made matters worse, I was relieved when Tahija announced that we would be leaving the party early, i.e., now.

We said goodbye to Millie Ellison, who promised to keep praying for us, and loaded everyone into the car. Once we were back out on Broad Street Tahija loosed her most stylized language in a tirade against her cousin Bailey and the music he'd put on — the cause of our early departure.

"He's S.O.L.* if he thinks I'm a sit still for that trash! I been told him don't put no rap on, but he got to go and put it on. What was the point of that? If anyone a my boys ever, *eva*" — she turned little Lamarr's seat so he was facing her — "call theyselves 'dogs' and catch theyselves talking some 'I'm a do this to you baby and I'm a do that' they going straight to boot camp, I don't care if they not but six years old. Ya'll hear me?"

Kaki and I looked at each other. Did she mean us, or the boys?

"A lot of rap isn't about sex," I said. "And even when it is, it can still be poetry."

"How's it going to be poetry when it say 'bitch' and 'ho' a hundred-fifty times a song?"

---

*Shit out of luck

"She's got a point," Kaki said.

"Now you know that's not all there is, that's what reaches commercial radio," I said. "It's poetry because it's rhymed, it's metered, it's urgent, and just like you when you're steamed it bounces language around like a superball in a handball court."

"She's got a point," Kaki said. Miss moderator.

"I mean, last week, I get on the subway," I went on, "and there's five or six youngbulls huddled up at one end, right? So I sit aways off, but then I hear this, this *language*, this poetry, coming from one, and I move a few seats closer, because it's *good*. I see some of them have notebooks open, waiting to read, and some of them it's just coming from memory — long long lines, like Walt Whitman, and rhymes? One guy said, 'niggas with diseases talkin' 'bout Jesus.'"

"He must a had some type of grandmother like my Grandmom Grealy dragging him off to church all the time," Tahija said.

"Exactly," I said. "He had something he *had* to say and he found an original, musical way to say it. That's poetry."

Tahija was not persuaded. Anyway, it wasn't about definitions of poetry for her. Was it about shame? Related to sex, to African American culture? She sure was mad.

"I asked him ahead of time, you heard me ask him, 'Put on some jazz.' He got a whole collection, it's not like he don't. Boo-boo the fool. *Then,* my mom's going to sit there and talk some, 'Why you not calling Millie anymore? Don't you love her any-more?' Do I look like I have time to be asking 'How far?' every time Millie say jump, the way my mom do? *Come* on now. If it wasn't for Millie I wouldn't be in all this misery. You know why we had came back from Colorado."

I knew, but this was one train that was going right on through.

"Because Millie was sick, is why, 'sposed to be dying. She not dead, is she? Do she look dead?"

"She looks quite chipper," Kaki said.

"And do you see anybody coming over to help me with these boys so I have *time* to be talking on the phone? People talk shit out they mouths but when you ask them 'can you drive me to the

WIC office?' you're S.O.L. They *have* cars, it's not like they don't have cars."

In this manner we proceeded down Broad Street through the brightly lit corridor of Temple University's floodlights.

"You know these boys knocked out already," she said after awhile. "It was an all right party though."

"Except for Bailey letting the dogs out," I said.

"Don't get me back started," she laughed.

"Don't nobody get started," Kaki put in, turning left and off the edge of Temple's artificial day, into our neighborhood.

By the time we reached Hancock Street Tahija had joined her boys in sleep.

Kaki parked in front of the house and turned off the engine, sighing.

"You tired?" I asked.

With fatigue her interstitial cystitis acted up more, which made her work more, which made her more fatigued. Her new three-fifths time job was taking all five fifths more often than not, and there were tensions — most pressingly with her new co-director, an Ivy-league educated black minister, her senior by ten years. He had criticized the AVP-style workshops she ran for young people, especially the way she used recovering addicts to facilitate. I'd seen them together. Race, class, religion, gender, gender preference — it was hard to tell which came first, but they sure did push each other's buttons.

We looked into the back seat. Mahad, in the middle, snored away, loud as his dad. Tahija's head was tipped back. A few hairs showed at her temples, fine as mustard-seed sprouts.

"Remember the first time she was in the car?" Kaki asked.

"Couldn't hardly get a word out of her."

We had walked a good distance with her. Opening the car door, turning to wake her and help get the boys into the house, I believed I could go on, as the song says, a little more.

Part Three

Jubilee

Chapter 23

One night Marcelle and Jorge walked over to have dinner with us. Tahija seemed to like them, and for years after will let me know if she's seen one or the other around. She joined us in the living room with little Lamarr, whom she entrusted to Marcelle. By way of introduction, I guess, he spit up on her. The cleanup done, he sat very straight on her lap examining her face and long hair. Then he turned his gaze on Jorge of the dark impressive beard.

"Look at dat," said Jorge, in his Ecuadorian accent, "It is he who is assessing us, not we him."

Damear began crying upstairs and Tahija suggested I go up and get him. When I came down with two, stopping on the stairs for the green light, Tahija said to the others, "Told you."

"Told them what?" I asked.

"That you'd come back with both."

It was a happy moment and a good night. In the writing that follows, about conflict in the Hancock Street house, I tried to keep in mind what Jorge had implied: in looking, we are looked upon; in assessing, we are assessed.

* * *

It had seemed like a good idea.

Tahija's friend Stefanie visited the house often. With Tahija's new schedule I was watching the boys three days a week. What if Stefanie came and helped me one of those days? She'd be an extra lap and an ally for Tahija, who was feeling the strain, I sensed, of living at such close quarters with two watching advice-giving middle-aged white women. And when Tahija moved out, someday, she'd probably need help with the boys. What better chance would I have to inculcate a probable helper with my methods?

Tahija liked the idea (not the inculcation part, which I kept to my sneaky self), and agreed to pay Stefanie seven dollars an hour out of the childcare money. By the middle of the first day, however, I wondered what on earth I had been thinking. Stefanie had a proprietary air toward Damear, Mahad and Lamarr that made me doubt my methods and my right to care for them at all. Seventeen, heavy, as the chronically poor are heavy, with dimples and a low laugh that licked the plate of any joke clean, Stefanie in the house felt to me not just like Tahija's proxy, but all black womanhood's. And what all black womanhood was wondering (in my self-conscious imaginings) was just who did I think I was trying to have any say about how these boys were taken care of?

Stefanie, anyway, seemed to think I was the one in need of inculcation, and herself just the person to do it.

"They're fine up here," she said. "Look."

I looked. They were in Damear's crib playing with a toy phone. I saw motor skills wanting more space and challenge.

I had suggested we take them downstairs. Stefanie was on the end of the bed watching *Judge Judy*. Though she didn't cover as Tahija thought she should, Stefanie was Muslim. She wore an orange T-shirt with "Rough Riders" printed across the front, an unhemmed black kemar, and navy blue jeans two or three sizes too small.

"You watch *Judge Judy*, Kathryn?"

The portable television sat on an end table in front of the diaper pail, between Mahad's crib and the door.

"I've seen it," I said.

Judge Judy was shooting spitball quips at an amenable plaintiff. She had a book out: *Don't Pee on My Leg and Try to Tell me It's Raining*.

"Come on, Stefanie. I have the whole downstairs baby-proofed. Looks like Judge Judy have some kid of attitude today anyway."

"This man lying from the gate, is why."

I roused myself and scooped Damear and Mahad from the crib. Stefanie sighed and lifted Lamarr by the arm (he knew to go limp, but I winced anyway).

"It's fun, you'll see," I said when we had them downstairs.

She fell back on the couch, readjusting her jeans, and waited to see.

"Hey, I've got an idea," I said, "when the boys take their nap why don't we have some reading practice?"

"We can," she said.

Stefanie seemed to have stopped learning to read at about third grade. At Tahija's suggestion, I'd been tutoring her a little. She liked it, but I was sure going to miss my nap.

As I was attaching the bouncy swing they loved to the door jamb, Wah-wah bonked his head and while I searched for the cut that must surely be there — with the way he was crying — Damear dashed for the kitchen, where he pulled down a flimsy rack that held our pots and pans.

"They love banging on pots and pans," I told Stefanie, who followed me into the kitchen shaking her head.

I put Mahddy down and gave him a wooden spoon. Still holding Marr, who *would* find any findable hazard, I put the cat food bowl up high, checked the childproofing latches inside the cabinet doors, and then set him down too. He took Mahd's spoon. Mahd took Mear's. Mear's hand darted out for an asterisk of cat food and before we could stop him —

"Nasty!" Stefanie smacked his leg. "Spit that out before I pop you good."

197

The smack, the words, the tone — this wasn't black woman-hood, it was my mother and her temper, it was my early childhood coming back to me. Once had been enough, thank you.

The phone rang in the shamrock room. As I was taking a message for Kaki, trying to hear over Damear's crying, Marr crawled in heading for the hula hoops — a safe destination, I thought. Done with the call, I went back in the kitchen to put on water for tea. Strong tea.

"See," I said to Stefanie, who was leaning on the counter, fore-head in her palm, "the trick is to keep them in one area, give them something stimulating to do, and — "

Just then a strange sound came from the shamrock room, a sound like a bowling ball heard from a distance, then a slowing oscillation, as of a metal lid waffling to a standstill. A paint can lid.

In two steps I saw what had happened. Lamarr stood beside his mom's chair as an amoeba of blue expanded outward from a tipped gallon of interior/exterior semi-gloss latex paint.

"Aaaahh!" I screamed (channeling my mother). "Who left an open damn can of paint, *paint for God sakes,* where anyone could get to it?" In my mind, blame slingshot to big Lamarr (he'd been painting trim, salmon-pink though), then to Kaki, who wasn't home, was *never* home, leaving me with — just then Stefanie came around the corner to see Lamarr plop down nice as you please in the paint.

"My my my," she said, slowly shaking her head, as I imagined her ancestors had been doing at the strange ways of whitefolks since before mine wandered in from Nova Scotia and Ireland. "How about I take the other two back upstairs now?"

And you insisted that the children come downstairs? I imag-ined Judge Judy peering down at me. *Is that right Miss Gordon?*

I held Lamarr at arm's length, letting him drip into the spreading inlet. "While I give this guy a bath?"

"Ba-ath!" said Lamarr.

"He loves baths," I said weakly.

He had better, Judge Judy said, *with the likes of you taking care of him.*

*   *   *

Stefanie let me know I was busted.

We were in Kaki's office, the boys and me on the floor rolling a ball back and forth, Stefanie leaning in the doorway.

"She saw broccoli in the diapers," she said.

Tahija had approved crackers and juice, but nothing more. I had been feeding them lunch.

"Am I supposed to eat in front of them and not give them any?"

"You gotta know to say no sometimes."

"And some people gotta learn to say yes," I said.

"Ball!" Mahddy said. I pushed the ball toward him. Damear had gone to explore the realm beneath Kaki's desk while Lamarr was trying to get a hand on Purrsilla the cat, who woke from a nap to find herself trapped in baby land.

Stefanie saved her from becoming a squeeze toy, and went to watch *Cosby*. Mahd, Marr, and I kept rolling the ball back and forth. It was 11:30. Almost time for the lunch I hadn't resigned myself to not feeding them.

Kaki and I had observed that Tahija sometimes did not eat for long stretches, and that when she did it was often in large quantities. Was this an eating disorder, a response to past deprivation? Both? We didn't know, but we worried.

In our first attempt to exert authority after being appointed legal guardians, we asked for a meeting with Tahija and her mother. I don't recall whose idea it was to gather at Friends Center, a campus of buildings that housed, along with offices, one of the largest meetings in the city. Probably it was my idea. I loved the place, how the red brick of the mid-nineteenth century wing contrasted yet somehow balanced the plate glass front of the newer section. At the entrance, where these two parts formed a wide angle, was a bronze statue of Mary Dyer, a Quaker martyred for the cause of religious freedom. Even before I knew her story

I liked to stand by the statue looking up at the figure seated in worship. The sculptor had rendered her hands long and slender. They lay open in her lap. Hold us in your peace, I thought as we passed her to go in. May the whole building hold us.

We walked through the lobby to the older part of the building, and a great balconied meeting room. It was empty, the rows and rows of plain wooden benches seeming a kind of gathering. I felt, as I often did in that worship room, and others as old, a presence, as of a misty convocation of elders from another century.

We sat on the benches nearest the door. They looked out and down on the rest of the room, facing benches Quakers called them. Did Tahija and her mother take peace from the room, from September sunlight angling in through a tall window whose shutter had been left open? Or did this feel like foreign territory? Anyway it was not, as someone pointed out to me later, exactly neutral territory.

Laura had put on weight. She and Tahija looked more alike now, though she wore only a loose copper-colored headscarf while Tahija was fully covered — pinned-at-the-neck kemar and outergarment.

"Lucretia Mott worshipped here," Kaki said.

"And Sojourner Truth spoke once, I think," I added, though I was vague on the point, having heard or read it somewhere. Perhaps I just wished it were so, as I wished for Quakers to always have been impeccable allies of Abolition and African Americans. I didn't know then about the back bench — the practice some meetings had of relegating Friends of African descent to the rear of the meetinghouse. In truth, whatever peace entered us through that room and its history was a complicated, a flawed peace, one which we were meant not so much to absorb, perhaps, as to carry forward into a season of repair.

Kaki and I opened the discussion by saying that we felt our new role as legal guardians gave us a responsibility to address the food issue. It had been troubling us, we said, for some time.

Tahija moved a little away from us, nearer the door. There had been no talk until then of legal guardianship giving us any new authority, though we had, I suppose, assumed so. A mistake, I realize now. It must have felt to Tahija as if we were changing the terms of the deal.

What we wanted, we said, was a solid lunch for them in the middle of the day, and healthy snacks.

"It must seem like they eat a lot, being there's the three of them," I said.

Kaki added something, an observation, and we waited; like people standing on ice they'd just heard crack we waited.

More than her words, Laura's tone added the weight that plunged us all into the frigid water. Why, she asked her daughter, was she disrespecting these ladies when we had taken her in? She had better start doing what we said.

Tahija jumped up, fighting tears, and ran from the room, her mother following. Kaki and I waited a moment in the echoing room, the rows of benches seeming to wait with us, then went out after them.

They stood face to face, shouting, on the walk leading out of the building. Passersby slowed to watch, one man saying something that made Laura say something back. Crying, more upset than I'd ever seen her, Tahija whirled around and sped away.

Hardly knowing what had happened it had happened so fast, Kaki and I went to Laura and stood watching with her as Tahija's figure receded down the sidewalk.

"People better mind their own business," Laura said.

Meaning us?

"Some man going to say, 'I'm watching you,'" she went on. "How's he watching me?"

Who else, I wondered, might be watching us, from the other side of the plate glass, say? In it I saw our reflection, Mary Dyer behind us, and behind and above her the reds of a changing tree.

There was a restaurant across the street. We went there to eat and had a good lunch, and a good talk, not about food but about our high schools being desegregated, and about mothers,

Kaki's, mine, Laura's: what they had done and not done, what had stood in the way of their doing better.

"All we can hope," I said, "is to do a little better than them."

I don't know if, called to play a motherly role, I did improve on my mother's performance. But I know for certain Laura did, and that the difficult girl who'd run away that day would come to the table before long, and share many meals with her mother.

Tahija had told me about groceries left on the front step by neighbors. During the hard hard times. About not being let to bring them in. Chronic hunger in childhood ... iron deficiency that makes ice, paint, dirt appetizing. I had seen it in the neighborhood, had heard adults talk about it, Sam with a kind of nostalgia: Remember summer days so hot you could pull chunks of tar off the road and eat them? (No Sam I don't.) And corn starch, one time I ate a whole box.... Toddlers so hungry they sneak down at night, seize any chance to gorge on whatever can be reached, flour, baking soda, lard, spices, uncooked grains — discovered by older children or adults who tell the story later not as a story of hunger but of the funny ways of children, or of *those* children, greedy and sneaky.

Not just hunger but denial of hunger, not just denial but insistance on the right to deny: an attitude born of necessity, yes, of genocidal centuries, but hard to live with, nonetheless.

It's Mahad's turn to ride in the front seat and superintend the radio. They're eight. Damear and Lamarr are in the back seat eating the snack we stopped to get after playing in the big park near their house. One Slushie, one cheese Danish, one bag pistachio nuts (no dye).

"If I was sick," Damear is saying, "you'd bring me things to eat."

"Yeah? What would I bring you?"

"Apple juice," Mahddy says, "and apples."

He's got me pegged. I love the way he says *apples: appulls,* popping the *pp*'s. "What else?"

"Tea," says little Lamarr.

"And toast," Damear puts in, "and soup, and, uh … carrots!"

"But I thought you didn't like carrots."

"Mahd doesn't like carrots."

Everyone thinks they know what Mahad likes and doesn't like.

"I do *too* like carrots, Mear."

"I like Oodles of Noodles!" says Lamarr, bouncing.

With the list of foods I would bring them if they were sick punctuated in this way by debate and qualification, we drive the mile or so from the park back to their house. After establishing whose turn it is to ride in front next time and whether or not Quickie-mart stops are a regular or a sometime thing, we go in.

I find myself thinking later about the food list, lingering over the image of spooning soup to little boys and setting down plates of sliced apples. Macintosh would be good and sweet, also Gala and Golden Delicious. And they should have Red Delicious too, and Empire and Fuji, Granny Smith and Rayburns, organic or low-spray if I could get it, peeled if not, cored either way. And then all those other fruits, the common and the less common, orange and grape, kiwi and mango.

My list went on longer than the boys'. Because I knew of more foods, because there was not one good food I could think of that I did not want to bring them and watch them eat, until even the remembrance of emptiness was filled, in them, in me, in Stefanie, in our parents and theirs. In all of us.

Chapter 24

I think the hardest thing about living on Hancock street was not being able to do whatever I wanted. I felt like I had parents all over again in some ways it was good because I could always talk about a problem I was having and whenever I needed help with anything all I had to do was ask and Kaki and Kathryn would help the best way they could, but it was also bad because I felt like I always had to answer to someone and I am not at all use to answering to anyone.

from the interview

The historian and philosopher Hannah Arendt has written that the only power we can have over the past is forgiveness. Through the years I would give Tahija much love and attention, gifts, money when money was what was most needed, advice, good and bad, but the most valuable thing I gave her may have been the chance to exercise that power over our past.

She had moved out several months before. We had been speaking only by phone. We met at the community college and walked to the Rodin museum, where we sat on a bench in front of his sculpture of the thinking man.

She had gained weight, and the blemishes that appeared on her forehead and the sides of her face during the bed-rest time had come back. I didn't ask about the boys. I felt I did not deserve to ask, felt a remorse that seemed to stretch back farther than I could see, into and through the American history that had scrolled before my mind's eye that long ago day in Quaker meeting.

"When you were living with us ... at the end?" I began. "I was angry a lot. That anger didn't start with you. It was from my own childhood. I think the boys crying, and your anger, brought it up. I wish I acted better. You didn't deserve it. I'm sorry. I got too attached. I guess I got too attached."

"You were watching them," she said. "It was normal for you to get attached."

This was something I had said once to her. Hearing it come back to me made me cry. Just then a tourist bus from Pittsburgh roared in and unloaded a hundred or so people.

"Busloads of people appear whenever I cry in public." I joked. "You forgive me then?"

The sightseers snapped pictures of *The Thinker,* but I like to think that what they were actually preserving for posterity was our scene of forgiveness and reconciliation.

"I think sometimes I was just mad at you and Lamarr for making me see how being poor and black affects people, babies even. I thought that was in the past, wanted to think it was in the past. I wanted to stay asleep."

"No one likes to get woke," she said.

"We think we do, we ask for it, but when we get it we don't like it."

The only power we can have over the future, Arendt also observed, is the power to make a promise and keep it. That day I promised to help Tahija and her family stay together. "Whatever you ask, whatever you say you need." She has not called in that promise but a very few times.

We each made good choices that day: asking forgiveness, giving it, promising, accepting, trusting. Before this reconciliation, however, came bad choices. Bad choices and hard times.

*   *   *

Kaki, Lamarr and Tahija were waiting for me down in the living room. I sat on the new queen-size bed in the formerly purple room listening to little Lamarr cry half-heartedly. It was Friday, early evening. My time to watch them wouldn't come around again until Monday 9:00 A.M.

"Kathryn," came Kaki's voice up the stairs.

I went to the window, from which I could see the nursery's side windows — where Damear's crib was. I couldn't see it though through them; what I could see was the backyard, or part of it, and through the window of my mind a day not so long before, a day in June, bright, when Tahija and I had made a sort of hut by hanging an old gold-colored drape over the clothesline's ropes. We played there with the triplets in a cove of filtered light. Damear made a game of running back and forth between us, falling in turn into each of our laps. Trying to teach us something.

"K.D.!" Kaki called (Kathryn Darling or, sometimes, Kathryn Darn-it, her nickname for me). It was time for the house meeting with food at the top of the agenda.

I got up and went down one flight, stopping before the closed nursery door. Little Lamarr had fallen asleep, I guessed. Was anyone awake? On the light-blue door, Tahija had taped a few small cutout fish left from crib mobiles she, Kaki and I had made. I touched one I remembered cutting and coloring. The open mouth seemed opened to feed, shark like. I went down the next flight.

Tahija was sitting at one end of the sofa, which had its summer cover on now — pale pink flowers and green leaves. I sat at the other end.

Kaki and Lamarr had pulled chairs up, close to each other. Kaki had a legal pad.

"Anything to add to the agenda?" she asked us.

"Nothing I can think of," Lamarr said.

"Good," said Kaki. "Then let's start."

I started with silence and Tahija continued in that vein.

Lamarr said, "You two, how are we going to get anywhere if you don't talk?"

Lamarr liked house meetings. Though never an addict, he had lived from time to time in the New Jerusalem Now recovery community, where house meetings were a daily occurrence. He was good at them. I was not, a fact which I was about to make clear to all concerned.

"She," I said, looking at the bookshelf, "has food issues."

"Can you phrase that as an 'I' message?" Kaki asked.

"No."

"Sure you can."

"If I have food issues she's got them worse," Tahija said, to the wall.

"'I' messages help us own our reactions to others."

I dove in. "When they're hungry and I can't feed them I feel like what was the point of me driving all the way past Broad Street to the supermarket somebody put on her WIC list when she could have put the one right around the corner."

"Because I thought my grandmom would be driving me and furthermore that's the supermarket she picked because it's close by her house!" Tahija shouted.

"Ya'll are way off the agenda," said Lamarr.

"Shut up," said Tahija.

"That's just the sort of language that makes open and peaceful communication difficult," Kaki said.

Open and peaceful my foot. I felt like an Irish-style house meeting: is this a private fight, or can I get in on it? Then I remembered I was trying to be Quakerly.

"I feel frustrated and worried," I said, looking at her finally, "when it seems like they're not getting enough food."

"But they're just playing you," Tahija said, "trying to be slick. They eat like grown men before I leave in the morning."

"Why would they fake being hungry?" I asked.

"Just *greedy* I guess."

The way she said "greedy" pushed some buttons in me, brought up reactions I'd had to how much she and Lamarr ate. They had both gained a lot of weight.

"So if you don't say they need it, they don't need it?"

"That's right," she said.

"And can't nobody," I said, "not even they own stomachs, tell you different?"

"Don't get smart, Kathryn."

"Don't talk to me like you talk to them."

"I'll talk to them any fucking way I please. They're my children — no!" She'd jumped up and Lamarr was trying to block her. "Let me finish. They're my children. If ya'll two want babies I suggest you go find some of your own!"

Whatever I said next caused Lamarr to have to hold Tahija back, but her words kept on coming, and then Kaki felt called upon to hold me back.

In this fashion the house meeting came to an end.

I took my anger into the kitchen and like so many women before me scrubbed until I could see it reflected back to me in stainless steel. Lamarr came in, big face all peaceful.

"I think she's just worried that the boys will get, you know, confused," he said.

"Get confused about what?"

"About who their mother is."

"About ... what?"

Lamarr looked at me in a way that made me want to show him my GRE scores, or some other proof of intelligence. I thought about it ... the boys crying if I walked past the room without going in ... Tahija slamming the door ... Mahd reaching for Kaki, Mear running to me.

"But they're bound to get attached to whoever's watching them, playing with them."

"Feeding them," he said.

Of course he was right. Why hadn't I seen it? Live long enough, my mother used to say, and you'll find out what type of stupid you are.

Nothing left to clean, I leaned back against the stove and looked at Lamarr. He was eighteen and a half. He wore a long 76-ers jersey, jean shorts, new-looking sneakers. (They might or might not actually be new. He kept his sneakers in perfect shape.

Growing up, he'd told me, he had a shelf for them over his bed. A sneakershelf.)

Well I was glad he had clothes he felt he could face the world in. On the wall behind him was a small painting. I hadn't been thinking of him and his family when I bought it, but then a friend remarked on the symbolism. It showed a close-in view of a squar-ish hand — a brown, male hand with the cuff of a striped dress shirt showing. In the hand is a nest, in the nest four speckled blue eggs, and perched on the nest, looking in, two pale-red cardinals.

"You know, when I was a kid," I said, "I used to say I'd never have children, used to *fight* the boys who said, 'You will too.' I was going to be the first female quarterback at Notre Dame. But finally I was forced to accept the reality — I was just too short to see my receivers over the linemen."

He laughed.

"I don't think I ever told you about my brother Joey. You remind me of him a little. He was born when I was fifteen, and I took care of him a lot, me and my sister did, and sometimes I think I'm trying to, you know, relive what I had with him."

"How old's he now?"

"He'd be twenty-six. He died when he was sixteen."

"Car accident?"

"No, a fire. Him and his best friend had an adventure. He told my mother he was sleeping at the friend's, and the friend told his mother he was sleeping at Joey's, but where they actually slept is in the cabin of a boat they sort of broke into. It wasn't locked. It was dry-docked in a boat dealership, a sort of hang-out."

"For kids."

"Right, from the high school. So while they're sleeping in the cabin of one of the boats a fire starts, we don't know how. Welded the door shut."

"He died in the boat?"

"In the emergency room."

Lamarr was leaning back against the wall, the hand with the nest in it just over his head.

"He would have visited me here. We were friends. Look at me," I wiped off tears. "Some dyke I am. All I'm saying, Lamarr, is I'm not trying to take them from her, I'm not. But I don't always know why I do things."

"Who does?" he said.

"Kaki."

We laughed.

He stood up straight, wanting, I sensed, to make an exit, but open too, if there was more. Maybe later I'd tell him more about Joey, what it was like for him being one of only a few white kids in first grade, and a redhead at that. Freckle juice, the bullies had called him. Maybe I'd also take that print off the wall, give it to him.

I promised to try to help only when asked and otherwise to back off. A dream I had that night made it easier. The triplets had been adopted by a well-to-do white couple and were living in a beautiful suburban house. I've come to visit, and am so happy to see the boys sitting in sturdy wooden highchairs, their trays waiting to be filled with fruits and vegetables. Now this is the right way to feed them, I think. But then I see something's wrong. Their adoptive mother is over on the other end of the cavernous kitchen. No food's being prepared. I speak to her, but she doesn't hear, she's preoccupied. Then she calls Damear George.

"George?!" I cry. "This is Damear, *Damear*."

But she keeps calling him George, and doesn't ever feed them.

We are fed by more than food. They had the names their parents had given them. They had their parents.

211

Chapter 25

I felt like you wanted me to be like you and I wasn't then and will never be like you. We were raised too differently to even consider it. You see if I act like you I lose myself in the process. I wasn't trying to be difficult I was being me. I felt like it was unfair for y'all to tell me in so many words not to be me when that is how I survived my whole life.

A 2005 e-mail from Tahija Ellison

Lamarr and Tahija had little good to say in my hearing about black people, family not excluded, family particularly *included*. It seemed an ugly dynamic operative in my own family: if you hate and feel ashamed of yourself you will hate and feel ashamed of those most like you. This is especially true if folks from the dominant group are hanging around. Judging or not it hardly matters; their existence in and as the dominant group is the judgment. It's divide and conquer at its most intimate, and lasts longer, sometimes, than the conquerors themselves: postwar landmines of the mind.

I remembered my mother's fierce *shushing* of us in public, though we were a fairly quiet five kids, and good (in public). White trash had big loud families, especially the Popish Micks. Still to this day I make nervous jokes about the rhythm method, Irish drunks, rusting appliances in the yard. Still I grow tired around middle and upper class people. It wears me out: repressing the shame at having been poor; envying, trying not to envy, or to judge; having to compete with people who have had so many more resources; trying to forgive their snubs and generalizations (about people who live in trailers, for example, or who love their pro sports teams); straining to see the crosses they may bear and with what grace; working to discern when in any one relationship all this is too much, and to walk away, self-esteem intact.

So I should have known that Tahija talking trash about Lamarr's family was not Tahija deciding to stay away from Lamarr's family. The stereotypes and fears I'd been raised with, however, had gobbled up her critical comments like candy. When she asked me soon after the house meeting to drive her and the boys to this place I'd heard so much about — Lamarr's family — I was alarmed. There? Today?

If I didn't mind.

It would be her first overnight away since the hospital, the boys' first ever.

We drove in silence. She had on the black outergarment she'd been wearing the first time I saw her, and the black kemar, pulled low on her forehead.

"We going to Lamarr's mom's house?" I asked after awhile.

"His sister's house."

"Oh. The dancer?"

"Yes."

When we got there, and she had taken two in and had the last, little Lamarr, halfway across the lawn of a nice-enough house with a closed-in porch, she turned and said "Thanks." Not, *Can you pick us up at such and such a time,* or, *I'll call you later,* or *We're staying a few days, a week, a month, forever.* Just "Thanks." Like you would say to a cab driver.

Didn't she see my face? That I loved them? That I was concerned for their safety, for whether their bellies were full and with what? She had seen my face. The love there must have looked like possessiveness, the worry like mistrust — of her, her family, her community. No wonder she hurried away. The thing to do then would have been to give her more space. Instead, I went home and waited by the phone, my worry a net poised to be cast.

"She just assumes I'll run to pick her up when she calls," I told Kaki.

"Well won't you?"

"Why should I?" I said.

"I can if you're busy."

I tried to be busy. The next day when Tahija called Kaki wasn't home, and I was busy. And furious.

"You think I have nothing better to do than drive you to every corner of the city and back!" What I meant, and wished I'd said, was simply: I was worried. I deserve to be told when you're coming home. If you don't think I deserve at least that, we need to talk. Maybe I shouldn't be watching them.

But I couldn't say or even think *maybe I shouldn't be watching them*. I was afraid she'd agree.

Lamarr met her and they took a cab home. From the kitchen I heard them carrying the boys up the stairs.

The next day was the fifteenth of the month: payday. The envelope of twenties appeared on my desk. I didn't think I'd be seeing it again come the end of the month.

What a lonely place a car can be.

Like my melancholy father before me, I began dealing with my emotions by slamming out of the house. I gave the finger to God: I can't walk with her, it's too hard.

Driving up eerily wide and empty American Street, a few people waiting for the 21 bus, the dark hulks of the dead factories behind them; then east on Lehigh into white Port Richmond and the superstores, the whole predictable palette of restaurants. If I drank I would have gotten drunk. If I smoked dope I would

215

have gotten high. What I did was veer into a fast food drive-thru and order a milkshake.

Back on the road I opened the bag and found, to my surprise, two milkshakes.

Blame it on the magical thinking of the Irish, but I saw that second milkshake as a message, and the message said: Go talk to Tahija, go straight back to the house up the stairs to the nursery door and knock on it, knock till it opens, hand her the milkshake and say (Dr. Huxtable or at least Roseanne style), "We've got to talk."

I didn't do it. I drove around with the gift milkshake sitting in the empty seat beside me. I got lost in the zone of highway overpasses where part of Fishtown had once been. I found the Avenue eventually and followed the fluted pillars of the El track home.

Anger is a furious narrowing. It never leads anywhere you'd want to be if you weren't angry.

Something in me knew what a dead end I was heading down when I came home that night and put the milkshake meant for Tahija in the refrigerator. It's too late, I told myself, she'll be asleep.

Is it ever too late for reconciliation?

The next morning Kaki, leaning into the refrigerator, found the soggy cup. "What's this, Hon?" she asked, holding it behind her.

An opportunity, a gift, a divine nudge.... "Just something I didn't want."

The boys were kept in the nursery more than ever. Tahija cut out all meetings and social activities, coming straight home from school and going straight up the stairs. I wrote her a letter trying to explain my view and asking for more for them — more food, water, exercise, encouragement, stimulation, affection. I wrote that childhood is like the eyepiece end of a telescope. If you move it the tiniest fraction, the view at the other end, adulthood, moves millions and millions of miles. She had the telescope in her hands, could point their future up at the stars, or down at cement.

The nursery began to feel like a separate house. A house with very thin walls. When they cried I felt I knew what it was they needed; felt it in my molars, in the cartilage of my spine: needs I could not meet, perhaps had no right even to want to meet.

I took to wearing earplugs to bed, as Kaki did in summer, when our opened windows let in the noise of the street. I had resisted it; plugging one's ears seemed to me an inauspicious symbol if ever there was one, but I could not sleep otherwise.

So their crying came to me as through water.

"This is why I changed my mind," I said late one night.

"What?"

We took our earplugs out.

"When I changed my mind, when she was in the hospital? This is why, this crying."

"Are you blaming me?" she asked, looking at the low ceiling.

I turned onto my side. I could see her profile by the light from the street. "I'm not blaming you."

"I feel like you're blaming me," she said.

"I'm not." I rested my head on her shoulder. "When I was fifteen, and my mother had Joey, he cried a lot nights. Colicky, they say. My mother was forty-two. Sometimes I got up and rocked him. Sometimes I didn't get up."

"So you're blaming yourself."

"My favorite pastime."

"Please don't. Don't blame anyone. Try to sleep. I'll talk to Lamarr tomorrow."

"Oh that'll be effective," I said, blaming Lamarr, which was getting to be my second most favorite pastime, and a dangerous one. It was so easy to fall into scapegoating … thinking that he'd stolen things that later turned up, that he was playing us when it turned out he wasn't. Oh he was a player, and styled himself a gangsta'. It was a role he thought gave him the only respect he could get. But this blaming him was an ugly thing to see in myself, and an ongoing struggle to resist.

I turned away from Kaki, but I could not turn away from myself. Nor their crying. It was worse because I knew each one's crying. I knew their very coughs apart. I tried something my spiritual director Marcelle had suggested the last time we'd met — an anguished session when she prayed with me and tried to help me accept that the boys' every need was not going to be met; that no one's every need is met and that I had unmet infantile needs that were crying out, from the past, and making the present so torturous. She suggested that I visualize going to them. They might feel it, she said, at the etheric level, and be comforted.

I pictured myself going down the stairs and into the nursery, comforting each in turn, walking him, singing as I sometimes sang in the day. *Hush little baby don't say a word, auntie's gonna buy you a mockingbird, and if that mockingbird don't sing....* And one boy at a time, like a lid onto its jar, they were threaded down onto my heart, so tightly, it seemed, that the only way to remove the lid thereafter would be to break the jar.

Chapter 26

won't you celebrate with me

won't you celebrate with me
what i have shaped into
a kind of life? i had no model.
born in babylon
both nonwhite and woman
what did i see to be except myself?
i made it up
here on this bridge between
starshine and clay,
my one hand; come celebrate
with me that everyday
something has tried to kill me
and has failed.

— from *The Book of Light,* by Lucille Clifton

I was fired. I received my notice in a long, lucid letter from Tahija that I wish I had saved. Among other things, it informed me that Stefanie would be taking over full time, and that I was not to help unless asked, by her, Tahija. I continued to tutor Stefanie in reading, and she repaid me by sometimes leaving the door to the nursery open.

One day I ventured in to watch *Let's Make a Deal* with her and empty the diaper pail. Damear stood up, smiled, and raised his eyebrows endearingly. When that failed to bring me to him he showed me how well he could bounce. Then he just looked at me. Then he plopped down and bowed his head, cutting his eyes at me humbly, expectantly. This posture was new yet somehow very familiar. It was the way Lamarr sat when he was being called out on the carpet, I realized. It said, *All I have as a defense is this humility, this meekness.* I liked Damear better bouncing and testing his limits, but maybe he was learning a way he needed to learn. Who was I to say otherwise?

But oh how I wanted to go to him and show him that he could be however he wanted, whomever he wanted, and I would still love him. But I couldn't. As he had had to wean himself of his mother's breast and her full attention, he would have to wean himself of his baby-sitter now.

"Lay down, Meana," Stefanie said, "you supposed to be asleep."

Meana. A new nickname. I had never heard it. Maybe that was the point.

One thing that made me happy during this time was that I'd started cooking for the weekend workshops Kaki ran through her AFSC job. These were for teens and meant to be a cross-cultural experience — kids from our neighborhood and middle class white kids working together on conflict resolution. I loved it: two and a half days of straight cooking. I especially loved watching those kids eat. When a few dozen of them were sitting around big round tables causing salad or hoagies or chicken or the pizzas they'd helped make disappear I could almost forget the triplets.

At last the season of lunch began. Because she was not unkind, and because pulling those stairs hot as it was was about to kill her, Stefanie let me help with lunch. It was two sandwiches each: peanut butter, peanut butter and jelly, or jelly alone. No carrot sticks, no apple wedges, no rice, no beans, no greens, no bananas, no raisins, no avocados, no peaches. Tahija didn't want them getting used to a diet she wouldn't be able to maintain. It felt to me as if she was stubbornly insisting that they were poor, and going to stay poor. But the fact is they *were* poor. There'd be times later when she and Lamarr couldn't afford even potatoes.

With the boys' six sandwiches, I'd make two for Stefanie: turkey, or turkey and cheese, a little lettuce slipped in. It was my pleasure to also deliver apple juice in their little primary-colored, spill-proof sippy cups. Stefanie spread a blanket over the carpet and set the boys on it. They knew not to crawl off. They sat watching the door, and when the sandwiches appeared (with some fanfare when I was waitress), Mahddy did his food dance and kept his eye on those sandwiches until a sizable portion of one was inside his mouth.

Each had his way of eating. When they'd been babies propped on a pillow watching the spoon their mom or dad held go just as fast as it could from mouth to mouth, Lamarr, always at the right end, would have whatever was being "served" (think Wimbledon) all over himself. Mahad, on the other hand, in the middle, would vacuum in any edible particle within an eight-inch radius of his mouth and remain fairly clean. Damear always went for the spoon, and later, when he got to feed himself, took to disassembling his food — his mother's habit (I once saw her strip a whole order of tempura of its batter).

It was wonderful to watch them eat. Soon their blanket looked like a hail of bread balls had fallen on it. When they were done and de-jellied, Damear and Lamarr crawled off to play, while Mahad, cheeks bulging, took cleanup detail.

With lunch done I had no excuse to linger. I'd go up to the third floor and work on *Climbing the Walls,* the magazine that an imprisoned writer and I had started. The prisons hold a lot of talent. I had skills and, thanks to Kaki, a wealth of technology (computer, printer, scanner). Why shouldn't these form a ladder on which some of that talent climbed out, and the imaginations of readers on the outside climbed in?

Working on the magazine, I didn't use earplugs. I wanted to hear the sounds of the street as I typed a poem or scanned in a line drawing of a management control unit, one of the stainless steel boxes where about 10 percent of American prisoners live, 22–24 hours a day, often with no access to libraries, work, education, collective religious worship, the outside world, or other prisoners. I typed the unit dimensions beneath the sketch: five feet wide, seven feet long, nine feet high. This wasn't "the hole" — short-term solitary confinement for disciplinary reasons; it was home, 24/7, for years. Or decades.

I stood up and went to the window to stretch. The park pulsed with children. I raised the screen so I could check the street, left and right. Stan was on the corner of Hancock and Diamond, working his shift. Angelina was leaning in Barbara Parnell's doorway, going on about something (or somebody, most likely). Bryan, a shy ten-year-old from the street next to ours, ran with his friend Fester back and forth between telephone poles. Bryan had dyslexia and couldn't read. He'd once run from our house at the start of a game of Scrabble. He was tall for his age and very shy. He had a great special ed teacher at the elementary school, but I worried about junior high. A friend of ours, a Catholic sister, taught there and told horror stories about the crowded special ed class sometimes assigned to her. What would happen to Bryan when he went to high school? — "Badlands High" they called it.

I looked at the scanned-in drawing on the screen. It was good. The recessed toilet, the steel bunk, the tiny corner sink — all well done. The artist was Ojore Lutalo, who has lived in such a unit in New Jersey since 1986.* I'd learned that more and more control units were being built, in some cases whole prisons — supermaxes,

---

*According to Bonnie Kerness, director of the Criminal Justice Program of the American Friends Service Committee, Lutalo has never been charged with any infraction of prison rules. For more about control unit prisons, see www.afsc.org/control-unit/

they were called — of nothing but: stacked and rowed containers of people who never see one another, who eat and exercise, sleep and die, alone. It made you think of *The Matrix* ... people used for batteries, a few pennies a day from each body for the prison corporations, and no one who wasn't family complaining much, because they were violent criminals, weren't they?

Most in fact were not. I was learning that the majority of U.S. prisoners were in prison for nonviolent offenses, many of them drug-related. Thousands were being transferred without re-sentencing or appeal to the new supermaxes, which having been built needed to be filled. Batteries.*

I added the sketch to the file for our second issue and headed downstairs for tea. In the nursery *Gilligan's Island* was on. Little Lamarr was asleep, thumb in his mouth. Damear and Mahad were playing on the carpet, with Stefanie looking on from the edge of the bed.

"How you doin', Stefanie?"

"Bored."

"You want me to drive you home later?"

"You can."

"Just yell when you're ready," I told her. "I'll be upstairs working."

Because what else was there to do but work? That these three not become batteries powering some malevolent machine.

Home for Stefanie was Palethorpe. People called it that, not Palethorpe Street, just *Palethorpe*. A mile deeper into the Badlands, Stefanie's block was in an area the police department had been sweeping the city's drug trade into — Operation Sunrise, they called it, though on what horizon the sun was supposed to be rising it was hard to say. Driving slowly around

---

*In 1999, the Corrections Corporation of America ranked among the top five performing companies on the New York Stock Exchange. On its website, www.correctionscorp.com, CCA boasts that it "innovatively seeks new methods and technologies to reduce incarceration costs."

potholes and slow-moving people, I felt like I was in a city that had suffered aerial bombardment. More row houses than not were abandoned, and many had been demolished. All the gaps should have left a more spacious feeling, but they didn't. Even the weeds in the lots looked desolate, too straggly to screen the rusting car bodies and shopping carts, mattresses and burst trash bags.

I pulled over where Stefanie said to and shut off the car. From three narrow houses standing together like the last teeth in a ragged mouth came the sound of crying, "Shut up!" came a voice, "You not hurt."

A girl was getting her head done, sitting in a doorway in front of a woman.

A door opened and Stefanie's mother, in housedress and slippers, leaned out. She'd been by our house a few times.

"Hey Miss Fields," I said. "How you doin'?"

"Oh I'm all right." Not forty, she shook as if with Parkinson's. "How you doing'?"

"All right."

"Thanks for dropping my baby home. She do good?"

"Sure."

"She gives you any trouble you tell me, hear?"

"All right," I said.

A voice came from inside the house where the girl was getting her head done. "See now, somebody finally called DHS on your stupid ass."

The woman smacked the girl on the side of the head. "You act like you hurt, you not hurt."

Afraid my presence was aggravating matters, I started the car and said goodbye to Stefanie. She watched with her mom as I drove the white Chevy in reverse — it seemed the only way in that maze of one-ways and dead-ends — out to the cross street. Waiting to merge backward into the traffic, I attracted two dealers, grown men in tank tops and chains, tattooed muscles.

"Don't want none," I said as they came toward the car.

"Then what the fuck you doing here?"

I'll tell your leech ass what the fuck I'm doing here, I *did not* say. I darted into the traffic and put the dealers behind me. So easy with a car, with someplace else to go, with the recollection of the many places one might go. Stefanie and her mom could not escape so easily.

Stefanie had confided to me that the one thing she never wanted to see again was her mother walking the street, another desperate smoker. I wondered if she'd first seen that sight back when she stopped learning, stopped learning to read and write, anyway; as for learning how to keep her mother off the streets if not off drugs, Stefanie was pretty smart, and a hard worker.

"How you doin', Stefanie?" you'd say, and she'd say, "Fine, I have my mom home. We're waiting on the settlement."

When she was little, Stefanie had been struck by a city bus. Her family sued, winning a small settlement to come due when Stefanie turned eighteen. She dreamed of buying a safe house she and her mom could live in. But just as with the fifty-thousand dollars in stock Tahija was supposed to inherit from her paternal great-grandmother, something happened to that hope money. When Stefanie turned eighteen the city sent her a letter informing her that it was garnishing her settlement, all of it, to recover welfare her mother had received in her name.* Or maybe that letter came before I met her, and the dream survived the letter, forgot the letter even.

Last I heard Stefanie still lives on Palethorpe. Tahija told me she stopped covering and found work assisting strippers. At house parties, she gathers up clothes and dollar bills. And she's discovered a sure way of keeping her mom off the street. She brings the crack home and they get high together.

Cornel West has said there is a sadness only American black people feel. Dropping Stefanie off at Palethorpe, I felt a variety of sadness that was a cousin, I think, to that African American sadness. I felt enough of it, anyway, to find myself wondering if the crack cocaine that had been in the little blue-tinted baggies you saw everywhere could lift my spirits, and, if so, for how long.

---

*In this manner the state routinely "garnishes" child-support payments made by fathers.

Chapter 27

I wouldn't change for anyone but myself and that was my right.
Although I appreciate all that you have done for me I can't let
you change me. That is not for you, it is not for anyone.

A 2005 e-mail from Tahija Ellison

Not too long ago, near the end of the boys' first year of
school, I was at Tahija and Lamarr's house sitting in the deep sofa
as Tahija braided big Lamarr's long hair, him sitting on the floor
between her knees.

When he complained she was hurting him she told him sit
still or she'd hurt him for real. And anyway, tight braids make your
hair grow faster, everybody knew that. The two boarders, Shawn
and Craig, tall and short, were around, Shawn just home from
work and Craig in a low chair under a big new hat. They joked
about Tahija's hair braiding.

"Remember that time she did me in puffballs?" Craig said
rapidly — he had a way of running his words together that
had taken me awhile to get used to. As a child he'd been badly
beaten by a gang. "Couldn't shut my eyes for a week."

I'd seen Craig's puffballs: about twenty of them, inch-high
mushrooms of hair, each in its square of scalp.

"You looked like a jumping jack," I said.

"Or a depth charge," Lamarr put in.

"Least he's not no pumpkin head," Shawn said.

"Shut up," said Lamarr.

"Couldn't fucking *blink*," Craig went on. He pulled up on the skin of his forehead, showing us.

"Mm-mm-mm," Tahija shook her head, "something truly wrong with that boy."

Shawn, who was six foot four and a triplet himself, said that was nothing. When his sister braided your head ...

It was all playful, and a kind of display, I sensed, the dancers moving in slow motion so I could see the patterns and step into them; a display and a healing, or a fingering of the wounded place to see if it was healed. For the very worst time during her stay on Hancock Street, Tahija has told me, was the fight over little Lamarr's hair.

The longer the boy's hair got, the longer braiding it took, and the longer and harder tender-headed Wah cried. Cries that sounded like screams. Screams you just felt you had to do something about.

One day Kaki walked uninvited into the nursery and asked Tahija if she could be gentler with him. Tahija told her to get out.

Kaki sat down on the floor and wouldn't move. "I'm a bear," she said, meaning that she was strong in her passive resistance and would not be moved.

This enraged Tahija. She put Lamarr in his crib and tried to force Kaki up and out of the room. Kaki wouldn't move, and she wouldn't fight back when Tahija began to hit her.

I'd seen Kaki intervene in conflicts. She'd use surprise, humor, and faith in the Light within each person. One night when a dealer was doing noisy business in the alley behind the house she flung open a window and bellowed "The Battle Hymn of the Republic" into the night. It worked.

But whatever she was trying with Tahija now, it wasn't working.

I was upstairs when I heard a spike in the crying that made me reach immediately for the car keys, for surely crying of such magnitude meant a trip to the emergency room.

I ran down and into the nursery to see Tahija dragging Kaki toward the door.

"I want you to see this!" Kaki yelled. "I want you to see this."

What I saw was three crying babies. I ran to the nearest, hugged him, and turned to Kaki and Tahija. Kaki had gone limp.

"She won't leave!" said Tahija.

"Not till she agrees to be more gentle with them," Kaki said.

Tahija wasn't about to agree to anything. I asked Kaki to leave the room.

"Look at the boys," I told her.

She did, pulled herself up, and stumbled out.

"She wouldn't leave," Tahija cried. "I told her leave and she wouldn't leave."

I took a step toward her, wanting to be the ally, the confidant, but the emotion rippling out from her made me feel like the "good" cop in some cold manipulation. In his light-blue crib by the window overlooking the alley, Damear stood gripping the rail, silent sobs quaking his chest. In his white crib in the alcove of windows Lamarr sat crying unrestrainedly, tears streaming. And in the unpainted crib against the inner wall, Mahddy stood tense and tearless, looking across at Damear, who heaved one more big sob and fell back, turning away from us stupid, stupid adults.

I wanted to pick up and comfort each of them, but I was afraid; suddenly I felt the nursery was not my place, had never been my place, and that Tahija had just announced that in the language she knew best.

I went downstairs to the kitchen, where Kaki leaned against the sink sobbing. Unless you counted fouls in college basketball, she had never been hit. I tried to comfort her. From upstairs we heard "Fix your face!" and knew the boys were not being comforted, as their mother had not been after the violent experiences she'd told us about. I could only guess at all she had not told us, and at how long it would take her to uncover and release the repressed emotions. Fix your face. Though everything behind it be crashing down. Fix your face.

Maybe this was a necessary lesson, for the baby in a corner of slavery's kitchen, for the toddler under hay in a wagonload of runaways, for the feverish child waiting hours in the E.R., for the grown man humiliated among white men whose pleasure it is to humiliate him. Fix your face. Straighten the mask. Survive, and measure the cost later.

Kaki had repressed her fair share too. The violence she'd been exposed to in the neighborhood and the prisons, her family's judging her, the old childhood hurts, and the new hurt of loving babies your love couldn't protect ... these all surfaced and broke her face apart.

She cried so loud. She cried for us all. I can only hope the boys and the young mother above us heard and rode the wave of her emotion a little ways out from their own pain, toward some kind of release.

Years later, when the boys are seven and have finally talked their parents into letting them walk unescorted the few blocks to school, Tahija will call me with news of three fifth graders, "*fifth* graders, Kathryn," two boys and a girl, jumping Mahad one day on the way home. When she found out she slid a bat up the arm of her outergarment and went around to the house of one of the boys.

"Nobody beats on my baby," she said on the phone. "I told this little boy, and his mom was right there, 'See this bat? This bat has your name on it. Next time you take it into you head to mess with any one of my babies, trust me, that head and this bat going to meet up.'"

It turned out the boy's mother knew Tahija's mother — they had lived on the same street — and she chastised her son right there.

What I don't think Kaki and I realized was how that bat had been up Tahija's sleeve all along: the bat of maternal instinct in a dangerous world. Kaki had supposed herself intervening on behalf of a crying child. To Tahija she had been a threat, we both had been, then and other times: because we might put her out (hadn't we once?); because we might call DHS; because we had all the power, and she had only the triplets. And the more we came to love them, the more of a threat we must have seemed.

Chapter 28

It's just too late for someone to start all of a sudden bossing me.
I've been on my own too long.

from a conversation

Tahija wrote a qualified apology and bought a chain lock for
her door. We confronted her with the bruises on Kaki's leg.

"If you can do this to me," Kaki said, "what might you do to a
baby?'

"They don't provoke me," Tahija answered.

"Oh they will. You think they won't? Provoke you and test you
and defy you. Of course they will."

"Then they might as well pack their bags and head off to boot
camp, because I'm not having it. Furthermore, I don't believe in
hitting, I believe in time-out."

We had become the enemy, to be told what we needed to be
told.

We tried to persuade her to begin counseling. We would pay for
it. I told her about a good counseling experience I had had. She
refused. I think at that point that if we had asked her to keep breathing, she would have asphyxiated herself right before our eyes.

Friends who knew the system advised us to file a police report so that there would be a record of Tahija's outburst, should one be needed in the future. We didn't like to think about a future in which such a record might be needed, but we saw the point. Not wanting to increase the tensions between us, we didn't file a police report.

Tensions increased nonetheless.

Exercise was a walk around the park, shopping a walk to the Avenue, and recreation a game of kick ball down at the lot. Even when we left the neighborhood for Quaker meeting, it was usually to attend a small, struggling one just a few El stops north. And even there we usually did childcare, not so much for the children of the meeting, there being only two, but for the children lured from the surrounding streets by their world's only wide lawn and overarching trees.

I should have gotten away more. I wasn't eating right, or doing much of the meditating and writing that centered me. I thought of the boys all the time, and in the older boys on the block saw, or feared I saw, their future. As I grew more tired and took less care of myself I swung farther between extremes: hopelessness, manic helping; finger-pointing, debilitating guilt; and such a sadness, like every day was a funeral.

And in a very real sense every day was. A handsome, good-natured country boy just off the plane from Puerto Rico was arrested with twenty dollars worth of crack and sentenced to five years. Little Hakim's favorite aunt hung herself. Plainclothes policemen raided the rooming house next door and a man fearing deportation jumped out a third floor window. Falling, he broke his leg, the leg became infected, and he died.

When Tahija was in the house we might see the boys fleetingly, through the opened nursery door or on their way down the stairs to a doctor's appointment. It was July now. Every sunny day was a grief to me. I'd sit in the park and watch families, toddlers running laughing over the spongy rubber surface of the playground, babies in the baby swings, bigger kids in the big-kid swings, going so high....Why couldn't the boys have this? What had happened to Tahija that a park seemed so dangerous, the outdoors so uninviting? I remembered Lamarr saying, "Those boys won't leave this house until they're four years old." They weren't two yet, and I could feel them aching to stretch and climb and know the world. A nurse friend of Kaki's gave us articles about brain development, which was crucial during these years and depended on external stimuli. We gave these to Tahija; she dug in. Should we call in DHS again? If we did that, any trust Tahija still felt would be destroyed. We'd be the enemy, the circling hawk, the system.

But weren't we the enemy already? Wasn't everyone, eventually?

Nearly nauseous with guilt, and not without some fear, I spent one afternoon on the phone trying to get through to Mrs. Chissom at DHS. She had told us we could call them back in if things weren't working out. Returning my call, she left a vague message on the answering machine that I played, unwittingly, while Stefanie and Tahija were both sitting right there in the Shamrock room.

"Busted," Stefanie said, not looking up from her cheesesteak.

"What makes you think...." I started in on some lie and then gave it up, seeing their faces, feeling foolish and petty. Strangely, Tahija didn't seem worried. She had defeated the hawk twice already; she knew what would bring down its wrath, and what wouldn't. We had been arm wrestling over the boys' care, and I'd kicked her under the table. She seemed amused.

I deleted the message, acted like I'd found something on the bookshelf that I'd been looking for all day, and scurried upstairs like the snitch I felt myself to be.

When Mrs. Chissom did reach me she seemed impatient with my call. Were the boys being abused? she asked. I said no, I wouldn't say that. Neglected? Maybe. In what way?

"They *never* get to go out to the park, or anywhere."

Silence.

"I mean it's summer, it's *July*."

Mrs. Chissom was aware of the season, and the month. Unimpressed by my complaints, and irritated, it seemed, at my trying to hand the hot potato back to her, she agreed to send a caseworker around.

That caseworker appeared at the front door three or four months later, after everyone had moved out. I knew where to by then, but didn't say.

It wasn't the day for our worship group, but we walked over to Jorge and Marcelle's anyway. We needed to tell someone how bad things had gotten.

We sat in their kitchen and talked about the conflicts over food and the fight Tahija and Kaki had had, about the closed nursery door and the crying. Marcelle, tall and serious, with large, penetrating eyes, had known me for nearly twenty years. She was a respected Quaker and spiritual director. My time in her small room at the top of the house, time praying and striving to open to God's will and accept God's help, had kept me tethered to the leading that first brought me to the city. Jorge too was a respected Quaker as well as a family therapist. He was also the model father of a wonderful teenaged girl. Jorge and Marcelle had been to our house often. They knew the stress we were under and respected our efforts to do the right thing. That did not, however, mean they felt we were doing it the right way.

We had isolated ourselves. Why? Tenderly, Jorge invited us to consider whether our guilt as white people living in a racist society had affected how we interacted with Tahija and Lamarr. Were we reluctant to exert authority and hold them accountable? He thought we had done a poor job of setting boundaries and should have drawn more upon existing social services.

I felt defensive. DHS had opened and closed two cases. Tahija had been judged a fit mother, with our cooperation. Or was it collaboration? In walking with Tahija, had I taken on her perspective to the point of self-deception? Or was Jorge seeing the stereotype "teenaged welfare parents" and not the strong, determined, wounded, complex young people I knew? Ought we to have insisted the boys go to day care? In asking for better care for the boys were we imposing the dominant culture's ways, or defending the basic human rights of the triplets? Or were we simply facing the fact that there were some things we could not live with?

We came away from the conversation with the determination to set conditions. If Tahija and Lamarr refused to meet these, we would ask them to move out.

"*I* should move out," I said as we left our friends' house.

"For Pete's sake," Kaki said, "the things that trouble you trouble me just as much. We need to confront them. Being willing to accept that they might move out gives us a new freedom. We can say what we feel has to change, and let them decide."

We walked along a broken and tipped sidewalk past American street's closed warehouses. I felt fear at the very thought of confronting Tahija; not fear for my safety, but a visceral fear rooted deep in my childhood, a fear of facing and expressing strong emotions. It was the legacy of growing up in an alcoholic family.

We crossed American's four underused lanes and took the slow way home, following side streets we knew to have rose bushes in bloom or one of the murals Philadelphia is known for. It was evening, the hot day just cooling off.

"If she leaves," I said, "they'll have to start living on what? She gets $248 every two weeks, $200 in food stamps. Listen to me, I sound like Barbara Parnell. I know what she gets, too. She's always telling me. She's down to ten dollars every two weeks in food stamps. Ten dollars!"

"They'll have the childcare money," Kaki reminded me. "You know people keep part of that to live on sometimes. And it may be that without us pressuring her she'll take them out more, loosen up. I think she needs to be away from us to exert her authority over them."

We had reached one of the newest murals — *La Mariposa.* Rising above a well-tended community garden was a three-story-high butterfly, a twinkling mosaic of tiles and mirrors. We stopped and leaned against the fence, inhaling the garden's oxygen-rich air.

"'All is seared, smeared with toil,'" I quoted, "'and wears man's smudge and bear's man's smell. But for all this, nature is never spent. There lives the dearest freshness deep down things....'"

"Hopkins," Kaki said.

"Right." We both loved poetry. Would we enjoy it again, and hikes in the woods, and dancing?

"So, the conditions," she said, "what has to change?"

"More of this," I pointed to the garden. How I wanted Damear, Mahad and Lamarr to have this — peace, fresh air, art, a good world. And they weren't going to, I was afraid they weren't ever going to, and I couldn't accept it.

We settled on four conditions that we felt would make the house livable: that the boys be taken out of the room once a day, and out of the house three times a week (we'd compromise on once); that they be spoken to more gently; and that Tahija begin counseling or some sort of anger management program, to be paid for by us.

"She won't go for it," I said.

"It's not our job to complete the work," Kaki quoted a poster that hung over her desk, "but neither are we permitted to lay it down."

"I'm afraid, Kaki, that this is a back door way of laying it down. If we exert the least authority, she won't stand for it, she never has, from anyone. She'll leave. And you know what?"

Kaki massaged around her nose and under her eyes — sinus pain. "What?"

"It would be a relief."

"On some level."

"From her and Lamarr and most of all from always wondering if we're doing the right thing. I feel like I'm a bumper car: hurt, anger, guilt, bam bam bam. I can't take it anymore. So, we give them the conditions ... and then?"

"House meeting."

I groaned. "Couldn't we just get root canals instead?"

She didn't laugh. She seemed very tall to me then, looking down at me, and I wondered if she still saw in me what she had seen at first.

A motor scooter zoomed past down the sidewalk, a pit bull puppy giving chase (or trying to keep up, it was hard to tell). You could almost see the exhaust churning up the clean garden air. Like childhood, I thought, like love. Like the dearest freshness deep down in things, so soon disturbed, thinned, dispersed.

Why did we give the conditions to Tahija alone? Shouldn't Lamarr have been with her? He wasn't around much then, still in school, we hoped, and helping his sister with her kids, and keeping all his other many commitments, which seemed to involve hours riding on busses with his headphones on. And we had learned that while he might agree to do something, the follow-through left something to be desired.

For whatever reasons, it was Tahija alone reading the letter in which we laid out the conditions she would have to meet if she and the boys were to stay. She sat in the rocker where she had sat her first day in the house.

We watched, ready, eager even, to offer the compromises we'd discussed with each other. We never had the chance.

"*Ya'll* not my mother!" she yelled and jumped up. On the stairs she stopped, a hand on the banister, and looked over her shoulder to say, more softly, "It's just too late for someone to start all of a sudden bossing me. I've been on my own too long."

Chapter 29

I was already mad at the fact that me and Kaki fought..., the protest was the straw that broke the camel's back. I almost never talked to either one of you but Lamarr said not to take it personal that you were only voicing your opinions. I didn't care where we went at that moment just out of there.

from the interview

Tahija told me later that they'd been looking for a place to move out to for awhile. So maybe it was too late, but at the time it seemed a reasonable, if desperate, attempt to hold things together.

We fasted. For three days and three nights Kaki and I camped in the living room, neither eating nor speaking. We prayed. We put up signs saying what we were doing. We waited.

During Ramadan, Tahija and Lamarr fasted from dawn to dusk. We hoped that our lesser effort communicated how strongly we felt and how committed we were to finding a peaceful solution. Our signs read, *Fasting for Peace. Praying for Sunshine and Fresh Air. We Want You to Be Healthy and Happy. We want you to stay.* The biggest sign, high on the wall facing the front door, addressed those who might join us. It read,

> Thank you for coming and joining us in prayer. We are in the first day of a three-day fast and prayer vigil (longer if led). We are fasting for the rights of the triplet boys who live here, specifically and most urgently for their right to be taken outdoors and to play outside their small rooms. We are also praying and hoping their mother will meet us with a mediator to seriously discuss the terms we set for her and the boys to continue to share the house. We are fasting and praying for the strength to persist and to faithfully discern and follow God's will in this matter.
>
> Here is what we are asking: The boys get out for 2 hours a day; take a walk 3 times a week; be spoken to respectfully, meaning no *shut-ups* or other such language; and mom takes an anger-management class or parenting class and counseling, with us paying the cost.
>
> We are fasting for a change of heart and believe it can come and that conflict can be transformed into loving cooperation. Thank you again for joining us today. Please hold us and the boys and their parents in the light of your prayers.

We placed a notebook on the dining room table and wrote messages for Tahija and Lamarr to read. We read at length in the Koran and the Bible. A book about Gandhi's nonviolent resistance sat on the table. I prayed for the Light to shine within Tahija's heart and mine. I prayed for the mercy God promises through every religion that our mistakes be forgiven, both those we had made and those we had yet to make. I prayed not to make too many more mistakes.

On the first day, Tahija stopped on her way to the kitchen, read our signs, and looked at what we'd written in the notebook.

She seemed to soften a little, or maybe I only imagined it. We heard her on the phone in her room. Lamarr came quickly, left his CD player on the bookshelf, and hurried up the stairs. We heard her demanding that he get a job so they could move out.

On the morning of the second day, Marcelle walked over to sit and worship with us. She spoke to Tahija with tenderness, but, as I learned later, it felt to Tahija as if we were ganging up on her, especially when Jorge joined us later.

On the afternoon of the second day, Laura Ellison arrived. She stood between the front hallway and the foot of the stairs berating us. I was glad she came and glad she shouted at us, her voice rising like arms to comfort and protect her oldest daughter. She struck a nerve though when she accused me of abandoning her daughter for weeks at a time.

Abandoning! I'd gone away during the college's winter break to write and rest. In another setting, I might have gotten into it with her over that word. But the vigil had centered me in my more peaceful higher self, and Marcelle's prayerful presence entrained me, in a sense, caught me up, as I sensed my own presence sometimes did Tahija. At any rate, I surprised myself with my own gentleness when I broke the silence to say we didn't want Tahija to stay if she didn't want to stay, we only hoped to find a way to make it work.

Laura seemed disarmed, or maybe only deflected. Maybe arguing would have been more effective, more suitable. Was it, Our way in our house? We're white so we're right? Was the goal to disarm Laura, or engage her?

"Ya'll two are the ones need counseling!" she said, and whirled and was gone.

She was right. Kaki and I needed counseling, as a couple; as individual women who'd grown up in dysfunctional, alcoholic families numb to their own pain and to the pain their white privilege and pretense of superiority caused. We also needed more support than we had — a peaceful community to help ground us in our values and better selves, quiet hours to dip our gourd into the source of peace. I should have been sitting in silence part of every day Lamarr, Tahija, and their boys were in the house, centering myself in my best self, praying for guidance about how to walk this walk.

On the afternoon of the third day, we decided to break the silence and talk. What we talked about was houses.

We had talked before about houses. When she visited once, Kaki's mother had implied to Tahija that she would help her buy her own house someday. And Kaki had contemplated liquidating a portion of the money in her 401(k) retirement account for that purpose. This money had been troubling her for some time. She had already moved it to a lower interest, socially and environmentally responsible fund, but still it was there, doing nothing but providing the security her faith told her God had already provided for her. The lilies of the field, neither sowing nor reaping — she wanted to be like those. Reading the Gospels, she could not help but hear in them the call to redistribute her wealth and work for the beloved community.

On the evening of the third day, with the late-June sun still bright and the surf of voices from the park breaking against the house, Kaki opened a Bible and read from Leviticus.

"'You shall count off seven Sabbaths of years, seven times seven years, and you shall make holy the fiftieth year, and proclaim liberty throughout the land to all the inhabitants thereof.'"

She was lying down, head on the arm of the sofa. I sat at the other end massaging her feet. She read on,

"'It shall be a Jubilee unto you; and ye shall return every man unto his possession, and ye shall return every man unto his family. And the land shall not be permanently sold — for the land is Mine. You are strangers and visitors with Me.'"* She closed the Bible. "I'll be fifty in January."

"I know."

---

*From Lev. 25: 8-23. "Proclaim liberty throughout the land to all the inhabitants thereof" is also on the Liberty Bell. Both the bell and the phrase were made famous by the abolitionist publications that featured them on their masthead.

"My Jubilee year."

"What does that mean to you?"

She closed her eyes. "I think it's about redistribution of wealth, about realizing that what we have is not ours, but God's, to be dispersed according to God's plan. We don't know for sure whether it was an ideal or an actual practice, but in ancient Israel every fifty years all debts were to be forgiven, land returned, slaves freed. Inequalities that had developed in the community were leveled out."

"So if you buy them a house, or help them get one, it'll level things out?" I asked.

"Look, Section 8 is all but dead. There's a two year waiting list for PHA housing. Rentals are ridiculous."

"I couldn't afford to rent around here."

"But they could get a decent house for maybe $20,000."

"Are we trying to buy her love?"

This was something Agnes Grealy had once said of us.

Kaki closed the Bible and rested it on her chest. "Is that what we're trying to do? Is that what we've been doing all along?"

"I don't know," I said.

I myself had next to nothing in my checking account, no savings, no car, no furniture to speak of; only my good looks (that and two bucks would get me...). So it was hard for me to imagine having that much money, let alone giving it away. I could, however, imagine how hard it might be for Kaki. One of her jobs at Penn Mutual had been selling 401(k) plans. She knew how wise it was to invest money, how foolish to withdraw it. And she knew too the fines and penalties liquidation of shielded assets entailed. The very phrase "liquidation of assets" made her queasy. She was, after all, her frugal father's first child. She knew what he would say were he alive, and what her mother, two brothers, and sister, who were alive and hoping for relief from the inheritance tax, would say. In addition, there was the question of her poor health. She had no health insurance. The problem with more and more of the safety net being removed is that many of the people in place

to offer some amelioration to the women, children and men suffering in extreme poverty don't have a safety net, either.*
How to celebrate Jubilee in a season of greed? Vehemently.

At dusk of that third day we didn't move to turn on a light. It was quiet upstairs, a wakeful quiet. Feeling light-headed, impatient — for closure, for a plan with some otherworldly zing to it — and really really hungry, I took up my King James Bible, shut my eyes, and opened to a page.

Okay, I said to myself, if the sentence I put my finger on has the word *house* or *home* in it, or any word connoting a dwelling, I'll take this to mean we should help Lamarr and Tahija buy a house.

I opened my eyes and read: "Their houses will be taken from them."

Whoa. That tossed the question right back in my lap. Was this a simple yes, a warning, or a test of our willingness to give unconditionally? There remained a fourth possible interpretation, one that didn't occur to me until well after the fast: that "their" referred not to homeless receivers but to home-owning givers, whose houses would be "taken from them" — if wealth was not redistributed. (Even if it was?) The fire next time.

On midnight of the third day we took down the signs, closed the notebook where we had written messages during the fast, and gave signs and notebook to Tahija — the only reason they still exist to be quoted here. Because she saves everything. Because maybe the fast moved her, at some level, settled like a coin into the pool of her consciousness, to shine there, a wish. For peace between us.

Though she did not write in the notebook during the fast, when Tahija typed and e-mailed the messages in it to me at my

---

*If we have indeed entered a new age of volunteerism, when "citizen servers," as Bill Clinton called them, are expected to replace much of society's safety net, then shouldn't people who feel moved to liquidate assets be exempted from penalties and taxes? Let those with the resources to work on this work on it.

request in 2005 she added comments and rebuttals. They are in bold below, with what Kaki and I wrote (we didn't distinguish between our comments) in italics.

I am going to extremes to help you see that you must make a strong effort to have a good future. You cannot ignore the needs of others. 1:27 PM

You must have no idea of how worried and upset we have been about this because we care about you so much. 8:47 AM

The babies have rights to Real food at breakfast, lunch, dinner. No disrespectful or degrading language or tone of voice. No hitting, slapping or other forms of physical reprimand. Fresh air and exercise regularly. Being read to, played with often, lots of individual attention. 11:19 AM

The boys always ate and they didn't get any beatings, the only thing they got hit for was when they tried to play with the outlets and I popped their hands. Was I suppose to say no-no and let them get hurt? And again, my decision.

Treat your children such that they will obey because they want to please you, not because they fear you. 2:25 PM

No child wants to please all the time and a child of mine does what I say when I say.

Your unintentional mistakes shall be forgiven, but not your deliberate errors. God is forgiving and merciful. 33.5 The Koran

You aren't God.

I love you love you deeply 2:31 PM

245

I love you also but that doesn't mean I do everything you say.

Allah put us here to help. You need help with three babies.

When I need help I will ask.

Distrust builds up when there's too much distance, insistence on barriers and lack of communication. 11:35 AM

You want to know too much.

I need individual attention from Tahija, Lamarr, Damear, Mahad, Lamarr Jr. 11:52 AM

You don't need it you want it and you can't get everything you want out of life.

You are doing very well, I am doing very well, I can do much better, you can do much better. 1:38 PM

Everyone can always do better.

Chapter 30

[W]e moved in a real bad neighborhood and a bad house but I
did my best to keep it clean and livable and I tried to keep as
busy as I could so that I could make sure that the boys never
really needed anything.

My Life as I Know It

The first time we talked with Tahija and Lamarr after the fast
was to tell them about the house idea. Tahija sat in the same chair
where she had read our conditions, the same curtain of distrust
between us. Talk of liquidating assets, finding a Realtor, and tour-
ing likely neighborhoods must have sounded like delaying tac-
tics, or a trap. She wanted out. She informed us that she had done
what she needed to do to become an emancipated minor. As I
would remind her at key times in the coming years, when she
was cussing too much or getting herself tattooed (Lamarr and the
boys' initials in a bracelet around her wrist), Kaki and I never did
see the paperwork on that, nor did we stand before a judge and
rescind our yes, or walk backward with her and her mother
around Swann fountain. But if she felt determined to move out
we weren't going to try and stop her. We gave her some cash that

we were able to give, enough, we hoped, to help them get a decent place, and steeled ourselves for the move.

On the day when Donovan and Dante came with a borrowed car to disassemble the cribs, Kaki gave Tahija a parting gift. It was a piece of driftwood, wider than long, varnished and set on a small stand. On it Kaki had soldered the made-up word *Eliftages,* with this beneath it:

"E" out of

"Lift" raise up

"Ages" the generation

Soldered onto the back was a page with part of Dorothy Law Nolte's poem "Children Learn What They Live" on it.

And then she had written, in larger letters, "Don't move out of my heart! Kaki."

I gave a gift too: a small toolbox, for the new place. I handed it to her on one of her trips down the stairs. Since she was carrying two (empty) infant car seats and several outergarments, I opened it for her to show her the tools.

"In case the new place needs repairs," I said, hoping she would offer some details about this new place — like the part of the city it was in, or the address even.

She didn't offer details. We found out anyway. And it made sense, perfectly terrible sense, now that Stefanie was watching the boys. They were moving to Palethorpe.

I doubted the toolbox had tools enough in it.

Lamarr had called a taxi. Kaki and I waited with him in the livingroom as he sat reading a magazine. Damear, Mahad and Lamarr waited at his feet in their car seats chattering away to one another like birds at dawn. Was this a language of their own they'd developed? They sure seemed to be communicating: agreeing and amending, seconding and thirding this and that, sort of singing — a heterophanous melody that lured even skittish Purrsilla. Out of range of their matching sneakers, she sat and gazed up at them, her gray tail patting the floor. From the sofa,

Kaki and I gazed too. We hadn't seen them up close for weeks. They looked good, they looked fine.

Tahija was at the new place already, along with the three cribs, the six other car seats, toys and clothes, her things and her clothes, Lamarr's few possessions, the stretch limo, and her stuffed animal collection. The bouncy chair in the shamrock room was too frail to travel, but the rocker, a heavy, well-made piece of furniture from Kaki's mother, went. So did Tweetie Bird, who had seen so much and said so little. I'd miss him.

You could see Lamarr had dressed them. I liked the look — relaxed, outfits color coordinated but not identical. Mahddy wore a red sweatshirt with a blue action figure on it, Damear a red and blue striped pullover, Lamarr the blue overalls with red pockets. More than ever they seemed separate persons. Damear had developed the habit of sucking in his lower lip. Mahddy's widely spaced eyes held a surprised look. The muscles in little Lamarr's forehead bunched above his brow, two thumbprints, giving him an adult seriousness. And new teeth abounded. Damear still had his two not-teeth, crowded now by newer, bigger baby teeth. Mahddy had the biggest smile; it didn't appear often but when it did — rainbow. Damear's smile was noncommittal. He'd restrain his lower lip with his upper teeth, then lift one corner of his mouth, leaving the other behind to wait and see. Marr's smile often had to work around his thumb, where a dark callous showed on the knuckle.

"They're getting better looking every day," Kaki said to big Lamarr.

He glanced down. "Wah, *get* that thumb out your mouth before you suck the black right off it."

Pop.

I knelt and went down the line pulling tight the Velcro straps on their sneakers. No one reached for me. That was good, that was better, they'd forgotten already. Their young hearts were resilient, and mine, well … wasn't it still in my chest?

When a taxi beeped out front, Lamarr closed his magazine and stood up.

"About time," he said, though I suspected him of having brought them down early on purpose. He lifted Wah's car seat, retrieved his CD player from the bookshelf, and turned to look at us, eyebrows saying, *Go on and do what you want to do.*

We jumped up and got a car seat each: me Damear's, Kaki Mahad's.

While Kaki and Lamarr buckled the car seats in, I set Damear and his seat lengthways on the front step's railing and leaned close, looking into the paired wells of his eyes. I smelled baby powder and hair oil, and something else, something sweet spilled on his shirt. Apple juice.

"This — " I pointed, "was your first house. And I was your first baby-sitter. Remember 'The itsy-bitsy spider went up the water spout'?" Holding the seat steady between one hand and my chest I did the spider climbing. "You came home first — "

"K.D.," Kaki called. The taxi was blocking a van.

" — and you had your mom *aaall* to yourself." At my "all" he smiled the half smile. "Then Marr came and you had to share her. You didn't like it, not one bit. So I said, 'Well let me do what I can.'" I was crying. "But don't *let* me hear you telling your brothers I love you better. I love you all three the same. With you I just ... *feel* it more."

I carried him to the car and tried then gave up on the stupid strap buckle thing, and Kaki did it, and big Lamarr got in front.

"Call when you get there," Kaki told him.

"All right."

"Don't be a stranger."

"All right."

Then she leaned in and kissed everybody on the forehead — Mahad at the far end, "dear Mahddy," Lamarr in the middle, and Damear closest.

"Tahija's going to be pissed," I said to big Lamarr, "we've got them in the wrong order."

He turned and smiled the smile that had disarmed me when first I'd seen it, through the bars of a wrought-iron security door. Mahddy let out a *yalep!* and kicked wildly, as if to show us how very far behind him he had put all that failure-to-thrive business.

And then they were gone.

The driver of the van that had been waiting leaned across his passenger side seat to look down at us.

"Sorry to hold you up," I said. He was a handsome bald-headed man in his forties.

"That's all right sugar." He nodded at the receding taxi. "Were those triplets?"

"Yep," I said.

"Boys, girls, what?"

"Three boys," said Kaki.

"Three boys?" he said.

"Three boys," I said.

Three questions out the window. But I would have been happy to answer ten more. He asked only one. It was a good one.

Looking from Kaki to me to Kaki, he said, "Grandchildren?"

"More like … godchildren," I said.

He nodded. "Well, have a nice day now."

"You too," I said.

"Have a *great* day," said Kaki, my cheery Swede.

"You too," he said.

Inside, we stood in the living room waiting to feel what it was we were going to feel. For me, the loss was too much to take in all at once, the remorse too fearsome. Relief looked like the just-right bed. Gone was the tension that had crackled so long through the house. Gone too the always listening for them, the trying not to listen.

We went up the stairs.

"I'm glad she took the desk," Kaki said, seeing the middle room. "I told her to take it."

We went in. With the bed moved long ago to the nursery and the desk gone, the only furniture was the orange chair by the window. I remembered Lamarr sitting in it with newborn Damear. I remembered sitting in it in the night and secretly feeding Mahddy.

251

I walked around the room, following the eye-level strip in the pink wallpaper: baby bear rubbing his eyes, sleeping on folded hands, rising and shining.

"I keep expecting to find a spot where the bear's doing something else," I said, "touching his toes or something."

"Revising already," Kaki said.

"That's me."

But I was trying *not* to revise, not to alter a second of Tahija's time in the house. I remembered the day she had come home from school and run up to her room in tears. I had followed. The English teacher she liked so much had argued with her, saying teenagers could never make good parents, they just weren't ready. I hadn't taken a side, had only stayed with her as she tried to look her reality square in the face. But that had been months before. How often since had I been in her room, listening, supporting? Not often. Maybe I just wasn't ready.

I turned to Kaki, her tanned, oval face, the pencil-sketch mouth from her mother, hazel eyes like mine. Her hair was up, locks of it loose around her ears. I saw gray in it, and the lines at the corners of her eyes. The top of her head came nearly to the ceiling fan. I remembered that fan turning above us the first time we made love, in this room when it was the guest room and I was the guest. Would we ever get back to that Christmas-morning joy of new love?

We backed out of that room and turned to the nursery. Empty of cribs, dresser, and the cabinet where the requisite canned food had been kept, the room seemed huge. Though the plastic diaper pail was gone, its odor lingered, cut by the scent of baby powder and body lotions. Along the walls where Damear and Mahad's cribs had stood, handprints smudged the school bus yellow paint, and the blinds against the back wall's windows had missing and bent slats — little Lamarr's work.

Kaki went around opening the long-closed windows while I stood taking in the emptiness.

What did I feel?

More relief, guilt for feeling relief, curiosity: what would life be like now? While the triplets were in the house, we had done what we could to make their lives better; we had struggled daily with difficult questions of how our race and class affected our ideas of what better meant. We had tried, and as long as they were in the house we felt obligated to keep trying. But now they were gone, and what I thought I heard in the silence was the sound of a great weight being set down.

"It's so quiet," Kaki said. A bus roared by, kids jumped rope to the rhythm of a jumping song, the old guy in the rooming house next door cleared his sinuses. Yet I knew what she meant. Emotional noise, a steady din for almost two years. We'd gotten used to it, but now, the way you do when a refrigerator motor finally cuts off, we heard, by contrast, how noisy it had been.

In the crib-sized shadows of dust, a few keepsakes: black rubber bands, small and round, a puzzle piece with curling edges, a latex nipple with a split tip.

I picked up a wooden block.

"I'm always picking up these damn things," I said, holding the tears in.

An El train pulled in, gave its disregarded cautions about doors, and pulled out.

253

Chapter 31

After awhile, with bookshelves and a desk, a chair in the sunny nook, the nursery began to feel like just any other room. Sometimes my eye would fall on a powder-blue windowsill and I'd think, that's the windowsill Damear could reach. Or I'd forget and try to pull down the blind Lamarr had torn, and which we'd never replaced. Or I'd cut on the light and remember holding Mahddy up to the switch so he could work it — up down, on off, up down....

Would they remember the Beatles songs I'd sung them? And the drinking songs from my Irish grandmother's old 78, "I'm a rambler, I'm a gambler, I'm a long way from home," and the dirges, "When you look in the heart of a shamrock, sure you're dreaming of I-er-land, and home." And that one from my Scottish grandmother, the words I couldn't recall replaced by made-up ones:

Hush little baby don't say a word
Auntie's gonna buy you a mockingbird
and if that mockingbird don't sing
Auntie's gonna buy you a diamond ring
and if that diamond ring don't shine
Auntie's gonna give you this heart of mine
and if this heart don't tick long enough …

I'd make up things I'd buy and ways they might not work and other things I'd buy instead. If I could rhyme it I could buy it. My grandmother had sung it "Momma's gonna buy" not "Auntie"; I'd felt the need to change it though, felt guilty using "Momma." Which should have told me something, been a warning.

Ach, I thought, indulging a bit of the melancholy I come by honest, as Tahija would say — from the Irish as well as the Scottish side — if you're always looking for warnings surely you'll find them at every turn. It was by God's grace that our paths crossed, and it would be by God's grace should we meet again.

To be sure though, my heart was broken, and no comfort for it.

Was I a racist? Had my racism caused Tahija to feel she had to move out? Were there different kinds of racism? How did you know when you were done, free, clear, *clean?* What were my deepest motives? What were Kaki's? Were hers different from mine? Had we done too much, or too little? Exercised too much authority, too little, or the wrong sort? Had I damaged the boys? Would Tahija always be harder on Damear? Would I ever see them again? Would they remember me?

In the days that followed, these and other questions weighed upon me. I didn't like walking in Fishtown anymore. I felt angry at the way some there might treat the triplets. I remembered the Rite-Aid lady and her, "Well I hope she's done." But I didn't like walking in our neighborhood either. Too many mean or suspicious looks, from strangers mainly, but there were many strangers. One day two men I thought might be from the Dominican Republic abruptly stopped talking when I neared. Then one of them spit on the sidewalk inches from my shoes.

Is that what the white race had earned for me and mine? I felt ashamed to be white. I had felt ashamed, I realized, since I was a child first learning whiteness. Had that shame motivated me to move here, to give of my time and labor? Only to find now, in the quiet house, yellow walls gleaming like a sun whenever I passed the still-empty nursery, that the shame stung as much; more, in fact. Or perhaps it was just nearer the surface.

I could not love myself, or forgive myself, and of course, in many small ways, the world collaborated in confirming that I was unlovable and unforgivable and perfectly correct in assuming the worst about myself. For example, one day while driving I nosed out into a busy street, trying to turn left with the light. When the light changed and I tried to back out of the crosswalk, I couldn't because a car pulled up. An older black man trying to cross was forced to walk around the front of my car, dangerously close to traffic. He glared at me with such hatred that I rolled down the window and said, "I'm sorry, I couldn't back up there's a — "

He cut me off. "Think they own the whole street!"

And the whole world, his scorn implied. You and your kind. As he stepped up onto the curb and strode on — his day ruined, I feared — I began to cry. I wanted to run after him, tell him about the triplets ... all the diapers I'd changed, the prayers I'd prayed, the inner changes I'd tried to make. I wished I had the boys in the car, or the King sisters — black faces to show him, to testify to him, to prove ... what? That I was not a racist. But I could never prove it finally, totally, to anyone but myself, and my maker. There would always be hurt and bitter people who would see only my white face; and cynical others who would see and try to make use of my guilt. That was on them. But what was on me, my responsibility, was not to use people in some confused subconscious drive to redeem myself. Wasn't that just another form of racism?

The light changed and I pulled out, driving past the man's rigid back, past other folks, women mostly, standing on corners waiting for busses, looking at me in my car as centuries of serfs had looked up at landowners on horses, their looks seeming to say, *Yes, however you care to intellectualize it, you are just another racist.*

It was better then, wasn't it, that they had moved out? Better that I should never see them again.

*   *   *

"You know what one of my favorite movies is?"

"What?" asked Kaki.

We were up on the third floor, on the couch in the front room, looking out over the telephone wire where the white leather sneakers still hung, no more worn out, it seemed, than on the night when I'd changed my mind about Tahija and the babies living with us. The trees in the park look pale and dry. The grass needed mowing.

"*The Mission.*"

"Never saw it," she said.

"It's about Jesuits in South America, when Spain and Portugal were carving up the land. There's this mercenary and slave trader, Rodrigo Mendoza, played by Robert DeNiro. He walks in on his brother in bed with a woman he loves, and kills him. In jail he's tormented by remorse. A Jesuit priest visits and converts him. Mendoza not only converts but decides to become a priest himself."

"Now why is this your favorite movie?"

"Well, Robert DeNiro for one. But mainly it's the waterfall scene. The head Jesuit is going above the falls, where the Guaraní people went to escape enslavement, and he takes the converted mercenary along. They have to climb up this cliff face, under, around, through the waterfalls, for like a mile."

"Okay."

Purrsilla padded up the stairs, appraised the possibilities, and jumped into Kaki's lap.

"Here's the amazing thing. Mendoza's hauling behind him, up this cliff, a full suit of body armor, his old body armor, see — helmet, shoulder pads, boots, all that — dragging it about thirty feet behind him by a rope tied around his chest."

"Wow."

"Yeah. So they get to the top of the cliff, the Jesuit first, Mendoza trailing, with his armor dangling over the cliff, swinging in the air, pulling him backward, so you think it might just yank him back over the edge. A Guaraní man, maybe the chief, embraces the Jesuit, but when he sees the former slave trader he starts yelling, because not only did this Spaniard terrorize the tribe for years, he captured and enslaved the man's own mother. We find that out later."

"Good plot. So what does the man do?"

I scratched behind Purrsilla's ears.

"Well, he takes this machete-type knife and heads for DeNiro, with the Jesuit explaining something in the native language. Or maybe he explains it first and then the man gets out the knife. I forget."

"So what happens?"

"The man walks past DeNiro and looks over the cliff. He says something — the Jesuit translating — about Christ and forgiveness, then he cuts the rope. He cuts through it and the armor crashes down all the long long way they've just climbed, and sinks into the river."

"He forgives him."

"Yeah."

"So why are you crying?"

"I don't know." I picked Purrsilla up and squeezed her and put her back down. "Tahija will be seventeen next month."

"On the 8th. If we had her address we could mail her a card."

"They don't have addresses on Palethorpe!"

"Of course they do."

Twilight had come as we spoke. The white sneakers were shadows now. "We said we'd be her legal guardians until she turned eighteen."

"It was her choice to move out," Kaki said. "Is this the suit of body armor you're dragging up the cliff?"

I went for some tissue and came back blowing my nose. "Oh what do you Protestants know about guilt?"

But she did know some things. I could tell that by her next question.

"Do you believe a white person living today is to blame for the crimes of the past? For things like slavery that happened before they were born?"

"Collective karma? No, I don't think so. But I think you can choose to carry the responsibility, to sort of take on the debt."

"Doesn't that thinking lead you down the road to some kind of sick, egotistical martyrdom?"

"Or maybe to some kind of healthy, spiritual martyrdom?"

"And how would you know the difference?"

"Good question. I think if you're miserable, it's probably the first kind."

"And if it's the second kind?" she asked.

"Um, you radiate peace and joy."

"So, how do you feel?"

I blew my nose again, leaning into her. "Point taken. But I know one thing. All this talk about forgiveness, and self-forgiveness, self-acceptance ... I know they're steppingstones on the way to emotional health. But I think there's also humility, and patience, and self-awareness. I think you can't just turn around and cut the rope your own self. That's not forgiveness; it's evasion, escape. No, someone has to come and cut the rope for you. Someone who wants to cut it, who can't stand the idea of that weight, that burden, on you, on anyone."

"But who?"

"Well," I stood up and went to the window. The lamps in the park had come on. "When I look back on all the mistakes I made, all the anger when love was called for, all the failures to open to another's humanity — and not just here with Tahija and Lamarr, there's other failures, things I haven't told you about, from way back in middle school — when I look on those and past those into American history, it seems like it can't be just one person cutting one rope."

"No?"

"It has to be millions and millions of opening hearts boldly, bravely forgiving, when nobody would blame them for doing otherwise. I mean, who would have blamed the chief for killing the man who kidnapped his mother? Except oh, what power, what peace when he strides past hatred and bitterness and vengeance and slashes that rope with one stroke."

"And what relief for DeNiro."

"To be sure." I sat back down with her.

"But if it's not one person forgiving another, how will you know, how will you feel it, when the armor's been cut away?"

"I don't know," I said, "You just do, the universe just shifts."

"And how do you know it hasn't already shifted? That the armor isn't lying rusting on the bottom of the river? I mean, we've had the civil rights movement, Martin Luther King Junior preaching brotherly love, peace, nonviolence. I come back to my worry about unhealthy guilt."

"But how can there be forgiveness," I asked, "before there's been the apology, or even an admission of wrongdoing?"

"You mean, the chief can't cut the rope if DeNiro doesn't climb the cliff?"

"You're getting pretty good at extending those metaphors."

"Thank you," she said.

We sat thinking about our extended metaphor as night came on and the empty quiet in the house grew emptier.

When I have the chance to teach, there's a short story I often use, one I like as much as *The Mission* for the way it grapples with guilt and responsibility. The story is Ursula K. Le Guin's "The Ones Who Walk Away from Omelas." Omelas is utopia with a twist. Life there is perfect — peaceful, beautiful, joyful, *full* — but for one thing: In a small room in a cellar of the city is locked away a wretched child — hungry, abandoned, frightened, and from years of deprivation stunted in every way. The citizens of the shining city know the child is there, and they also know that for the city to continue in abundance and peace the child must ever remain so. "There may not even be," Le Guin's narrator tells us, "a kind word spoken to the child." It's a law of nature there in Omelas, like gravity.*

---

* This story appears in many anthologies, including the collection of Le Guin's stories, *The Wind's Twelve Quarters*: Bantam Books, 1976.

Well this is a tremendous burden to the Omelassians. Many feel it deeply. As children, they visit the child, clambering down the narrow steps giddy with the outing, returning home older, somber, particularized in a way that girds the great city and gives it the philosophical bent for which it is known. Some come back to stare through the door's barred window and examine their inherited rationalizations: the child was defective to start with; the child is now too damaged to appreciate better; the child has adapted; the child and its suffering are regrettable necessities; the child will be with us always. None of these rationalizations begins with "The city is" or "We are"; in this they resemble the rationalizations of America's middle and upper classes, where so often the effects of chronic poverty are seen as causes.

A few Omelassians drop through the rotted floor of rationalization into the basement of empathy and, finding such misery far heavier in the balance than the happiness of the bright city, walk away; they walk away into the mountains, never return.

Many of my students say they would walk away too (into crowded mountains, if intention was action). Others say they'd fight to free the child even if that meant the end of utopia and greater suffering. A few honest pragmatists argued for resignation, while more than I'd like to admit drew on their own experience (as I was always advising them to do in their writing) and said, in effect, forget it and party. To their credit, though, I think the more common sequence is party, then forget.

But there's a fourth option, one not in Le Guin's story. It is to stay in the basement with the child. Take the old mop out of the bucket in the corner, turn the bucket over, and sit. After I had lived four years in North Philadelphia, and spent four more in country solitude writing this book and continuing to develop my relationship with the young family central to it, I came to see this fourth option as no less immoral than the option of enjoying a suffering-dependent utopia, for this reason: In sitting with the child, in living among and purporting to "serve" poor African Americans, I had the hidden motivation of redeeming myself from my family's, my country's, and my own racist past.

So what? some will say; in these times when we're having to form a safety net out of bare fingers all hands are needed. Clean up your motives as you go. This advice comes from those who are in the trenches, in the beleaguered schools and the under-funded drug rehabs and the food banks, who know and deeply feel the need, and whose motives have probably been burned pure by exhaustion, if nothing else. However, when redemption from guilt or shame exists as a motive, it will usually remain hidden, because we hide from shame, and, more damningly, it will likely make all "help" "given" dependent upon or, to use Shelby Steele's term, *contingent* upon a continued need for that help.

Those who take the fourth option are as culpable as those enjoying the pleasures of the bright city. Each group uses the child, one blithely, the other self-righteously, both with the same requisite condition: that the child remain alone and miserable, an everlasting victim. But there is perhaps more hope for the ones who sit on the bucket. Down in the noiseless basement, separated from utopia's glittery distractions, confronted by unending, unjust suffering, they may get past using the child to alleviate their own moral pain and arrive at seeing the child for who he or she is: not a symbol in an allegory, not a victim representing a class of victims, not an icon the guilty genuflect to for redemption, but an individual, a human being whose muscles may be withered from disuse but whose will to live remains. Hope a seed buried within that will.

Are the only choices then complacency, violence, exile, or a more dishonest victimizing? But isn't it arrogant to think the choice is ours alone? Isn't it the child's too, or, in the end, the child's only? In a sense there are two children in the room: one an image projected out of the collective mind of the city, which includes the mind of the sitter who hopes to be redeemed by sitting with the child; and the other — the living, breathing child. Only the second can get up and climb the stairs. The best the sitter can do is hold open the door, or at least keep out of the way.

I came to sit with the child and found that I was the child. If I choose to remain in the basement of paralyzing guilt, well then — as Tahija and Lamarr would phrase it — that's on me.

Chapter 32

I liked going to college, but first of all I couldn't afford it, and second of all I had to go to work to support my household.

from the interview

A few times that summer and fall I drove past the small paved park near Palethorpe longing for a glimpse of the triplets; they were never there. A friend of Kaki's told her about a law giving visitation rights to any adult in whose house a child had resided for a year or more. We appreciated this validation of our relationship with them, but didn't want to demand visitation rights. It was hard to imagine Tahija cooperating, and I think, too, we were afraid of making ourselves vulnerable again. The boys were young, they would forget us. It was better this way.

That New Year's Eve, the last of the millennium, we were surprised by a call from Miss Millie Ellison wishing us, "you girls," as she always called us, happy New Year. A few days later Laura Ellison called to see how we were doing and say hi. We hadn't spoken since the fast, but it felt as if we'd been playing roles then, and now we could play ourselves.

I told her I was worried about Tahija. "You know welfare cut her off." I'd heard it from Stefanie, who came still for reading practice. I dreaded the thought of Miss Congeniality coming up against a new roll-cutting caseworker without us watching her back. Not that she didn't know the system much better than Kaki or I knew it; it was just that she had this bad habit of assuming herself worthy of a basic level of respect.

"She told me," Laura said. "It's hard times all around. They'll be alright. She's been acting grown so long, let her find out how hard it is."

And if it was too hard? I'd seen enough of the walking wounded to know the answer to that.

"But three two year olds!" I said. "What if it's all too much?"

Laura answered with words I had heard many times from Tahija.

"Well then that's on her."

And if she wasn't in our house, it wouldn't be on us? On me?

I'd known Lamarr walked a dangerous edge, being a young black man in an America whose leadership is just now apologizing for its failure to outlaw lynching.* But as I woke up more and more to reality, I began to see the edge Tahija walked. I had thought it was poverty. Though poverty, to be sure, is a cold, gusting wind that buffets her nonstop, the edge she walks isn't poverty. God help her, I fear it's insanity. Over the years, Tahija would be diagnosed with depression, paranoia, bi-polar disorder, and obsessive-compulsive disorder. She agrees with the last diagnosis and is seeing a psychiatrist regularly.

Walk with her. It's what I had been guided by. But how far, for how long, to where?

Once, standing beneath a cherry tree in the park, I was asked by a little girl for a boost up. I made a stirrup of my hands and she stepped into it, grasping the forked trunk. Just then

---

*To be fair though, and give credit where credit is due, the Senate did, as early as 1908, make the mailing of postcards containing photographs of lynched bodies a violation of postal regulations.

266

something in my lower back gave, but I wasn't about to drop her. I held her until she'd found her foothold.

Did I pull back too soon from Tahija's higher-stakes climb? Was Palethorpe a dangerous fall, or the lower branches of a long climb? When we said yes to her living with us, and yes to legal guardianship, Kaki Nelsen and I took on the responsibility of asking such questions, and, if they couldn't be answered, of carrying them with us forever.

In early spring Millie Ellison surprised us with another phone call inviting us to family and friends day at her church. We accepted gratefully.

The appointed Sunday was a rainy day. We'd given up the car, and so went by bus to Millie's church, which was about eighteen blocks west of Palethorpe. We wore our best — dresses, hose, and heels, my shortish hair blow-dried into something semi-feminine, Kaki's held back by side barrettes.

Once in the church, we had trouble finding Millie Ellison because the white-gloved woman usher who greeted us knew her as Miss Mary. When we had that clarified and she was leading us up the middle aisle — all the way up, to the second row — I worried she might think us presumptuous, using the family name as we had. And did Mary Millicent Ellison even want us to sit with her so far up? Did we appear to be expecting special treatment? Were all guests led to their seats in this way?

We were reminded of the mindfulness and humility members of the dominant majority need when we accept invitations into the places that have been havens from us, and which, like the African Methodist Evangelical (AME) Church, arose in response to segregation and exclusion. And if we should find ourselves excluded, for a time, or in some cases forever, we can choose to see that as payback or we can take it as a test — an opportunity to show that yes, despite our dismal record, we from the excluding class can bear up under a little exclusion. Humility goes a long way, and opens doors in what had appeared to be walls.

When we found Millie Ellison, Miss Mary, near the front, it seemed appropriate to sit in her row, but at the outside end. We admired her beautiful hat (she's known for them) and greeted Laura and her husband Jules. Little Laura, who was close to Tahija and had stayed over at the house a few times, was happy to see us. We also knew and greeted the four-year-old twin boys — the triplets' uncles.

"This does feel a little like family," Kaki whispered to me.

"I guess we earned it," I whispered back, speaking not out of pride so much as fatigue. When we met her Tahija's life was an island in the path of a hurricane, and we had stayed.

The men's choir processed slowly up the center aisle, its resonant cadence raising a "that's all right" from several in the congregation. As the pews filled and the women's choir entered singing, "I will glor-i-fy the name of the Lord," Kaki and I looked often to the back of the church hoping to see the faces we knew so well.

Even without her great-granddaughter Tahija, born Shannon, and her great-great-grandchildren Damear Donovan, Mahad Dante and Lamarr Lamont, Miss Mary Millicent Ellison had more members of her family in attendance that day than any other family in her large congregation. Kaki and I had supposed we were there as friends on this "Family and Friends" day, but when the minister called for the Ellison family, Millie gestured for us to follow her into the center aisle. And so, with scores of others, we promenaded past the altar to be counted among four generations of the Ellison family.

It was a moment and a day I will treasure forever.

The first time I saw Tahija again was at the post office. We'd talked by phone a few times, and Lamarr had been over (with nary a triplet). I was working full time on the magazine and most days walked or biked to the post office to pick up submissions and subscription orders.

So one day on the phone I suggested to Tahija that we meet there, and she said, "We can," and we did.

An alley ran behind Palethorpe's few houses and ended alongside the post office. Tahija was waiting there with Stefanie. She wore her biege outergarment, black kemar pinned tightly under her chin. It had been six months since I'd seen her, two years since we'd first met.

We hugged, and stood in the alley catching up.

Big Lamarr had been sick, back and forth to the emergency room, and had finally been diagnosed with Type II, or adult-onset, diabetes. The doctors couldn't get it under control. He allowed himself to be admitted to the hospital, where, with his sugar levels perilously high they had put him on an insulin drip. In the middle of the night his insulin level crashed and he woke with every muscle in his body paralyzed. A nurse who noticed tears on his cheeks may have saved his life.

This did permanent damage to his liver, and still nothing seemed to work to keep his levels stable. One day of manual labor took him three days to recover from. And the pay was so low after taxes and mandatory transportation costs (you were required to take the company van to work), seeing his paycheck made him feel, Tahija told me, as if he'd been raped. His months at Phame helped him secure a good factory job, but he passed out one day while operating a metal-stamping machine. His supervisor liked him (nearly everybody does), but said he couldn't keep him on without a doctor's note verifying that he was fit to work around heavy equipment. Lamarr's doctor would not sign such a note. He encouraged him to apply for social security disability insurance. He did several times and was rejected each time.

Tahija was not well either. Heavy hemorrhaging and pain, caused by her polycystic ovarian syndrome, had led two different doctors to recommend a hysterectomy. I phoned the mother of the boy whose nanny I'd been — she was a gynecologist now — and she told me she had never heard of a hysterectomy being recommended for that condition in a woman so young.

"That's what they said," Tahija insisted when I asked her. "And they said I need to stay off my feet, told me I can't work. But I have to work."

After moving out, she had managed to complete fall-term classes. Then her benefits had been cut, because she'd changed districts, she was told. It took two months to get the paperwork in place, and when she did the new caseworker informed her that she had to leave school and find full-time work if she wanted to keep benefits. She began a nine-to-five training program that mainly involved designing a resume. Design it to death, I thought, still it wasn't going to have a high school diploma on it, or the AA degree that had been within reach, or any job other than the flower-shop job she'd had in ninth grade.

This pulling her from school seemed to me symbolic of so much, and frighteningly arbitrary. The new act behind TANF dictated that states could allow up to 20 percent of those on welfare to count college as work-related training. But which 20 percent? Didn't an enrolled sixteen-year-old with two semesters of good grades behind her and three children to feed look like a good bet? Apparently not. And when I later saw studies indicating that education and other discretionary benefits, such as travel stipends, were given more to white welfare recipients than to black, I was angry, but not surprised.* All along my walk with Tahija I had seen how the broken glass of racist bias littered her already difficult path. I had heard about the caseworker who said — the first words out of her mouth when Tahija sat down in her cubicle — "Three? You must be one of those girls can't keep her legs closed." And then there was the one who cut off her cash benefits and neglected to inform her that the family still qualified for food stamps.

---

*See Susan Gooden's article, "All Things Not Being Equal: Differences in Caseworker Support toward Black and White Welfare Clients," published in the *Harvard Journal of African American Public Policy* (1998. 4: 23-33). In her study, Gooden found that welfare caseworkers did not offer similar levels of support to black and white welfare recipients. Specifically, black welfare recipients received less transportation assistance, and, Gooden found, less support for pursuing education.

A five-year entitlement didn't entitle you to anything more, Tahija has said, than "five years of being hassled down." I could see the effects of it on her face, in her eyes. There was a deadness to them. The whites were veined with red, and the dark rings were back, wider and lined. She joked that no one at her job believed she had just turned eighteen. She could have passed for thirty.

Tahija wasn't philosophical or political about having to leave college. She was realistic. "I liked going to college," she wrote, "but first of all I couldn't afford it, and second of all I had to go to work to support my household." She'd keep her textbooks, and later encourage friends to enroll, coaching them through registration and placement tests. But it just wasn't possible for her.

I took her out for a belated birthday dinner and heard about her new job in an elementary school cafeteria. She liked it. One of the women there was truly psychic, the scary supervisor turned out to be softhearted, and the kids were adorable. She told me about a little freckle-faced boy who asked for a peanut butter sandwich every day.

"I mean *every* day, Kathryn. Now you know those sandwiches, how we make them is we lay out the bread when it's frozen and spread peanut butter on, going down the row."

"Easier that way," I said.

"Right. But the bread thaws out all soggy and them sandwiches *nas*ty. So I tell him, I say, try something else, Baby. But he won't."

"Hardheaded."

"Exactly."

Tahija worrying what this hardheaded little white boy ate made me so mad. What was going on in her that nurturance flowed so easily in his direction? What was going on in this country that a young, intelligent black woman in poor, rapidly deteriorating health was commuting *three hours a day*, gone from can't-see to can't-see, in order to feed the well-fed children of white women while her own children languished, underfed, underweight, under the weight of decades of policies that moved

271

the jobs to the suburbs while segregating hourly wage workers in the inner cities.

If I sound angry, I am. Head Start's few incredibly effective federal dollars threatened by "restructuring."* Library funding slashed all over, by 50 percent in Pennsylvania, when so often the library was the only safe place the kids in my neighborhood could go after school. College grants and loan programs slashed, rungs in the ladder out of working poverty cut away by people who took college and grad school as givens, and don't seem to intend to give anything back. Making cuts in not enough leads to less than not enough, and less than not enough has a face for me now. Three faces.

If those who drop the bombs and order the bombs dropped were on the ground when they landed, if they could walk through the rubble of the home of the small boy who lost his whole family, or nurse the stumps of the same boy's lost arms, they might try other means, or like the ones who walk away from Omelas abandon their posts. Believing in the Light in each person, I believe that.

Likewise, if the leaders dis-assembling government safety nets lived in rat and roach infested homes, or consigned their children to schools without sports or art or music or — as in the elementary school in our neighborhood — even usable drinking fountains, if they looked daily into the eyes of children listless with chronic hunger, they might try other means. Maybe I make a mistake when I assume that unawareness, rather than indifference (or worse), is behind their policies. Maybe seeing what I

---

*The latest Head Start bill, proposed in 2005, does not include the shift from federal funding to state block grants that created such a furor in 2003. Originally, Head Start dollars were delivered directly from the federal government to local public agencies to circumvent state government resistance to educating African American children. Today, 31% of enrollees are African American, 26% white, 31% Hispanic, with the remainder Native Americans and Pacific Islanders.

have seen would not change them. But I believe seeing *as* I have would. Which is why I write, and why I write with hope. But it is, as Cornel West has phrased it, a hope that is not hopeful. It is an open-eyed hope.

It was so frustrating to believe, as I did, that life is good and love real, and to try to impart it to these teens, that belief being more valuable, I felt, than any experience or material thing I might be able to give them, and to be handed back for my offering very difficult to refute proof that this just was not true. Why was it so easy for them to find proof that things would never get better, that there really was no inner flame to find and feed and share with their children? That love was a ruse?

Were the pressures of poverty and racism so great that Tahija and Lamarr could never heal from their various traumas? It was like they were being told to take up tools and learn a trade while their hands were occupied holding a great crushing weight off their heads.

How was I to use my freedom? Was I to stand with them beneath the crushing weight and loan my two arms, my back, that theirs might be freed up for a time? Could I do that, or did my privilege rescind the very force of gravity, so that what seemed crushing weight to them would be light for me, a source of shade? And what, morally, did it mean for me to stand in the shade of their suffering, bearing so little of it, or none at all, but feeling nevertheless enlarged by it, inspired by it to write this book, which though I should give every penny of profit from it to them still enlarges me — my career (perhaps), and certainly my sense of myself as a productive person?

Obviously the right thing to do would be to go around to where the weight came from and chip away at it. At racism and injustice, and their sad progeny: neglect, abuse, mental illness, addiction, imprisonment, debilitating anger, hopelessness, despair. Kaki was chipping away at the weight, with other Quakers fighting for drug law reform and effective treatment.

Was there some legislation I should be supporting? Resources I could be procuring? Groups of white people whose consciousness I ought to be trying to raise?

Laws, resources, reparations ... my witness is sorely lacking if it inspires no new or renewed efforts in these areas. But my main work, I began to see, was to be opening the heart: mine, and (I hope with a hopeful hope) yours.

Sweet Honey in my head again, as led by its founder Bernice Johnson Reagon, who was one of the founders, as well, of the SNCC Freedom Singers:

> We who believe in freedom cannot rest
> We who believe in freedom cannot rest until it comes ...
> Until the killing of black men,
> black mothers' sons,
> is as important as the killing of white men,
> white mothers' sons....

For me now it is as important, and if I rest I rest fitfully. I know the Light of divinity shines in each soul, and I believe what a marrow-weary black man born in Jim Crow 1935 once told me: Every time a white person thinks that, by virtue of their whiteness, they are superior to a black person, something in the universe shifts. We live in a universe that has so shifted millions and millions of times. Maybe you are one of the white people who knows this, who has learned it without going through what I had to go through, without making the mistakes I made. I suppose, then, that you are already acting on this knowledge, within your spheres of influence? Do you think you could do more? I ask on behalf of Damear, Mahad, and Lamarr — three lights on three stacked and beeping heart monitors, three hearts headed home.

Chapter 33

After a year of living like that I finally took Kaki up on the offer
of helping me and Lamarr get a better house for us to raise the
boys. We still go through different ups and downs but I can honestly say I know they both care about my family no matter
what. I can also say that we care about them just as much.

My Life as I Know It

I went to a nurse's aide school, I studied hard and eventually I
passed. I started a new job and I stayed there for four months.
When I finally got certified they fired me — they said I wasn't
Christian Home material. I think I wasn't, I was better, and that is
what they didn't like. They couldn't tell me not one thing I did
wrong so I will leave it alone but I will learn from it. Also I learned
that not everyone cares if you're good at your job — if you don't
look and act like them you are bad in their book. But it's wrong.

from the interview

Kaki was first to see the boys again. I think Lamarr may have
arranged it, a way of letting her know how things were. At any
rate, one day when she came by the Palethorpe house to give
him a lift downtown, he said she could come in. Tahija was at
work. Stefanie was next door with her mom. Lamarr's brothers

and Craig, a friend who was staying at the house (and would live with them for years), were asleep on the living room floor.

Kaki stepped over them. The house was so small: downstairs was a tiny living room, its one window a mat of plastic and hung blankets, and a smaller kitchen, where the only light was a shadeless lamp placed in the middle of the floor. The bit of counter space seemed to quiver: small roaches, she realized, roaches on the uneven floor too.

Between these two rooms was a short, narrow staircase. It had been poorly built, with the risers too high and the span too short, so that it was more like a ramp than stairs. These were hard to walk up, harder to walk down. Or maybe it was what she saw upstairs that made the walk down so hard.

No banister, only the unpainted sheetrock Lamarr and Tahija had hung before they moved in. The landlord was in prison. His elderly father came for the rent, $250 a month; as for repairs, they were on their own.

At the top of the stairs, two rooms. To the left a bedroom with a bedroom set taking most of the floor space; to the right, down a short hallway, a smaller bedroom. No windows, three cribs, one powder blue, one white, one unpainted, and not a crib's width of floor space between them.

She went in, happy to be seeing them again. A brief happiness. They lay on their stomachs, soaked with urine, awake but unresponsive. It was mid-afternoon. Eight hours earlier, well before dawn, Tahija had left for her cafeteria job in the suburbs.

She said their names, eventually got them to their feet and played with them a little. She saw no diapers nearby to change them into, and downstairs in the kitchen little food, only cases of Pediasure from the doctor. Lamarr assured Kaki he had been feeding them. His explanation for why they were so listless was that the diapers had run out that month at about the same time the money did, and they tended to lie very still when their diapers were soaked.

Kaki came back the next day when Tahija was home and persuaded her to accept daily help. Tahija agreed, and for all of that

August, while I was renting the attic of a friend in the country, Kaki came every day to play with and feed the boys, and to try to cheer up Tahija, who returned home from work exhausted and fell into bed without eating.

Again the idea of buying a house came up. This time Tahija was more open, and Kaki more determined. She put herself on the rack of computing exactly what withdrawing $20,000 from her 401(k) would cost her. There would be early withdrawal penalties, back taxes due on disbursal, and more taxes due at the end of the year because the disbursal bumped her into the next income bracket. She researched ways to buffer these penalties, such as giving the money to a tax-exempt organization and letting them purchase the house, but there didn't seem to be a legitimate buffer. She decided to pay the fines and penalties out of the retirement money.

She and Tahija began looking at houses. Within weeks, on a day when I happened to be with them, we found a freestanding two-story house with a garage, a pale-yellow stuccoed front, a (relatively) large backyard, and a side yard that might be purchased later. The El was in sight and hearing, with an elementary school a few blocks away and two Quaker meetings within walking distance.

The house was owned by an elderly Italian widow who with her housepainter husband and very little English had raised eight children in it. We liked the paneling, the drop ceilings, the wall-to-wall pink carpet, the extra bathroom in the basement and the deep backyard. From the low ceiling of the dining room hung a huge wedding cake of a ceramic chandelier. The many tiers of bulbs radiated heat like a space heater, which was a good thing, given the short life expectancy of the furnace (not to mention the plumbing and the appliances).

Philadelphia is more segregated than most American cities, and this neighborhood, known as Frankford, had been a working class white one until the mid '90s, when African American and

Latino families began moving up from the crumbling housing projects and, later, from gentrifying areas of the inner city. It was about half white then, with a fair number of derelict white people who wandered about or begged on corners, looking befuddled and betrayed. Where, they seemed to ask, had the middle class gone to? Where the Catholic schools, and the churches where their babies had been christened? Too poor, too broken, too rooted or to stubborn to leave — they now became, for the people who had been oppressed by it for centuries, representatives of the white race. Some filled the role admirably; some became friends and allies of the family that had become family to me. Others demonstrated yet again how fear and hatred can warp the soul and abort community.

There were trees and parks though, and the dry cleaners where Lamarr's mother had worked for years was nearby, so that he knew the neighborhood and felt fairly safe there. And it was closer to Tahija's job, giving the boys an hour more of her each day. The main problem with the house was the asking price, $40,000. We'd found that houses in the $20,000 range tended to be in higher-crime neighborhoods like Palethorpe and in need of major repairs. What if Kaki held the mortgage and Lamarr and Tahija paid back part of the cost? Say half? We took a deep breath and made an offer of $33,000, cash.

It was accepted.

The plan had originally been to buy the house in Tahija's name. Kaki and I had second thoughts though, fearing back taxes or some other mishap might cause them to lose the house. In an echo of my sea change when she was in the hospital, we met with Tahija days before the closing and told her about the new terms. She agreed. What choice, she asked me years later, did she have? It was Palethorpe or our terms. She chose our terms. But she predicted that without her name on the deed she'd be ineligible for programs that offered assistance, with heating bills for example. This proved to be true. For this reason, and because they'd kept up well enough with taxes and the many major repairs needed, we transferred the deed in 2006.

Tahija and Lamarr agreed to pay Kaki $200 per month at 3% interest until they had paid off half the selling price of the house. Kaki soon dropped the interest, and the minimum payment was adjusted, as circumstances seemed to warrant

The final cost to Kaki Nelsen of accessing that $33,000 was $12,000, for a total withdrawal of $45,000, or almost half her retirement fund.

At the closing, Kaki and I both signed our names to the papers. As when we had become Tahija's guardians, this legal recognition, with its significant, if arid, ceremony, felt like a kind of wedding. Even the octogenarian widow who had sold us the house smiled as we walked hand in hand from the Realtor's office, giving us a few kind words. They were in Sicilian, so I didn't know the literal meaning, but because of their tone and her smile I chose to receive them as a handful of rice.

When the school year ended, and with it her cafeteria job, Tahija found and enrolled in one of the for-profit training programs springing up in the wake of welfare reform. In eight weeks, the brochure promised, she could become a Certified Nurse's Aide. Then she'd be able to earn the state-mandated minimum for CNAs — $11.00 per hour. While still in this program, she found work through a job fair at a nursing home in the suburbs. The starting pay was only $6 an hour, but there would be opportunities for overtime, she was told, and once she was certified the higher wage would kick in.

She woke before dawn and rode two busses out to Christian Home. She liked the work, and the residents liked her; she indulged them in small ways: a foot rub, lotion for their hands, a few minutes of listening.... They had so many stories, so few visitors. Though she often worked twelve-hour shifts, occasionally double shifts, because of the way the hours were allocated the promised overtime rarely showed up in her check, which hovered just under two-hundred dollars.

The day finally came for her certification examination. She called us from the new house to tell us about it. Kaki and I listened on the same phone.

She'd been very nervous. She arrived at the testing place early and waited with about ten others from her training program. She did well on both sections of the test — practical and written. Although everyone else who took the test that day failed, she passed on the first try with a near perfect score, and the one question she had missed — Kaki and I both agreed — was a judgment call, plain and simple. You might tell a resident that another resident had died, or you might not, depending.

She was so proud. I worried about a training program that managed to pass only one of its students, but I was glad she had been the one. She thought she might go into nursing, or maybe counseling, something where you helped people.

Then the blow came.

The week after the big test, at about the time she was expecting to see the higher wage boost her paycheck up over two-hundred finally, she arrived at work to find her name missing from the schedule. Was she fired? Laid off? No one would say. When pressed, her supervisor, a Karen, told her she simply was not Christian Home material.

Last week she was but this week she's not?

Tahija thought it was because she was Muslim. Several times this Karen had remarked on the white kemar Tahija wore with her uniform. It seemed to me that the higher wage might have had something to do with it too. Kaki researched it and encouraged Tahija to go to legal aid and fight the firing. But Tahija was too disheartened to do it, or anything, in her own behalf. It was same-old, same-old — the strong exploiting the weak, the system outdoing her at every turn.

I had often felt that Tahija's hopelessness and defensiveness aggravated or even caused most of her problems. If she could only be more positive, more cooperative.... But then a Karen came along, and her hopelessness seemed logical, her defensiveness sensible. Tahija and Lamarr operated in a dimension where gravity had a far greater force than the gravity I knew. Really, in the end, I could not know what they were going through. I could only listen when they tried to describe it; listen and resist the urge to jump into that mightiest of North American rivers, De-nial.

We tried to advocate for her at the nursing home but were stonewalled. The human resources office blocked unemployment payments for months by refusing to file the needed paperwork. This also kept the family from getting TANF benefits reinstated, since Tahija couldn't prove she had been fired. The unemployment office launched an investigation, got nowhere, and then caught someone from human resources lying during a three-way phone call. Declaring that Tahija had been unfairly terminated, they awarded her back benefits. These were extended twice during the recession that followed September 11.

A teacher at the CNA training program told her she had had a similar experience with the home.

"I had them two years in court," she told Tahija, "and lost. Just forget it."

Tahija couldn't forget it. That day when her name had disappeared from the schedule she'd felt so betrayed. They wouldn't even let her get her things from her locker. She sat on the stone steps of the home for a long time, crying and crying, looking out over the lawns and winding walkways she knew well. The residents liked her, they said so. She had tried so hard. She remembered washing the body of a dying woman ... the breaths coming at longer and longer intervals, the sunken chest barely moving. The head nurse had looked in, telling her to hurry up, the family was on its way. She chose the best nightgown, slid it over the pale, thin shoulders, working the cloth down, as she'd learned to do. And when the last breath came, she was there.

She stayed a long time on those steps. All the disappointments came back to her, the abandonments, broken promises, betrayals. Security would come soon and escort her off the premises. But for now she sat. Had you been driving by you might have noticed her, a heavy-set young black woman in a white uniform, waiting for no one, expecting no ride home.

281

Epilogue

In the summer of 2001 I rented an apartment in Pennsylvania's Endless Mountains, to write. That September a former professor of mine asked me to fill in teaching a writing workshop at a unique school she was helping found in Brooklyn, New York. Bard High School Early College let students do two years of college-level work and then transfer on, at sixteen, to a four-year college. And best of all, it was part of the New York City public school system. Step team shaking the auditorium. Hip hop in the hallways. White kids learning to be in the minority.

I was thrilled to find myself present for the first days of this school, the more so when I saw my classroom's spectacular view: just across the East River, lower Manhattan, twin towers so tall and bright. And that's what I was looking at, in the company of fifteen or so ninth graders, when the second plane hit. Many things changed in the world that day. In me, two: I knew I had to write this book, and I knew I had to live alone in the country.

In this frame of mind I drove to North Philly to find Kaki up at the new house babysitting. Tahija was over at her friend Jackie's helping her and her kids move out on an abusive boyfriend. Lamarr, left all week with the triplets, had cried uncle, or rather aunt. That's what they called Kaki, Aunt Kaki.

I knocked on the door. Kaki poked her head out the second floor window.

"It's not locked."

I let myself in and the boys came down the stairs, Mahd bounding, Marr stepping gingerly, Mear holding back until I had greeted the other two.

"I see three boys," I said, "but I only got two hugs."

He came forward, the crowded, tipped smile. Though they looked more like two-year-olds, they were three and a half, and beautiful; beautiful and perfect, each an auricle of my now three-part heart.

I had rushed, trying to make a special episode of *The West Wing,* but the TV reception was so poor, and the boys so distracting, I gave up. We went to their room. Out the window was a full moon. I pointed to it and told a variation on the story I'd told my nieces and nephews when they were small. About the child who wanted to go to the moon, and did.

Damear especially seemed to feel something like what I did for the moon. He and I are more alike. And he's the most hurt, I think, by whatever hurts them — the most sensitive. Is this sensitivity my fault, my imprint? But I had so little time with him. Yet the time I had encompassed his first experience of the world. Let it be so then. Let him carry the burden of openness, accept its gifts, that there are wonders untold all around us, that the moving light in the sky is a wonder never exhausted; that the light and wonder are there for us all the time, and if we don't notice, or allow anyone or anything to keep us from seeing, from opening, that's a tragedy.

After the show Kaki and I loaded everyone into the station wagon I had borrowed from my sister and we drove to Hancock Street. They rode quietly and were asleep by the time we arrived. We parked in front and each carried one in. Left alone for a moment Mahddy started to cry and Kaki rushed for him. How we hate to hear them cry. We put them in the room that had been their nursery, Kaki's room now. The single bed was still there though, and they fit fine, sideways. When Lamarr woke crying I sat with him until he fell back to sleep. He tossed and turned not at all. Now and then, though, he reached up, arms taut and shaking, and I was wrenched back into their first eighteen months ... the nights when I lay awake hearing them cry, the days when I walked past their closed door knowing they needed to be held, not holding them.

He put his arms down and lay perfectly still, eyes open. I saw the long curled lashes so like his mother's blink slowly, deliberately, as if he were doing a before and after test. Same ceiling, same room.... What was he thinking?

The next day in the playground Lamarr stands inside a swarm of day-care kids, concentrating in the same way, focusing inwardly. I call and call but he doesn't hear. I have the sense he is settling into a self he doesn't quite know, realizing that not all kids come in matched sets of two, like his uncles, or three, like himself/ves. Later when we go in he'll resist having his shoes taken off. I'll compromise and leave them on, but when I go on to Mahd's, Marr will fuss again, as if those are *his* shoes on *his* feet. "These not your feet," I tell him — Tahija's tone. But do they feel like his to him? Is that a problem?

Each needs more time away from the other two. To care for them Tahija has had to treat them as one: meals, baths, hair, clothes, trips out, always done as a unit and always in birth order — Damear, Mahad, Lamarr. It's made it possible for her to manage. But oh, I long for full-fledged spoiling-allowed bossy grandmotherhood, or at least official aunt status. I'd take them one at a time for shoes — any color, any style (or would they insist on matching?); I'd bring them to a wide meadow where each could run in any direction he liked, or stand and stare, or sit and roll.

Have they seen a meadow, a river, a lake? Had I taken them to a meadow, a river or a lake? No (not yet). Have they brushed their palms over the tops of dandelions gone to seed? No, though Tahija would say yes, knowing I knew it was not true and defying me to challenge her. Allergic to everything green, she shuns even city parks. And where she doesn't *want* to go, they don't *need* to go. Kaki has pointed out that I haven't asked to take them often enough, haven't tried hard enough to augment Tahija's care, which is the best she can give, we accept, far better than so many other children get. They live in a city. They are poor. Why should they have meadows and dandelions?

Why should they not? I have been a coward and a weakling. I must brave Tahija's wariness, risk the broken and re-broken heart, make it work. Make what work? My loving them without dislodging her. Maybe they're old enough now, well enough bonded with her.

I have found excuses to withdraw because I have been afraid to love them more, afraid to see and be pained by all they have yet to go through, all they will choose to create based on what they already believe to be true about themselves. I haven't wanted to watch as they grow to boys, and then men, trying in vain to meet their unmet infantile needs. For them the first years will be a for-gotten, loamy place — the long hours alone in a crib, arms raised to be lifted by arms that do not lift.... For me it will be a few years when I tried, and made so many mistakes, and longed more than I had ever longed, but for God and my dead mother, to be the arms that lift.

Damear is climbing up the slide. The day-care kids are gone so I let him break the never-climb-up-the-slide rule. I watch from the plastic bench on top of the platform, beside which Mahddy stands driving a play steering wheel and telling me about their two guinea pigs. The guinea pigs are named, unaccountably, Powder Comes With It and Neither/Nor.

"Who gave them those names?" I ask him.

"We did."

"But who thought of them first?"

He can't say, and when I ask big Lamarr later he can't either, claims they seemed to think of them simultaneously.

Lamarr meanwhile is running through the grass toward the cherry trees, Kaki close behind. Does he remember sitting under them waiting for his mother to come up the block from school?

Damear's halfway up the slide.

"Hold on!" I tell him, though he is, to both sides. How steep slides are, how far the fall backward if you lose your grip! He climbs with great concentration, the last few steps so hard. I want to pluck him up and zoom him to the top, but don't, and he makes it — two feet firm on the grating of the platform.

"I did it!" he says — a clear, cheerful voice I haven't heard from him that day. I want to applaud him grandly, but something in me keeps it to a "very good."

He hurries down the ladder and goes around to start the climb again. Mahddy turns us hard starboard, and I'm remembering Damear's first steps, four in a row across the rug between the cribs. He had fallen laughing into my arms and I'd raised him up high, *You did it!*

Why do I hold back now? Am I afraid to re-establish the bond that caused us both so much pain when it was broken? Those terrible days when I couldn't hold him, could only stand in the doorway looking at him looking back. Should I never have let the bond form at all? I hardly saw it happening. I had a need. He had a need. It seemed easy and necessary to give what I had so much of, what I had lived enough to know was inexhaustible, and only increases with the giving.

At the house meeting from hell Tahija had accused Kaki and me of wanting babies. Maybe she was right. Kaki always wanted a daughter, says Tahija is the daughter she never had. I always wanted to write and live in the woods. I've done that, and I've watched babies, and of the two I prefer the woods, the words ... but for Damear, for these three, I would give up all. I would stand in front of a bullet; would donate a kidney in a minute; would — will — conform to Tahija's methods, as far as my conscience will let me.

I don't applaud Damear's triumph because from his parents' perspective he is spoiled, and ought to be given less than the others, to wean him of it. He has to learn he can't always have what he wants, can't always do what he wants to do, can't be ... what he can be. So often it seems that what black children have to learn is to get by with less, way less than enough, and to get used to humiliation. I will not humiliate them. If it is really so that

287

the triplets must be prepared in this way for lives as black men in America then let it come from other hands.

All that weekend I am careful to be consistent with Tahija's methods. Such consistency is better for the kids, and I desperately want her to let them stay over again. And whatever I do, she'll notice, because however they play me they'll try and play her. So … no spitting the milk back into the cup, Mear (I know it's a fun noise), get that thumb outta your mouth, Marr, and if there's any fighting over that truck, Mahddy, it's gone! I even punish Damear once. I send him to look at the corner for as long as I can stand it. After, he looks at me differently. With more respect.

I missed most of the terrible twos, which happened back at the terrible hovel on terrible Palethorpe Street during the terrible year when I didn't see them at all. Tahija says Damear gave her the hardest time, with Mahddy a close second. What she must have gone through! After two days of watching them I am more impressed with what she's accomplished, and more accepting of how she's accomplished it.

May Allah/God/Christ/The Light/The Source raise each of them up one day and exclaim, "You made it!"

May they all make it. I love them so much.

They're five years old and I've finally gotten them into the country. I'm living in the house where Mahad defeated the mossy rock, working as a caretaker while I write this book. Big Lamarr and Tahija are getting a campfire going out back while I do the dinner dishes.

Little Lamarr walks past from the bathroom. He's the tallest, by a fraction, and with his big eyes and long, attractively braided hair is sometimes mistaken for a girl (that changes soon).

"Mr. Stevens?"

"Yes?"

I take a piece of firewood from the stack beside the cook stove.

"Could you bring this out to your dad please?"

"Sure."

He carries the wood like a whole arm load, strutting a little, in the style of his uncles Dante and Donovan. I go back to the dishes.

Seconds later Damear's at my side, eyebrows awry with dismay.

"You gave Marr a-a piece of wood for my dad but you didn't give *me* a piece for my-my dad."

I dry my hands and take a second piece from the pile by the stove. Damear's lost his round baby face. He's the thinnest of the three, with a sharp chin and nervous eyes.

"Thanks." Out he goes, hoisting the wood up to his shoulder.

I don't return to the dishes. I pick up another piece of firewood and wait for Mahddy. The triplet effect, big Lamarr calls it.

Sure enough, through the back door he comes, searching, but in his anxiety at being left behind not seeing me standing right there beside the stove holding the very thing he wants.

"Hey Mahd-man."

His big smile. It is, I realize, except for the missing front teeth, his great-great-grandmother Millie Ellison's smile.

He accepts his piece of wood and holds it like a cake on a platter.

"Thank you Kath-a-ryn."

"Thank *you* Mahd."

And he goes, out to the growing campfire.

Acknowledgements

My mother Catherine Zita gave me my first typewriter and my first stories. I know she would have liked this one. The triplets' great-great-grandmother Mary survived much and persevered that her family might do the same. I pray this book adds to their well being, and I thank her for welcoming me into her home and counting me among her family. God is good, all the time.

I welcome the chance here to thank poet Lucille Clifton for permission to reprint her poems, and also to thank singer songwriter and activist Bernice Johnson Reagon for permission to quote from her song lyrics. It means more than I can say.

To the triplets, and to their parents: Thank you for the chance to walk part of the way with you. Forgive if you can this book's flaws, errors of fact and of perception. Please forgive too the mistakes laid out here, and my many stumblings, past and future.

To those who gave me a place to work or support while I worked — thank you. Thank you Jean for precious weeks in your not-yet-lived-in house, where I started this book. Thank you Scott and Susan for a summer at the stone house, where I worked on the first draft. Thank you Alice and Wendy for the freedom five years at "Lucy" gave me. Thank you Cousin Bruce for reappearing as angel after so long.

I also welcome the chance to thank the people who read and commented on drafts. First come the triplets' parents and Kaki, for reading, suggesting changes, answering all manner of questions, and bearing with my attempt to tell their stories. Uda Braithwaite Bartholomew for knowledge and wisdom shared, and perspective-expanding criticisms. Maureen Mather for enthusiasm that carried me through the winter of the final draft. Marcelle Martin and Judith Fetterley for readings that called me to a deeper integrity.

This book would not be a printed book without Sue Clark's witness and Jeff Hitchcock's vision and tireless labor. Thank you both. I would like too to thank Jorge and Marcelle for being there with us in North Philly and for prayers over the years. And finally, without Kaki this book and its story wouldn't have happened. Thank you for walking this walk with me, for your dedication to peace and justice, and for being a resolute ally to the triplets and their parents.

Appendix

My Life as I Know It:

An in-progress autobiography

by Tahija Ellison

I was born on November the 8th 1982. I am not sure what time but it was a start to a long life. I was born in Temple hospital in Philadelphia. My mother was Laura Ellison and my dad was Juan Lopez, two crazy people that thought they were in love, but I will never know if it was true. About a year after I was born my two parents were separated. I guess they did the wrong thing because I hardly ever seen my dad after that. He came when he wanted to and my mom always made excuses for him. There was no reason for him not to come see me because I went to the day care center that my grandmom owned and ran. My grandmom was his mom so you would think he would come and visit, but he did not. I believe he wanted to, but he was scared to. I am not sure what he would have been scared of, but it was something. I was only a child, I would've thought whatever he did was great. I didn't know any better at the time, so whatever mistakes he would have made would have only been between him and my mom. The thing he screwed up on was the part where he didn't show up, even I knew that was wrong. I waited for hours for him to show up, my mom telling me all the time he just forgot. I knew it was more than that, but I didn't know what the more was.

I was at least two years old when my mom found someone new, his name was Gary Wilson. They had gotten very close. They decided to have a baby. And they had a baby a year later. She was my new baby sister, at first I thought I would love her and she was only for me but actually we ended up fighting for the attention. You see Gary had become the dad I never had. I started to feel like they didn't know I was there. I had to let them know I was special too. I had to let them know I needed them just as much as she did. I know it seems silly but I was so use to being the only child I was a little jealous. I knew they loved me because they told me, but I felt like I was on the outside looking in.

I don't remember much about when I was three but my mom says that I "was a good little girl." My mom said I was very smart and I use to ask a lot of question and I liked to dance and sing. My mom said that when she use to wash me up I use to say, oh Mom you are hurting my arm. I was a little performer I thought that I could do anything. I always liked for my mom to read to me. I started to learn Spanish when I was three, but when I got older I forgot everything I learned, because I never stuck with the lessons I was taking because when I was four we moved out of Philadelphia.

When I was four years old my mom and dad (Gary) decided that we should move to Colorado to have a better life. When we got to the airport it was crazy, it was going to be the first time I had ever been on an airplane. Before we could get to the plane I fell down the escalator with the little bag I had back then I didn't know what embarrassed was but now I do and I would have been just that embarrassed. I was so scared of the changes that were about to come into my life. I guess it was the thought of everything new. I was about to have a new place to live new people around me and more new things to expect out of life. It was like a new start in a strange place.

When we first got to Colorado we had to live with uncle Greg who is my dad (Gary) brother and his family. I think when we first got there we were quite a burden on them but they got use to us pretty quickly. I actually never remember a complaint about us not to say that there wasn't one. Everyday life became a routine of two families joined together.

I remember getting ready to start school. The school I was about to start attending wanted to put me back a grade because Philadelphia schools were behind Colorado schools on an academic level. My mom insisted that they give me a test to see if I was behind the other children and I passed it and I didn't have to be put back a grade. I was so proud of myself. I had passed the test that everyone said would be so hard for me being as though I was from Philadelphia. I think if my parents wouldn't have stayed on my case about my school work I wouldn't have passed the test at all.

We finally moved into our own apartment. I was happy on one hand and sad on the other. The happy part was I had more space and the sad part was moving from uncle Greg's house and moving away from my friends in his neighborhood. I quickly got new friends and I seen my old friends from time to time. I remember when I was younger there were always people trying to take advantage of me, they would also try to pick fights with me. Back then I wasn't the type that would fight you until I got fed up. You see on one corner I had them trying to fight me and on the other corner I had my mom hollering at me, don't let them bully you. I really didn't see it as bullying because they never actually hit me they just use to threaten me. My little sister use to act like she knew karate and start to kick at them and try to do flips on them. [That sister would earn a black belt later.] This is when it all had to come to a screeching halt. It was time for me to show them I wasn't afraid I just didn't want to go that route. After I showed them I wasn't afraid everything stopped. I know it seems harsh but if I would continue to let it get bad it would eventually get worse instead of getting better.

Not long after that my mom and dad separated. I didn't see him as much as I wanted after that but we talked a lot. Me and my sister started getting close with my mom's friend Steven. He was nice he treated us like we were his own children even though he didn't have any children. Steven wanted to adopt us but our dad wasn't having that at all. Steven got us two dogs, Caesar and Butch. At first I liked them but as they got older they got bigger and soon I became scared of them. He also had a big fish tank and we would help him feed the fish. We went everywhere together. I think he was taking up the space that my dad use to, but the difference was Steven and mom weren't together, they were friends. I felt like they should have got together but they never did. My mom was actually with a guy who called himself Hollywood. I thought he was all right at first until he got himself into trouble and went to jail. I met his mother Mrs. Johnson. I thought she was pretty nice, when we met her she showed me how to make crispy fried chicken. I never forgot her recipe even though I didn't write it down.

One day we received a call that my great-grandmom was sick and that we should come to Philly because they didn't know if she would make it so we came back to Philly on a long bus ride so we could see the sights. I remember someone on that ride was stinking real bad, we had to spray on the bus to try to get rid of the smell.

When we arrived in Philly I really didn't want to be here, but I also didn't want to hear that something happened to my great-grandmom and we didn't even bother to come and see her. The first day we arrived in Philly everything seemed to feel like it was permanent, no one asked how long we would be here, no one said anything about us even coming from so far for all of those days on the bus. We came to Philly in August I remember having a short summer there, you see in Colorado we had already went back to school. In Philadelphia school was still a month away. I wanted to know how long it would be before we went back to Colorado but my mom said she didn't know how long we would have to stay to find out what was going to happen to Millie. My second day in Philadelphia was a mess every one was in an uproar because I didn't like sunny side up eggs and bacon. They thought I was just trying to be more than them. They told me I was too hasaditty in other words I was stuck up you see they were already mad that the night before I had screamed real loud because I saw a mouse and they thought I was exaggerating but I had never seen a house mouse before except on television. My family just couldn't believe I was truly afraid. We ended up not going back home that year or any other year and it was never the same again for me.

That month before I finally started school I met a lot of people. I would just go and walk for a long time until I finally learned my way around the neighborhood that would now be where I called home. That year me and a girl named Jenny and my cousin Crystal got close even though sometimes me and Crystal would fight for no reason at all it was crazy. Me and Crystal would fight and argue, but if someone else tried that they were in trouble. It was my fifth grade year and I couldn't believe that I was really liking my school and my friends. I also liked my teachers. I remember my two favorite teachers, one was Mr. Jones and the other was Mrs. Jackson. I did a lot that year. I was a safety guard and I learned about peer mediation.

I guess that is about when I started to wonder about the whereabouts of my real dad. I called my Grandmom Grealy and she said that she would take me to look for him, but when we went we couldn't find him. I told my mom and she was determined to help me find him so we went looking. That was the first time I was glad to see him and mad that I found him at the same time. Seeing him that day made me realize that all the time I thought I missed out on something I was only fooling myself. I had actually been blessed with a better life after all even though we came back to Philadelphia. I was shocked at the way I felt. One thing I remember feeling is, how can I help him, but I had to remember he needed to help himself. It was nothing I could do at all to make things better. I tried my best to get some results. I at least tried to do his hair it was all knotty and nasty looking. When he left that evening I remember going to my room crying because I didn't understand why he would let himself go like that. I never really heard anything bad about him, even my stepdad tried to tell me that my dad was an all right guy. I was shocked to see him that way. I don't even know why I even cared but I did.

When it started getting close to the end of the school year I had to start getting myself ready to graduate. By then my mom started to slip on me and my sister then I really felt like I had no other choice but to make sure my sister was all right so we moved back to Millie's even though it was no freedom. I knew we would be taken care of. I really felt like I had no one. I started getting too grown hanging out with the wrong crowed but I never got out of control to the point where I disrespected Millie. I did what she told me no matter what it was but no one actually knew the pain I was going through. I graduated that June with the help of Millie, she was my life saver, she got everything I needed that year but I was still stressed and no one could actually help me because they never understood that relationship me and my mom had. Most people thought that my mom let me get away with too much but she just let me make most of my decisions, when she left I had no one. That summer I started to drink and smoke every day, 'til this day I don't know how I got away with it everyday without getting caught once but I did.

I started the sixth grade still smoking and drinking every day. I use to sneak off with a guy named Eric, he use to tell me to stop drinking and smoking but I didn't listen. One day I talked to him and when he pulled off from seeing me I never saw him again, his best friend who was on drugs killed him so I had no one to talk to again I couldn't talk to friends because I didn't think they would understand. I still don't know how I kept good grades with all the stuff that was going through my mind. I slowly began to spend time with my cousin Mia, we started to walk to school together and I talked to her a little bit but I still couldn't talk to her about everything.

That year in sixth grade I had a real chip on my shoulder. I had questions for everyone and everything. I remember asking a guy with a Kufi on in the hallway at school a bunch of questions [about Islam] and he answered them, I don't know why. I guess it was God's way of stepping in and just letting me know he was seeing everything and I wasn't alone, but I didn't realize it was a sign until the next year. I was walking up the back hallway and I see my cousin fighting some boys and I thought they were serious and I got into it with one of the guys named Lamarr. A few days later the guy Lamarr asked me if I would be his girlfriend. At first me and my cousin made a pact that I would go with him and she would go with his friend but we never told them that was why we said yes. We got together on October 28th and I remember that because it was exactly two weeks before my birthday, which is November 8th. After awhile my cousin and her boyfriend broke up so without thinking I broke up with Lamarr. I thought it wouldn't matter because I thought we could still be friends but I actually had feelings for him. I thought they would go away but they didn't. A few months later I asked him whatever happened to that guy with the Kufi, and he said, "Are you serious?" I said, "Yes." He said, "That was me." Now you see we were meant to be. I thought everything was ok for awhile then I started to think that he wasn't really into me so I broke it off again in the meantime I continued to smoke and drink. One day Lamarr seen me drinking he grabbed my drink and threw it away that same day he seen me smoking and he threw my whole pack of cigarettes in the middle of Broad Street I was so mad. I bought another pack and I hid them thinking that he wouldn't find them but he caught me taking it out and threw that pack away and after that I could have easily got another pack but I didn't I quit but it took a little more for me to quit drinking.

I remember we were split up and I started talking to a guy named Marcus but everything he did I compared it to what I thought Lamarr would do so we didn't last but a week but we remained friends. A few months after that people who wanted to go to Spelman or Morehouse had to enter an essay contest to win a ticket and free stay on campus. I entered and my essay won. I went on the trip and a girl that knew Lamarr kept on mentioning his name and saying how she liked him and he kissed her and I had him on my mind the whole time. I felt like if I talked to another guy I was cheating and we weren't even together at that point. When we returned back a lot of people lied on me to Lamarr telling him I hooked up with guys while we were in Atlanta. That kind a left us on semi bad terms so we really didn't speak anymore for awhile.

That year before my mom had a baby girl with her new boy friend Jules. We graduated soon after that and I didn't see Lamarr for a long time until that summer one of my suppose to be friends Kendra told me her and Lamarr slept together I was so mad I wanted to find him so I tried my best to find him and I couldn't. I had to go to a friend's house who lived in the neighborhood where Lamarr lived and when we went I seen him but I tried to avoid him and two pepperhead girls said are you looking for Lamarr and I said no I was so mad that the girls even asked me that simple question. I did what I had to do then I went home that night and my cousin Mia said that Lamarr was trying to get in touch with me. I was about to move back with my mom this time on the Boulevard. It was now me, my sister, little Laura and she had twin boys and all of us and her boyfriend Jess moved in and that day I finally called him back. We straightened out everything I found out Kendra was lying and we ended up getting back together. I finally let him meet my family but before he could meet my sister she had went back to Colorado. The next day me, him, Mia, my mom and the twins went to the movies together. My mom seemed to like him from the beginning.

That summer was a crazy and hard summer for me you see my mom started slipping all over again and I was forced to watch the twins who were infants and Laura and take care of myself. In the midst of all of that someone I thought that I could trust raped me and things started to go downhill from then on. Instead of telling my mom I told Lamarr. I told him not to tell and he did anyway and I started to feel like I couldn't tell him anything, but I also realized how much he cared about me. Later on that year we finally made love together for the first time together. Everyone had thought that we were having sex all that time but we weren't. The next September I started my first year at Dobbins high school and Lamarr went there too so we seen each other every day and we talked every night. We started getting real serious then.

I remember one day I came home and the locks were changed and everyone was gone they had left me so I asked my aunt if I could stay there and she let me, if it wasn't for her I don't know what I would have done. For the first couple of days I didn't call Lamarr and that made him worry but I was all right. Not long after that a friend of mine named Krissy asked me if I wanted to move in with her and her boyfriend Kevin and I said yes and I moved out of my aunt's house and Lamarr moved in with me. I started to work at a flower shop at night and I continued to got to school in the morning. We all had some good times when we lived together but it came to an end quick because Krissy's dad had to close the building down and I had to ask my other aunt could I come stay at her house. She said it was ok but I wasn't happy at first, I didn't know what was missing until I started sneaking Lamarr in every night. I knew it was wrong but that was the way I was happy because I knew he cared. We went every where we could and we had fun. We went to Wildwood and Lamarr won me all of these stuffed animals. We had so much fun just being together.

That October I thought I was pregnant. I didn't know what to do so I said I would wait to tell my mom, but before I could find my mom my aunt put me out her house at one o'clock in the morning and I had to go to Renee's house and Lamarr didn't know where I was again. At that time I didn't know what to do. Finally I got in touch with Lamarr and I told him where I was, he was glad to know I was all right but he didn't know what to do. A few days later we had to go to an ultrasound appointment and the doctor said "I see one, no two" then she said "wait I see three." When she said that Lamarr passed out. When we told everyone they thought we were lying to them but we weren't. I got in touch with my unreliable dad yet again. This time he was doing ok. By then it was November 7th. He was suppose to come and get me and finally take care of me but the next day I waited as usual and he never showed up. I was left hanging all over again. It was about two weeks later Renee's mom told me I had to leave so that she wouldn't get in trouble for breaking her lease by having me live there. So Lamarr asked his mom could I stay with them and she said yes, so Kaki and Kathryn picked me up with Lamarr and took me to his mom's house. I really didn't know Kaki and Kathryn back then, but I was glad that they were willing to help me move my things from Renee's mom's house. I was in Lamarr's mom's house for three days and his cousin nagged that I didn't eat and I was pregnant, and then one of his uncles said that I was a runaway and his step-father said I had to leave so I called my grandmother Agnes and asked her to come and get me. I stayed with her one week before I had a meeting with Kaki and Kathryn about me staying there until I could get something permanent. They agreed and I moved in right away.

It was a calm night. I felt as if I didn't have a worry in the world. I was sitting on my bed reading a book when all of a sudden I began to get sharp pains in the middle of my stomach. I couldn't imagine what was going on and why I had the pain. I waited for about twenty minutes but the pain was still there. It was a constant pain and it made me begin to worry, being as I was five and a half months pregnant I began to not only worry I began to actually panic. I was thinking to myself, why was this happening. It was too early for this to be happening. Was there in fact something wrong. I quickly ran to the bathroom to see if there was any change in my body that I could see, but there was none. I then quickly called the hospital and they said for me to come into the emergency room right away. If I wasn't afraid before I was surely afraid now not knowing what would happen next. The whole way to the hospital I was thinking, is it something wrong with me or is this a normal situation for someone in my shoes. You see I had never been in these shoes before. All of this was new to me so I was very confused and most of all scared.

The panic I was in when we got to the hospital. First they made me wait until the doctor could see me which seemed like forever, but was actually a few moments. I guess when you are afraid you lose track of time. Minutes begin to feel like hours and one hour seems like three. The thought of not knowing what was wrong with my babies began to make me feel sick with fear. All of the emotions that were coming over me were starting to overwhelm me. I had to know what was wrong and why. I had been doing everything by the book. I didn't smoke nor did I drink, and I took those big prenatal vitamins all to insure that the lives that came out of me would be as healthy as I could make it. I felt like I did a good job insuring that the lives that grew inside of me would have a good start, I promised myself I would make sure that I gave them something more then what I had for myself. A family.

I wanted my children to have a real family. Some people think that if there is someone who is there with their child it is a real family, but to me I believe that a real family is a Mom and a Dad it doesn't have to be a biological mother or father but someone to love you unconditionally. A Grandmother, Grandfather, Cousins, Aunts and

Uncles are all the extras that a child should at least have the option of having but is not necessary to complete a family.

Now don't get me wrong I was loved by many, but I don't think that anyone understood me the way that my mother did and at this hard time in my life I couldn't count on her the way I needed and wanted to. I know it sounds selfish and I put myself in the situation I was in however I still believe that I needed her more than ever before at that point and time in my life. I know that at that time in my mother's life she probably needed me too, but I didn't know how to help her. You see for so long I was able to count on her and only her because she was the only one that was constant in my life besides my little sister. Neither of us knew how to help her this was something bigger than us this was about her. It was hard to deal with but we had no other choice but to deal with it because this was our life too. Now it was my chance to put myself in my mother's shoes and try not to make the same mistakes that she did not because I didn't want to be like her but because I saw what she went through and I learned from it and I wanted to change the cycle before it started. I knew that their lives hadn't begun and I wanted them to at least start out right even if it might not last forever.

I was forced to stay in the hospital for six weeks. I had to insure that I was getting the best care and the only way to do that was to listen to my doctor's orders and the orders were to stay for observation. Those were the longest six weeks in my life. I got through the six weeks thinking I wasn't alone and also thinking about the fact that I was doing this for my children. I had to endure one hospital room no walking around and strict bed rest. I had little visitors but I had three regulars, my partner in life the father of my children who never left my side. He had been there from the beginning never missing an appointment, and now that I would have to be in this hospital for awhile he would be subjected to sleeping in a chair or on the floor for the whole six weeks. I know he was probably thinking, how long will I have to be here on this hard floor or cramped chair? You would think that being in a hospital they would have at least a cot or something for emergencies but in my case there were none to be offered. We did what we had to do to survive.

I remember Kaki and Kathryn use to bring me ice cream and movies. I would be waiting for them to arrive thinking at last someone has come from the outside to visit us. I would be so happy like a kid in a candy store smiling ear to ear you wouldn't even have thought that half the time I was having contractions. I just went with the flow. I was in the hospital so long I got to know all the nurses on my floor and some were much nicer than the others. I remember one of them use to bring us movies so that we wouldn't be bored and I really appreciated that. Some days I would be so bored that I needed to watch a movie so that I could keep my mind off the boredom. I mean it was the same thing every day doctors and nurses picking and poking in the middle of the night. I don't think I had a good night of sleep the whole time I was there.

After about four weeks Kaki and Kathryn told me that they might want me to leave because they didn't think they could handle me and the boys at their house. I got so stressed and depressed that I would have to find another place again I just gave up with everyone. To top off all the bad things that were happening to me someone called DHS and said that I was a runaway and I thought they were going to try to take my children away from me. When I found out I started contracting too much, and soon the doctors couldn't stop the contractions anymore so I let them go ahead and get me ready for the delivery of the boys. Lamarr had already left the hospital to have a meeting with Kaki so he didn't know what was going on and I needed someone in the delivery room with me so I called my cousin Mia and she came to my rescue and she was there the whole time I got prepped for my c-section.

On the fine day of February 19, 1998, my joy had finally come but it wasn't the right time. I mean it was the first time Lamarr had ever left my side. This day would be the first day that I would be alone at the hospital. He had to meet with Kaki for breakfast and this particular day I honestly felt bad. I mean my head hurt my back hurt I knew it was time. Everyone around me said they didn't think it was time but I knew. I never felt like this until today and about one minute after Lamarr left my water broke. I rang my emergency buzzer and by the time the nurse had came he had already got out the hospital. I didn't think it could get any worse than this. The whole time I was there we had decided on natural childbirth but today as if everything wasn't going wrong as it is they told me that I had to have a cesarean. I was totally against it, but my only choice was I either had the surgery or I would be going home with one baby instead of three so I had to think of them instead of me and I made the choice to have the surgery.

Lamarr made it just in time for the big moment to see his children come into this world. After the birth of my three boys Damear, Mahad and Lamarr, Jr. they sewed and stapled me up and sent me to the recovery room. After two miserable days they finally let me out of the hospital, it was the first time I was outside in six weeks. When I was first let out of the hospital I went to my Grandmom Agnes' house but the boys weren't released yet. A couple days of being there Kaki and Kathryn finally said that I could come back to their house. After two weeks passed Damear came home. The first night we went to sleep in the middle of the night I heard a loud scream and I fell out of the bed. Later little Lamarr came home and after that Mahad came home then we were finally all together.

Later I got such a hassle from DHS and I did nothing wrong they only came because I was so young. I think it should be against the law and I wish I could've sued for harassment. DHS tried to make me feel like I was stupid and I couldn't take care of my children but I proved them very wrong.

The same year I had to go back to school and when I went it seemed like it was nothing like when I had left before I had the boys. Everyone seemed to be so immature I had to get out of there so Kaki and Kathryn took me to take the test to get into Community College of Philadelphia and January of 1999 I started classes. That summer Kathryn, Kaki and myself had started arguing too much about the boys so I decided to leave. I didn't have any money so we moved in a real bad neighborhood and a bad house but I did my best to keep it clean and livable and I tried to keep as busy as I could so that I could make sure that the boys never really needed anything. After a year of living like that I finally took Kaki up on the offer of helping me and Lamarr get a better house for us to raise the boys. We still go through different ups and downs but I can honestly say I know they both care about my family no matter what. I can also say that we care about them just as much.

To be continued ...

Interview

Tahija Ellison's written responses to questions from the author, 2002

Q. Why do you think Kathryn and Kaki became involved in your life?

A. I think Kaki got involved because Lamarr asked her to. I think Kathryn got involved because Kaki got involved in the beginning. Later I think the both of them stayed involved because they cared about the well-being of Tahija, Lamarr and their new family. I also think that they figured that they could help and Tahija really needed the help and she wasn't getting the help from anyone else.

Q. What was it like in the delivery room?

A. It was kind of crazy in the delivery room because I had to have the c-section and I was trying to wait for Lamarr to come back and I was all by myself. I had to call my cousin to be there with me because I didn't think Lamarr would make it back in time to see the boys born, then I also had a lot of doctors and nurses in the room because every child had their own team of doctors and nurses in case of any complications.

Q. What is your happiest memory of the time covered in this book?

A. The happiest memory I have of being a mother is the first time I heard them cry, because the doctor told me that they might not cry because they were real premature and their lungs might not be developed enough. The second was when I held them in my arms at the same time. I knew they loved me just as much as I loved them from the little smirk they had on their face, like *joy I finally see who I was kicking all that time.*

Q. What was the hardest thing about living in the Hancock Street house?

A. I think the hardest thing about living on Hancock Street was not being able to do whatever I wanted. I felt like I had parents all over again in some ways it was good because I could always talk about a problem I was having and whenever I needed help with anything all I had to do was ask and Kaki and Kathryn would help the best way they could, but it was also bad because I felt like I always had to answer to someone and I am not at all use to answering to anyone.

Q. What problems did you have with Kathryn's care of the triplets?

A. The only problem I had was I didn't want them held all day because I knew I wouldn't be able to get anything done if they were too spoiled. Kathryn felt that they should be held more but if she sat and held them all day she would need a maid to cook and clean and she would need a nanny to watch the baby for herself to get washed. It was three of them not one which is totally different you can't even compare the two situations. I think we had a difference of opinion but it went as smoothly as it could get.

Q. Do you think race affected the situation? If so, how?

A. I do not think race affected the situation however I think the way we were raised was different and that affected the situation a little bit. I believe you shouldn't spoil a baby because it will be too stressful to take care of the baby's needs and your own if you are alone taking care of it and it would have been even worse if there were three like in my case you have to set limits because if you don't you will be crazy and there will be no time for you.

Q. What do you see as the causes of the problems with Mahad?

A. Mahad was said to be failure-to-thrive only because he wasn't the same weight as the other two. He was a small child then he's a

308

small child now and if I could I would sue them for discrimination of age because like the doctor said he wouldn't have given me a hard way to go if I would have been older, but I know I have always acted older than my age, and I am real responsible.

Q. Talk about DHS involvement in your life.

A. DHS never helped me and I wish there wasn't such a thing because they made me miserable and they didn't help me one bit. If I could go back I would sue them for harassment. I was a fit parent they just couldn't get past the age. I was in a stable home but they still couldn't get past the age. They need to start judging a person by the person, not the age.

Q. How will the boys' childhoods be like or different from yours?

A. My childhood was easy until I got back to Philly and then it got super hard and the boys' childhood is nothing like mine because I will never let it get super hard for them. I don't care what I have to do to make it a little easy I can't make it perfect but I will get as close to it as possible.

Q. What was college like?

A. I liked going to college but first of all I couldn't afford it and second of all I had to go to work to support my household.

Q. What were your reasons for moving out when you did?

A. I decided to move to Palethorpe Street to get away from the nagging and protest about not going to the park with the kids. I also didn't appreciate the fact that Jorge and Marcelle were protesting too, that was the day I decided to leave. I really don't care what they think but I don't want them in my business. I was already mad at the fact that me and Kaki fought …, the protest was the straw that broke the camel's back. I almost never talked to either one of you but Lamarr said not to take it personal that you were only voicing your opinions. I didn't care where we went at that moment just out of there.

Q. What was the job market like?

A. The job market itself wasn't bad but some of the people were very mean, snobby and religionist. I wasn't able to get a lot of jobs because of my religious beliefs, but no one can make me not be Muslim. I chose it for myself and if I ever leave it will be because I wanted to. Working affected the boys because when I was working I didn't get to see them much and when I did see them I was mostly tired but I kept going for them even if that meant no rest for me. I am only surviving for them no one else right now not even for myself.

Q. What happened after you became a certified nurse's aide?

A. I went to a nurse's aide school, I studied hard and eventually I passed. I started a new job and I stayed there for four months. When I finally got certified they fired me — they said I wasn't Christian Home material. I think I wasn't, I was better, and that is what they didn't like. They couldn't tell me not one thing I did wrong so I will leave it alone but I will learn from it. Also I learned that not everyone cares if you're good at your job — if you don't look and act like them you are bad in their book. But it's wrong. I am kind of glad now that I don't work there because I spend much more time with my children.

Q. What would you say if you could talk to yourself at thirteen?

A. If I could go back and talk to me when I was thirteen I would tell me be very careful how you trust because when you need help no one you know will be really willing to help you but when you get it all figured out everyone will be asking for your help. All that work you are doing, get your own place, don't share a place with anyone even if it is fun, keep your own.

Q. What do you see yourself doing ten years from now?

A. I am not sure what I will be doing in ten years but whatever it is I hope it is something good. Maybe I will be a successful writer.

About the People

Kathryn Gordon goes by Elizabeth now and lives in Pennsylvania's Endless Mountains, where she works as a caretaker and teaches writing at community colleges. She recently completed a collection of poetry, *The Pilot's Quick Prayer,* and has started a novel. She and Kaki remain involved with the triplets and their parents.

Kaki still lives in the Hancock Street house, which she shares with people in recovery. She runs anger management workshops and has served as a co-chair of the Philadelphia Affordable Housing Coalition, a group that works to end homelessness, repair low-income housing, and resist gentrification.

The parents of the triplets continue as a couple, living in the house Kaki helped them acquire. They have served jointly as block captains and have run their block's summer lunch program. Tahija attends college part time and plans to earn her associate's degree by July of 2008. Lamarr continues to develop his music while working part-time jobs and mentoring neighborhood children.

Damear, Mahad and Lamarr, nine years old as of this writing, attend third grade in a public school they walk to. They are in good health. They enjoy a large and nearby extended family. They have many friends and two dogs, Kayla and Moo-moo. They visit Elizabeth in the country.